Monmouth County

Through Time

ROBERT GILINSKY

America Through Time®

For Claire and Leyna

America Through Time is an imprint of Fontwhill Media LLC

Fonthill Media LLC
www.fonthillmedia.com
office@fonthillmedia.com

First published 2013

ISBN 978-1-62545-044-9

Typeset in Mrs Eaves XL Serif Narrow
Printed and bound in England

Connect with us:
www.twitter.com/USAthroughtime
www.facebook.com/AmericaThroughTime

INTRODUCTION

In the fall of 2012, Hurricane Sandy wreaked devastating havoc on our beloved New Jersey, with Monmouth County suffering the brunt of the worst damages. As a lifelong resident of Neptune City, I felt extremely lucky to have made it through the storm and the ensuing weeks of fuel shortages and power outages. The aftermath evoked a national media frenzy, with looped footage of disaster scenes, replete with star-studded televised benefit programs and concerts. As a local, I witnessed the damage first-hand, but I took great comfort in the fact that for every devastating loss I witnessed, there were a dozen cherished and dear locales that survived the storm without serious damage.

Shortly after the hurricane, a personal letter arrived in the mail from Alan Sutton announcing Fonthill Media's 'Through Time' franchise. Mr. Sutton was aware of the previous local comparative works I had authored, and asked if I was interested in completing a volume for the inaugural run of the series. With so much attention on what had been lost in the storm, I felt confident that I could put together a great volume on what had survived. Tales of triumph are so much more heartening than tragedy.

Monmouth County is rich in history. It was within these borders that George Washington waged a crucial battle that is considered a turning point in our nation's struggle for independence. It was on these enchanting shores that countless notables and seven presidents spent their summers during the crucial era of growth after the Civil War. It was the location of pioneering technological research done by Guglielmo Marconi and David Sarnoff. Lest we forget the work done at Bell Labs in Holmdel which led to seven different Nobel Prizes.

The children of Monmouth County have left an indelible mark on our beloved pop culture. Interestingly, the greatest portrayals of Batman's Joker hailed from bordering towns. Cesar Romero grew up in Bradley Beach. Jack Nicholson's second grade teacher at Roosevelt School in Neptune City commented on his report card, 'Jack's work is excellent, but he needs more self control.' Norman Mailer learned how to read and write in Long Branch Public Schools. Count Basie worked odd jobs in his native Red Bank while he waited for his big break. Bud Abbott told his first joke in hometown of Asbury Park, and Danny Devito was sent to boarding school to keep him out of the trouble he always found himself embroiled in whilst haunting the boardwalk. Bruce

Springsteen strummed his first few chords in his tiny bedroom in Freehold. Brian Williams bused tables at the Shrewsbury Perkins and became interested in journalism while attending Brookdale Community College. Deal native Ashley Tisdale was discovered by a talent agent at Monmouth Mall.

Please join us as we pass some time together taking in the sites of Monmouth County, not only as we know them today; but as they have been known by the countless others who have treasured them before us. Take in the advance of progress and appreciate the blessing of preservation. Home is where the heart is.

Robert Gilinsky
Spring 2013

ON THE COVER

Front: The Twin Lights and Highlands landscape is viewed in 1869 and 2013.
Back: The heart of Long Branch's business district on Broadway is pictured in comparative views from the 1890s, 1930s, 1950s and 2013.

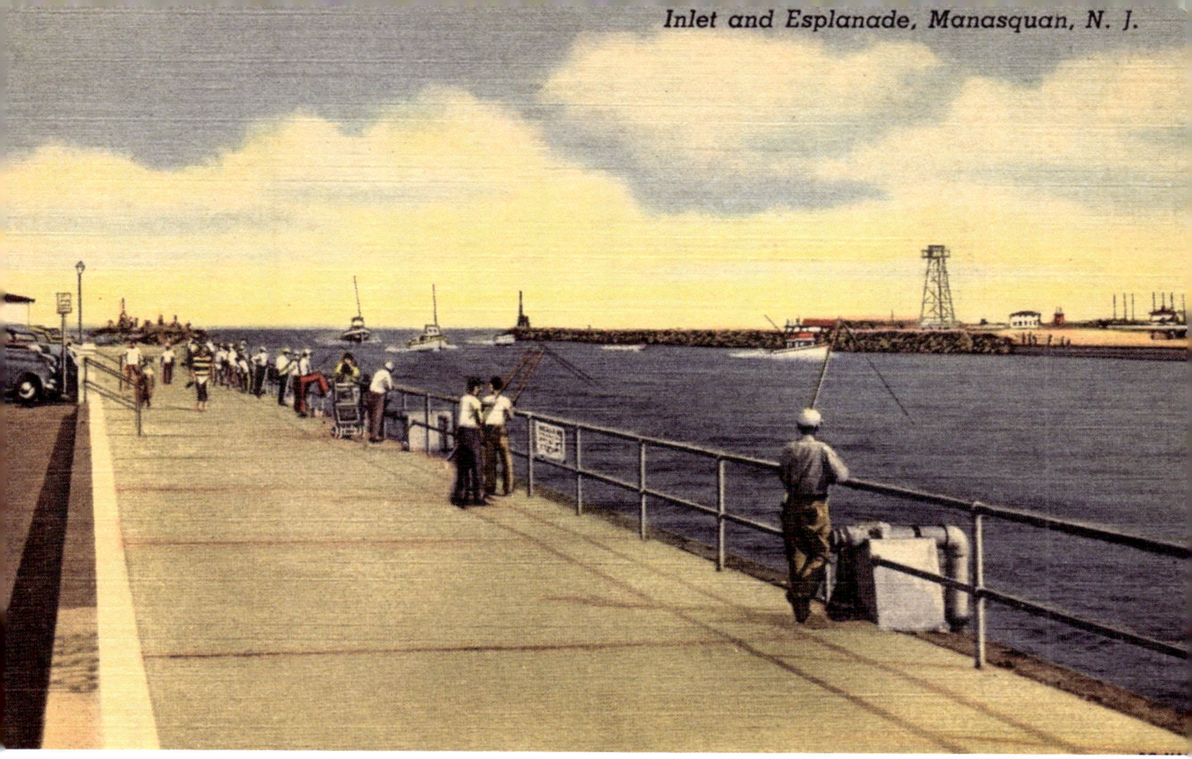

MANASQUAN: The ambience remains intact despite the sixty years spanning these images. On any given day one can find the dozens of resident fishermen waiting to reel in the prize catch of the day on the Manasquan side of the inlet. The southeastern corner of Monmouth County will always be a hub for those who love the sea.

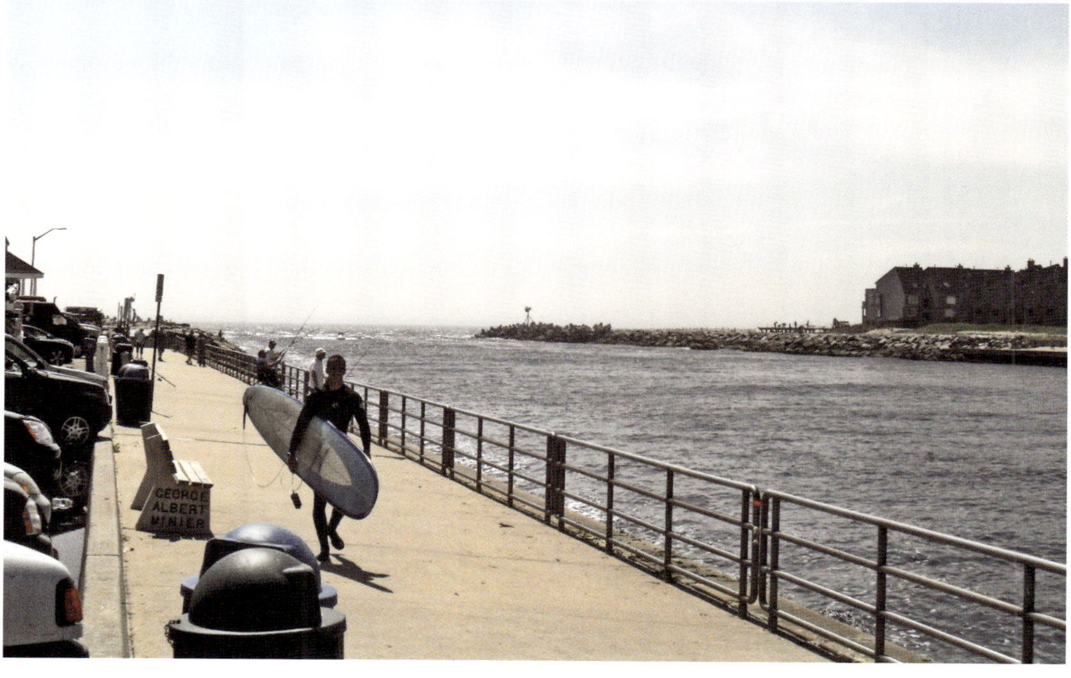

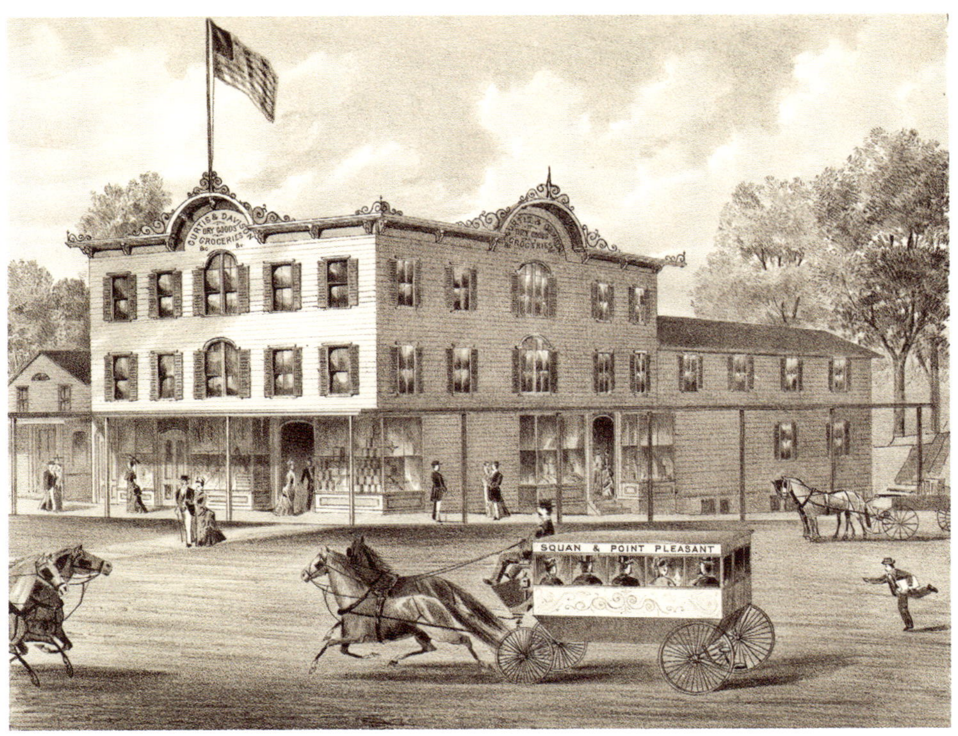

THE ORIGINAL GENERAL STORE: The store built by Jacob Curtis on Main Street in Manasquan in the second decade of the nineteenth century is actually the portion at the right in these images. Some thirty years later the building was moved to face South Street when the present edifice was completed. The comparison image here is from the landmark Woolman and Rose Atlas published in 1878.

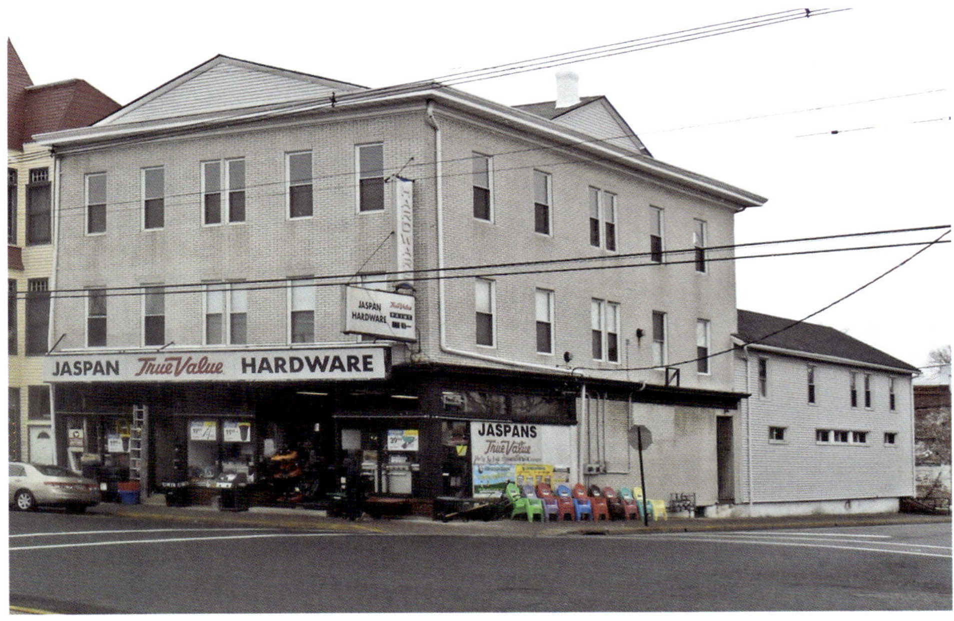

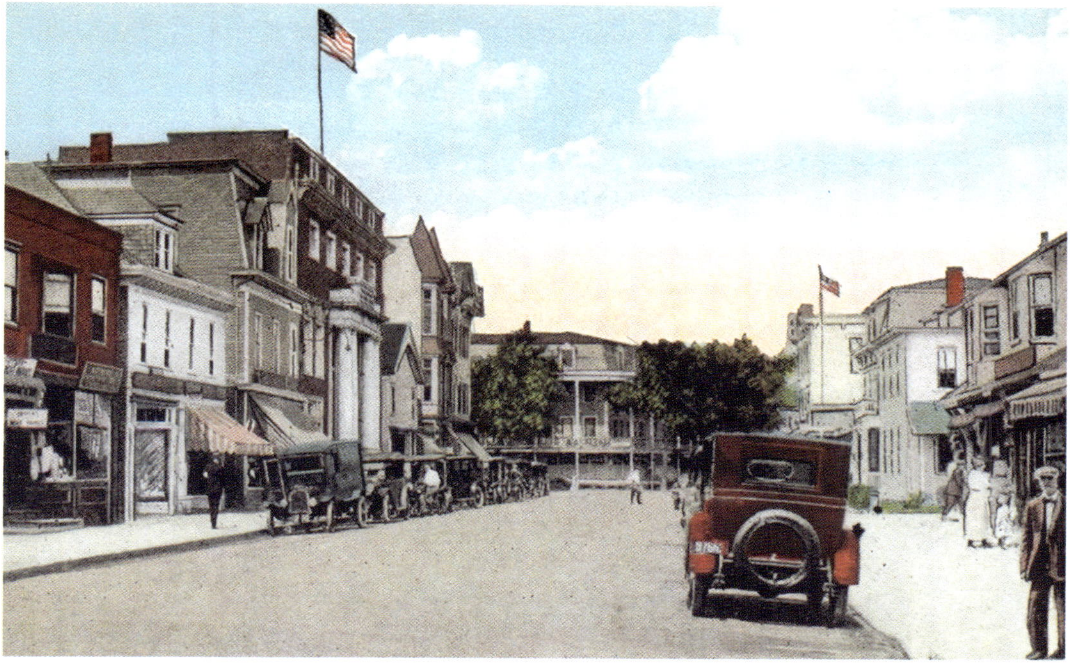

The Daily Bustle of Main Street: The business district of Manasquan has not changed pace since the scene depicted on this 1920s postcard. The columnated bank building at left center was constructed in 1883. Like any town square, the bulk of life's important necessities can all be had within reasonable walking distance.

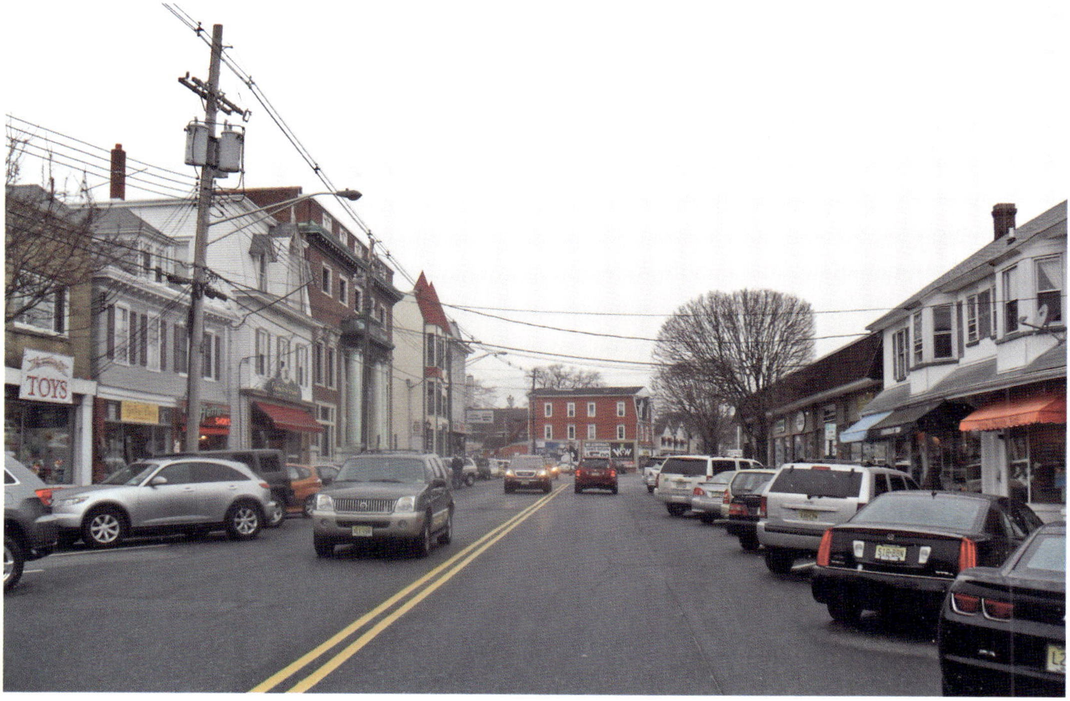

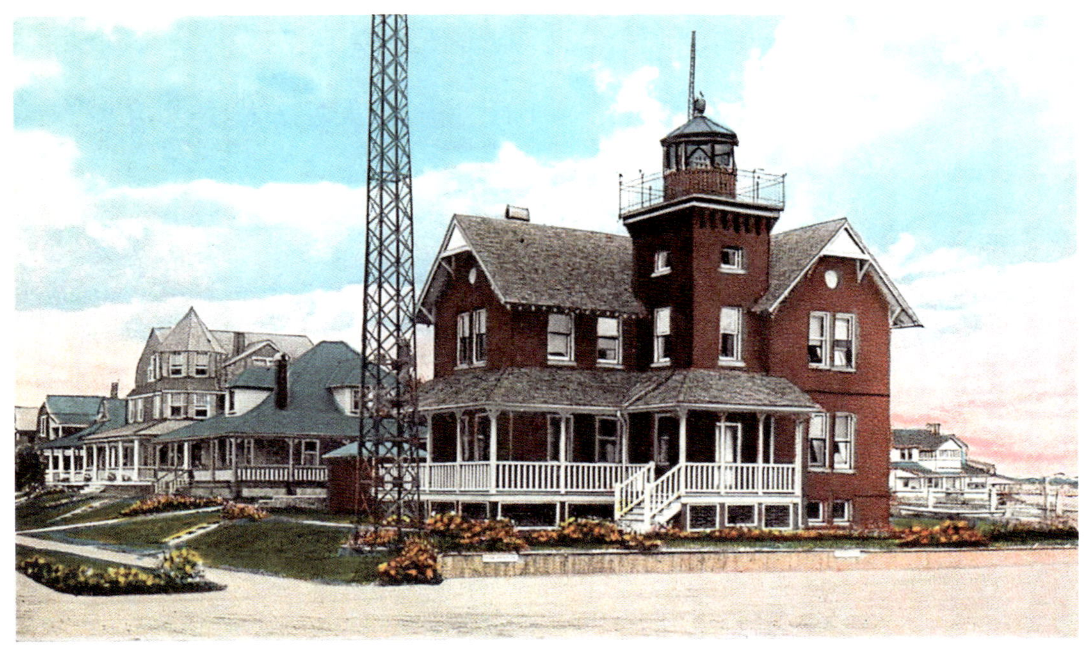

THE SEA GIRT LIGHT: The lighthouse was constructed in 1896 to alert mariners to the Wreck Pond inlet. Notably this building was the last east coast lighthouse built with a integrated keeper's quarters. It was also the first lighthouse in the United States to be fitted with a radio beacon, in 1921 (about the time of this postcard image). Members of the Sea Girt Lighthouse Citizens Committee, who have cared for the building since being deactivated as a lighthouse in 1977 meet daily at the foot of Beacon Boulevard.

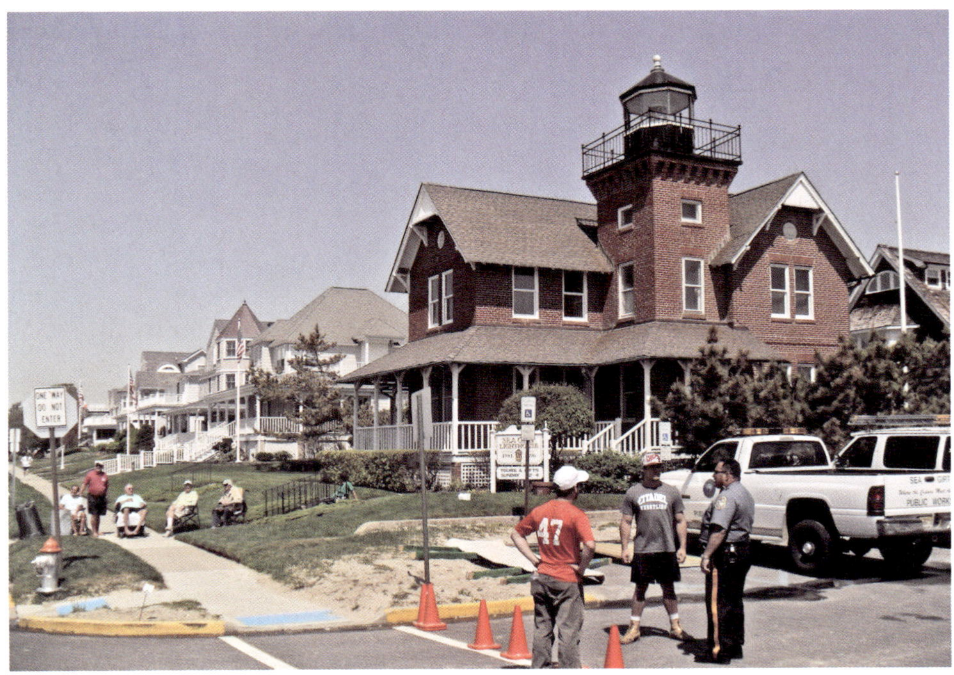

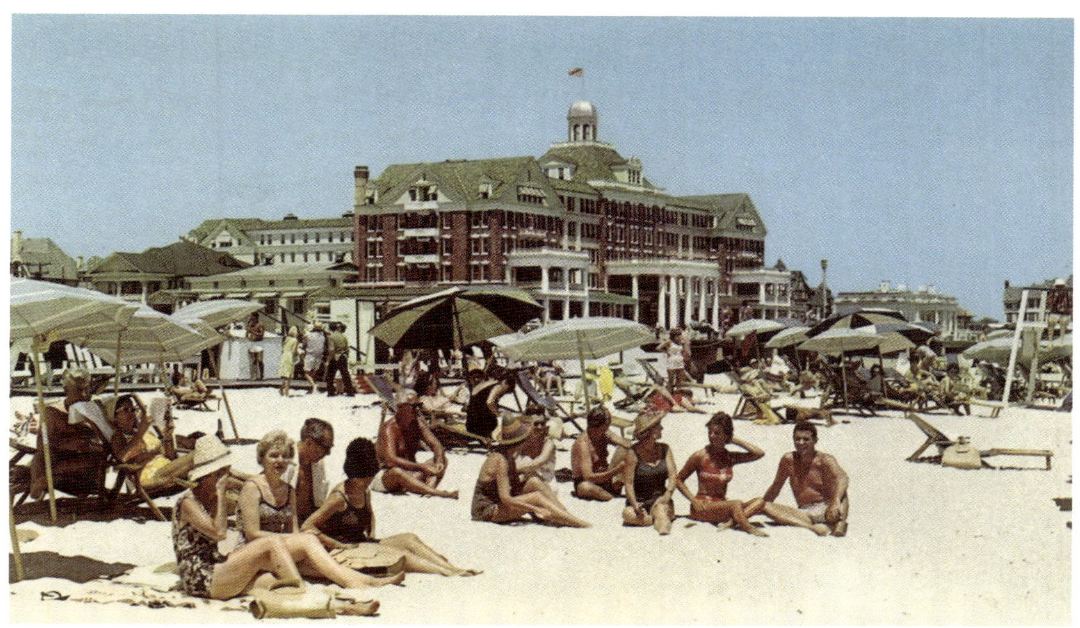

THE ESSEX AND THE SUSSEX HOTEL: The Hotel was launched from the radical reconstruction in 1914 of a much smaller conjunction of two different hotels which had been adjoined about two decades previously. For many years, the Spring Lake Hotel was the most exclusive of the elite oceanfront hotels in Monmouth County. Seen here from the beach in the 1950s, one can also get a good view of the concrete boardwalk pilings which were fabricated by the WPA in the late 1930s. The hotel was remodeled into condo units in the 1990s.

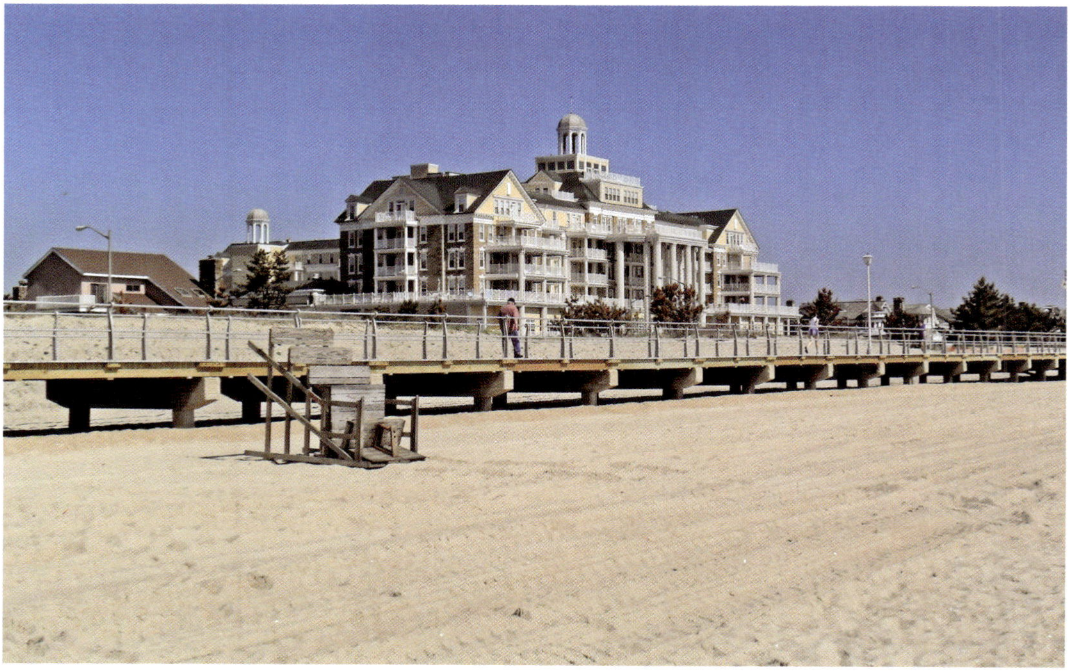

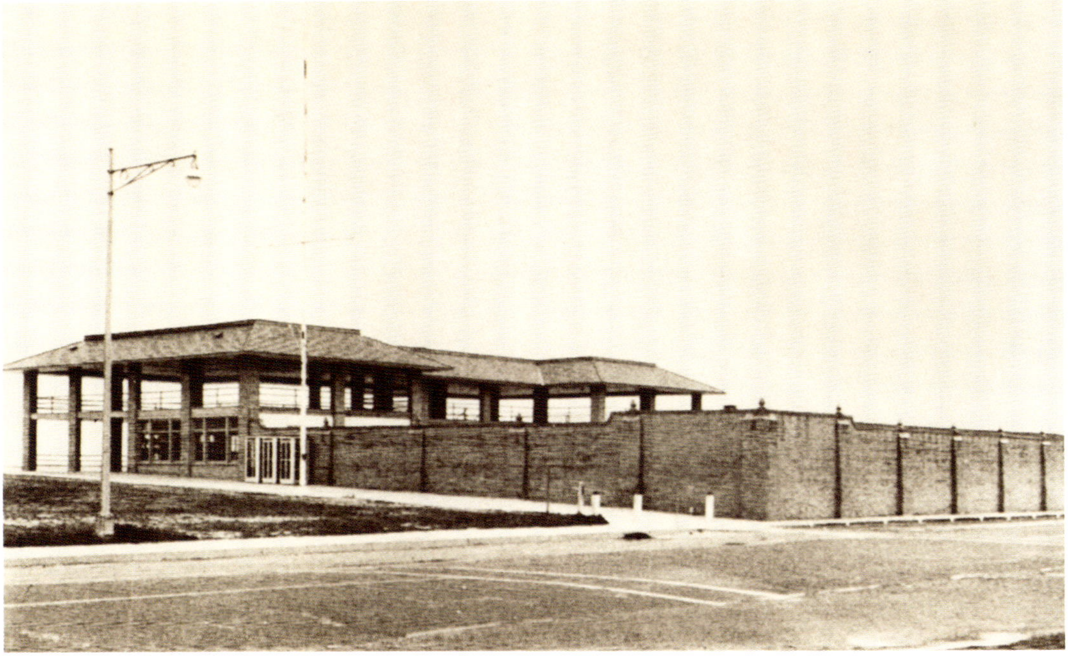

THE SOUTHERN SWIMMING POOL PAVILION IN SPRING LAKE: The Pavilion was built in 1928. Seen here in the late 1960s, the 'Southern Pavilion' as locals know it, was spared from the wrecking ball after plans were devised to replace the similarly-themed swimming complex at the north end of Ocean Avenue. The only remarkable difference to be found here is the absence of the bank of phone booths as the cell phone has rendered such structures obsolete.

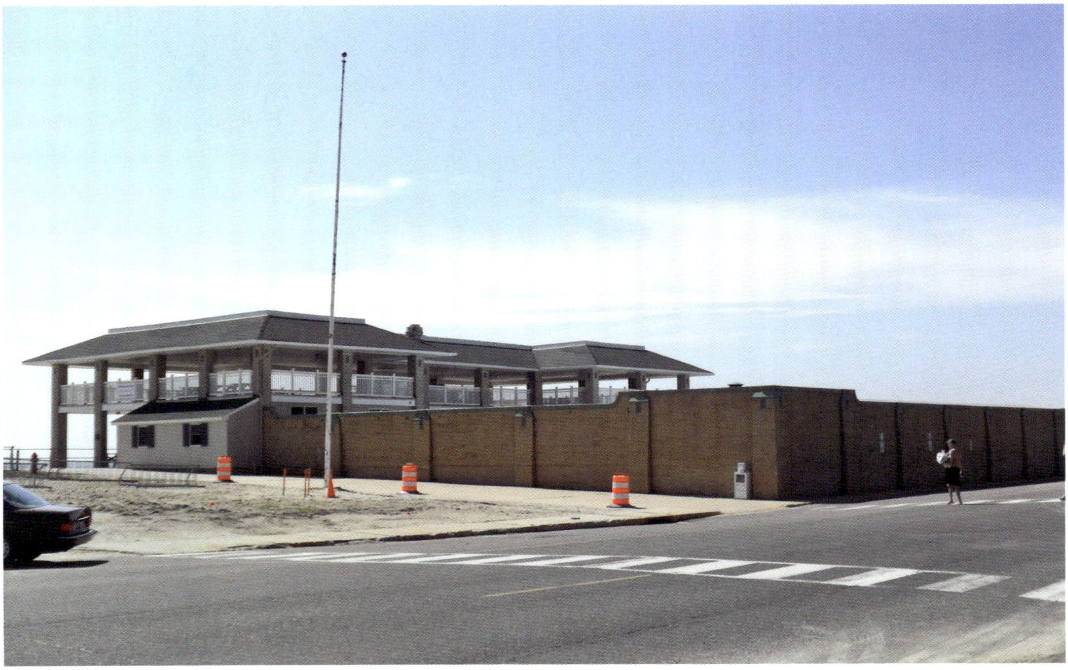

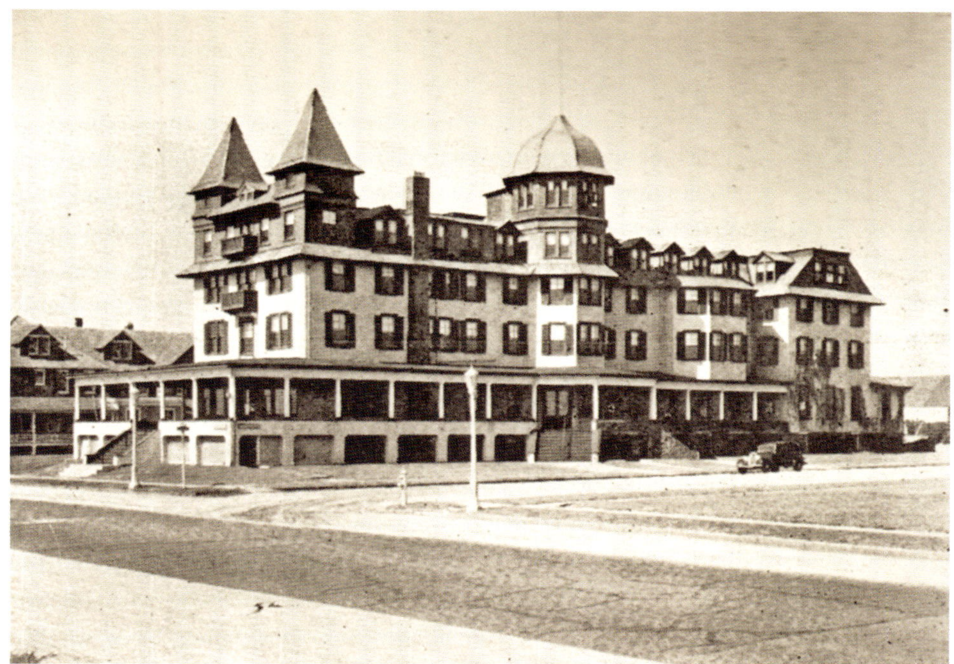

THE BREAKERS: The Breakers is the only grand hotel operating on Ocean Avenue in Spring Lake. Once populated by a wealth of extraordinary hotels which met with different fates over the past century, Ocean Avenue in this town has been redesignated as 'dream house' residential space. The Breakers was built in the late 1880s as the Hotel Wilburton, and has carried its present moniker since 1905. The image here dates from the 1920s.

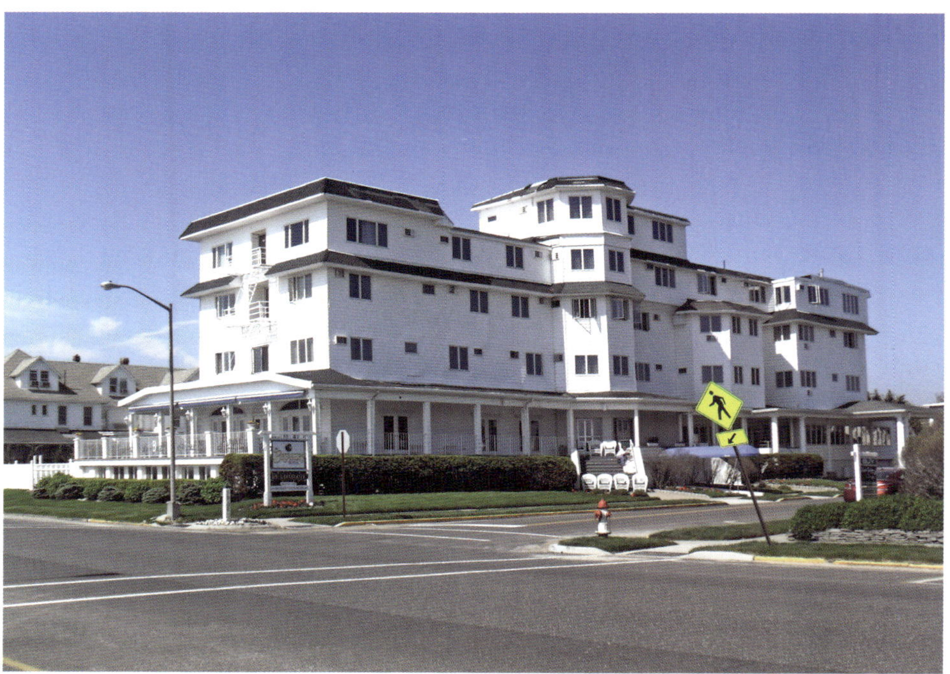

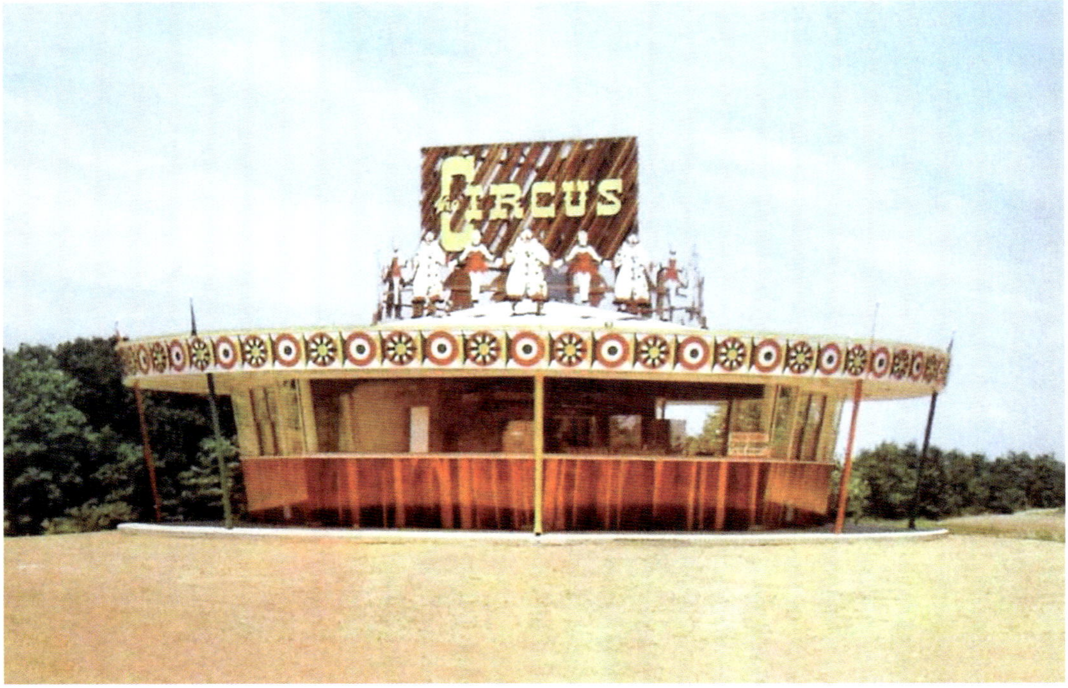

THE CIRCUS DRIVE-IN ON ROUTE 35 IN WALL: The drive-in was built in 1954 when car hop culture was at its peak. The establishment, as depicted on this early 1960s trade card, retains its authenticity as a drive-in and has added protection from the torrential elements that can pervade the Jersey Shore. Despite these upgrades, the Circus remains a seasonal operation, closing for the winter months.

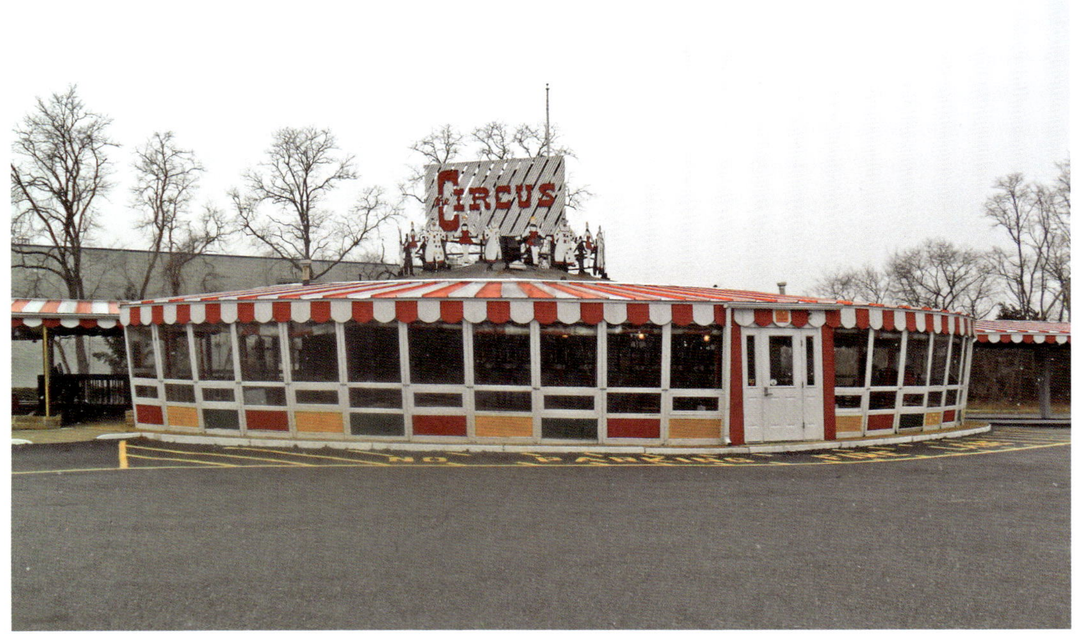

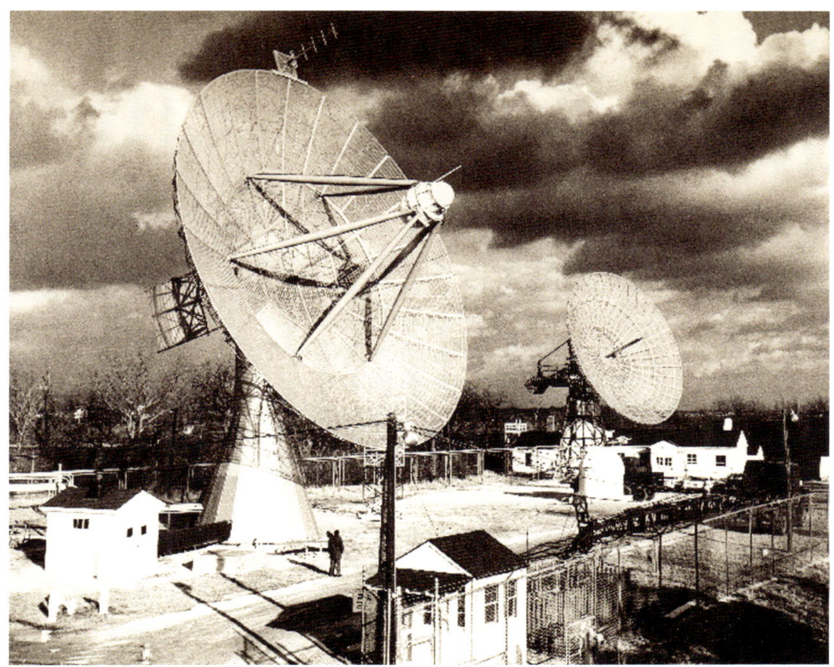

The Impressive Satellite Dish on Marconi Road in Wall: The dish is a remaining testament to the communications work carried on at the top secret army research installation, Camp Evans. The original dish on the right is actually a captured Nazi dish which was brought stateside after the war. This 1960 photo shows the site as the command center for the early TIROS weather satellites. The station is currently cared for by the Ocean-Monmouth Amateur Radio Club, who are having the dish restored, and hope to use it in conjunction with their radio club.

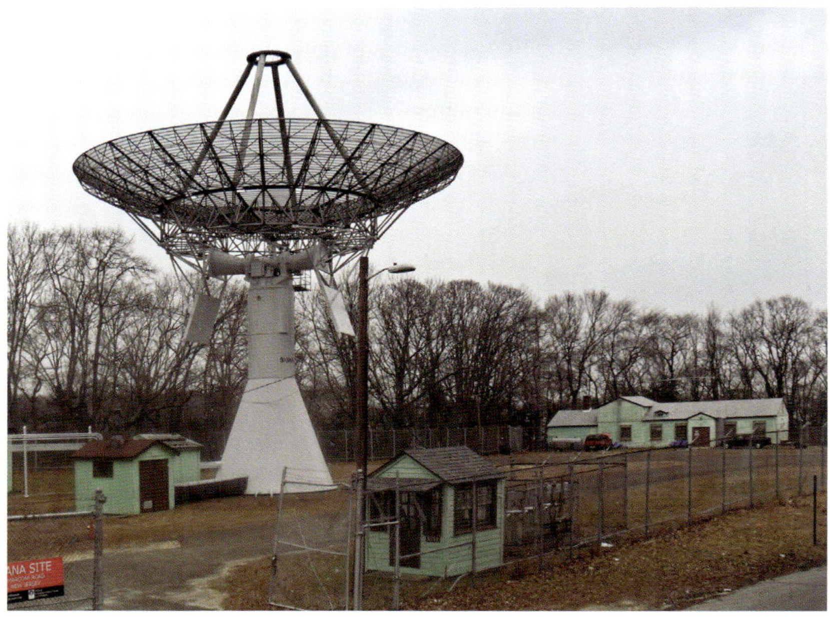

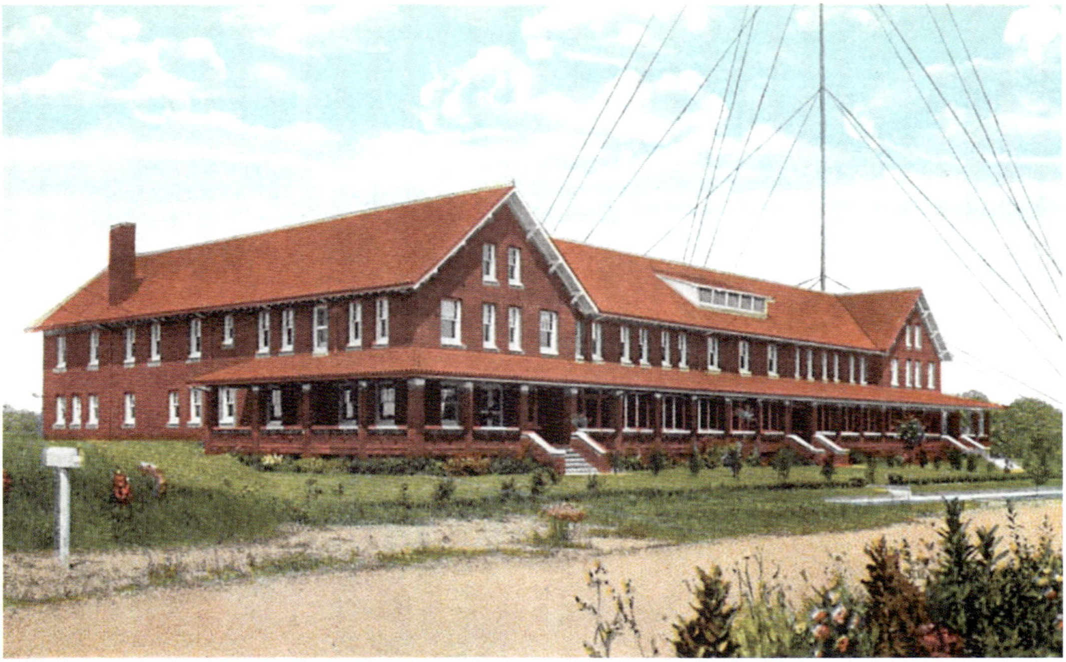

Marconi's Headquarters: Famed Italian inventor Guglielmo Marconi built his wireless research headquarters in the marshy southern shore of Shark River in 1913. The Marconi Hotel, which served as dormitory quarters for Marconi researchers is pictured here shortly thereafter. After the closure of Camp Evans, the non-profit organization Infoage has cared for the buildings and operate rotating exhibits of technological equipment, and a well-known 'Haunted Hotel' attraction during Hallowe'en.

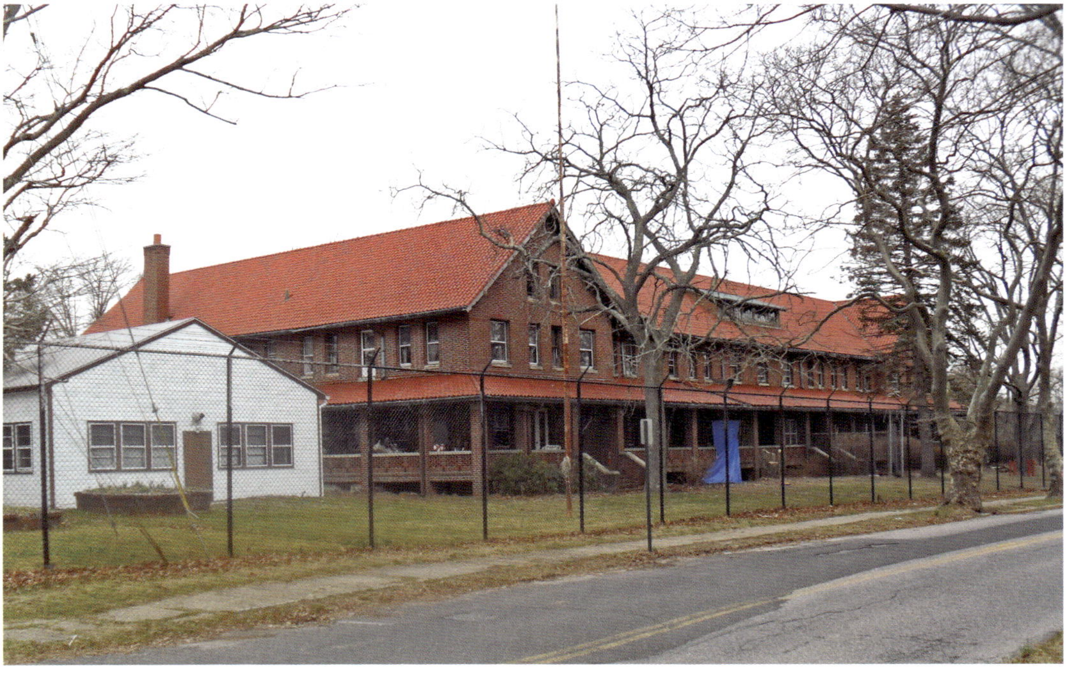

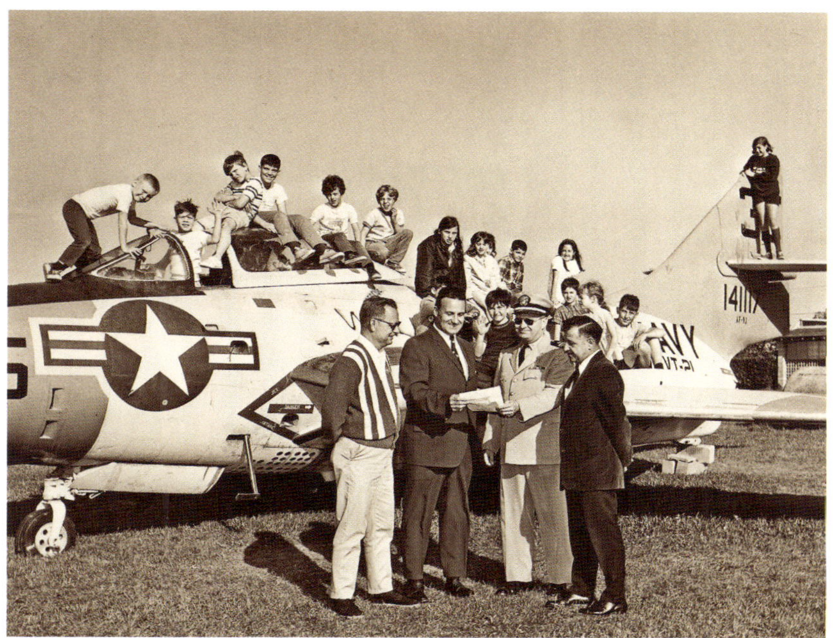

The Cougar F9: In 1969, a retired Cougar F9 was moved from Lakehurst Naval Air Station to the Wall Recreation Center at the fork of Belmar Boulevard and New Bedford Road. The plane was the park's principle attraction until it was removed in 1987 for safety reasons. After a lengthy restoration, the Cougar was brought back to the public in 2011, when it became part of the revolving display of aircraft at the Intrepid Museum in New York Harbor.

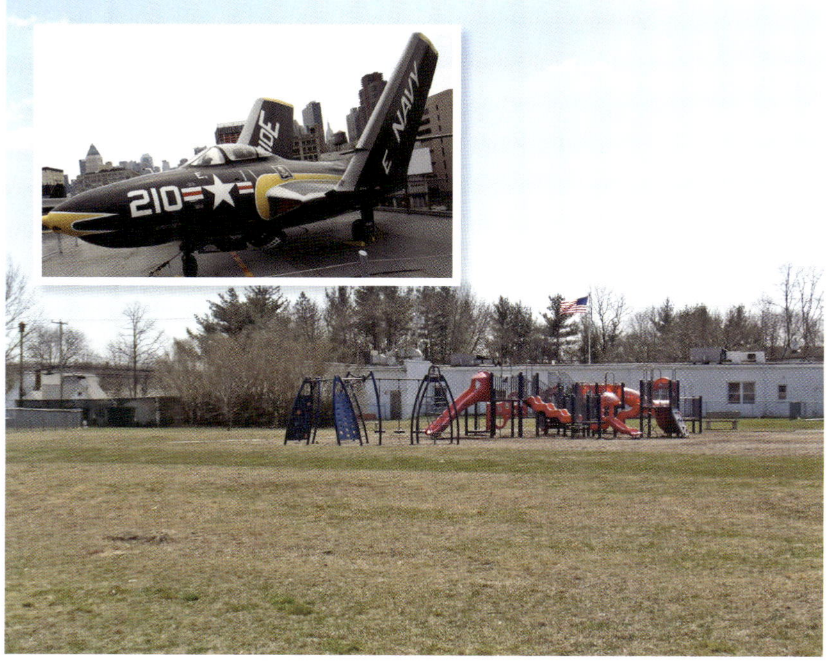

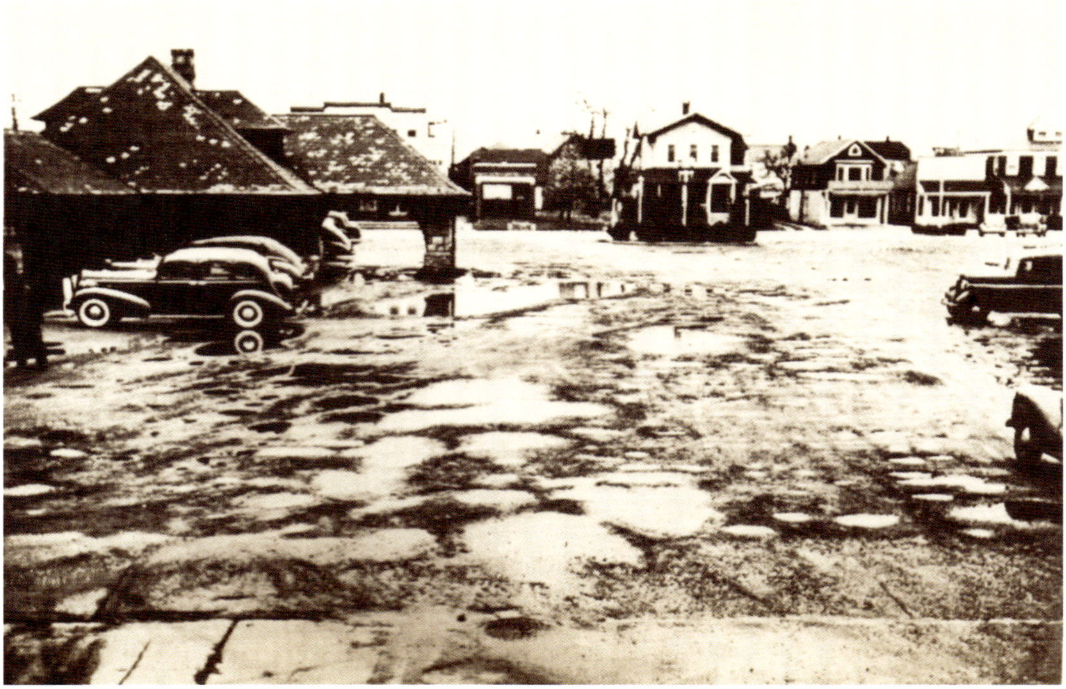

BELMAR TRAIN STATION: The station is pictured here in the late 1920s. The station building itself is the only recognizable feature of the plaza located in the heart of the downtown Belmar business district. It appears that the local seagulls have learned some etiquette while conducting their business over the past century when one compares the cleanliness of roof of the station in the images.

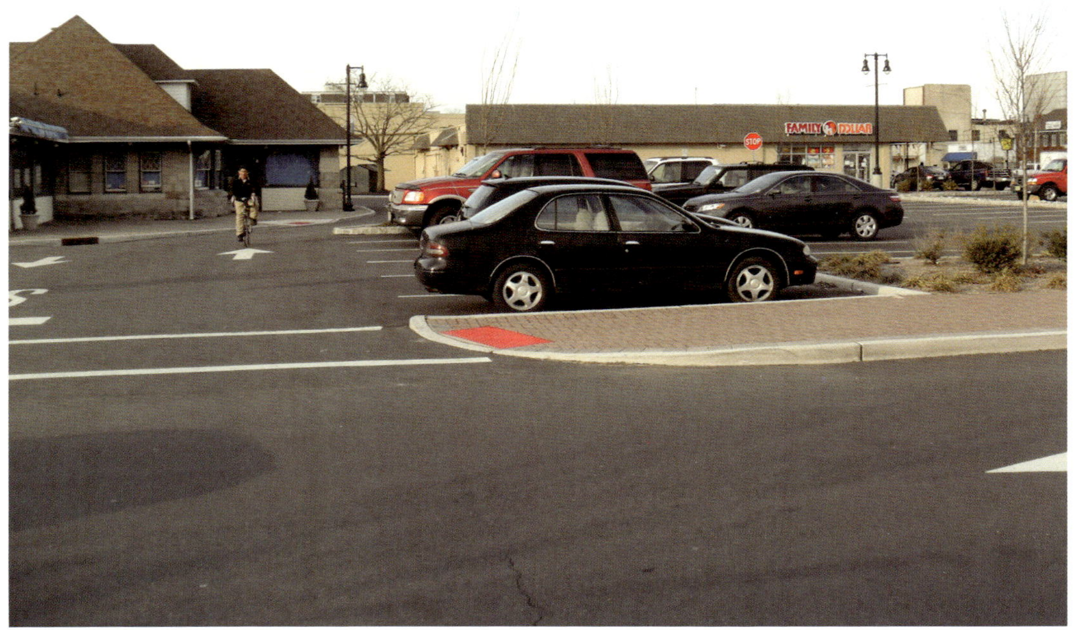

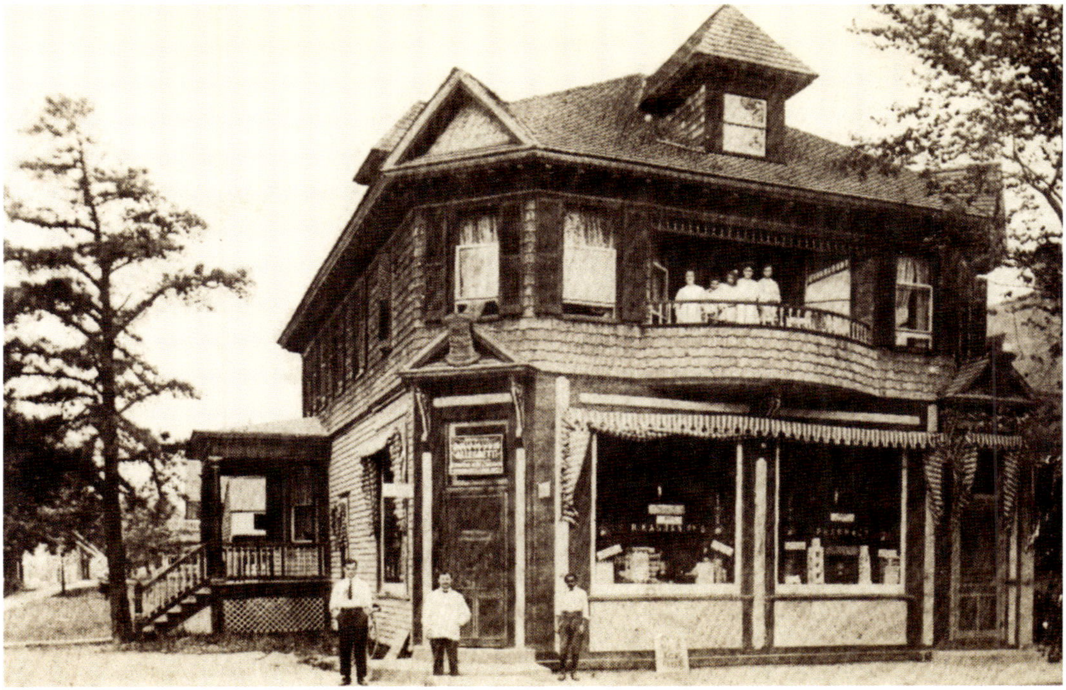

THE KASDAN PHARMACY: The pharmacy was one of the original Main Street structures in Belmar. Pictured here during the first decade of the twentieth century, the building has undergone significant structural changes, most notably the removal of the second floor. The basic layout of the first floor, with its signature corner entrance, remains intact.

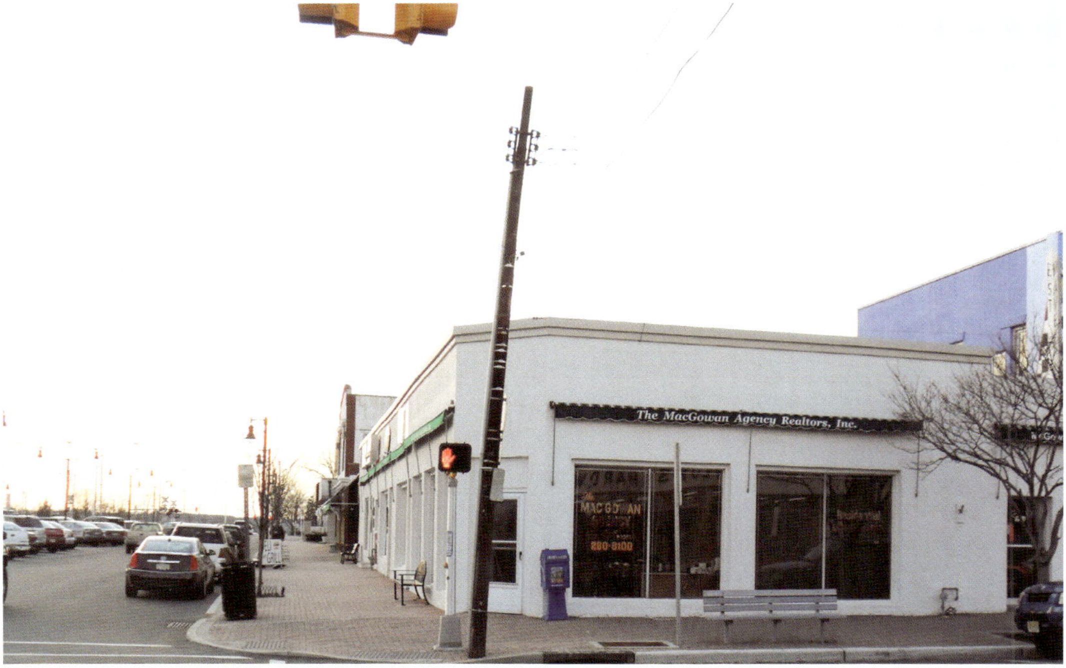

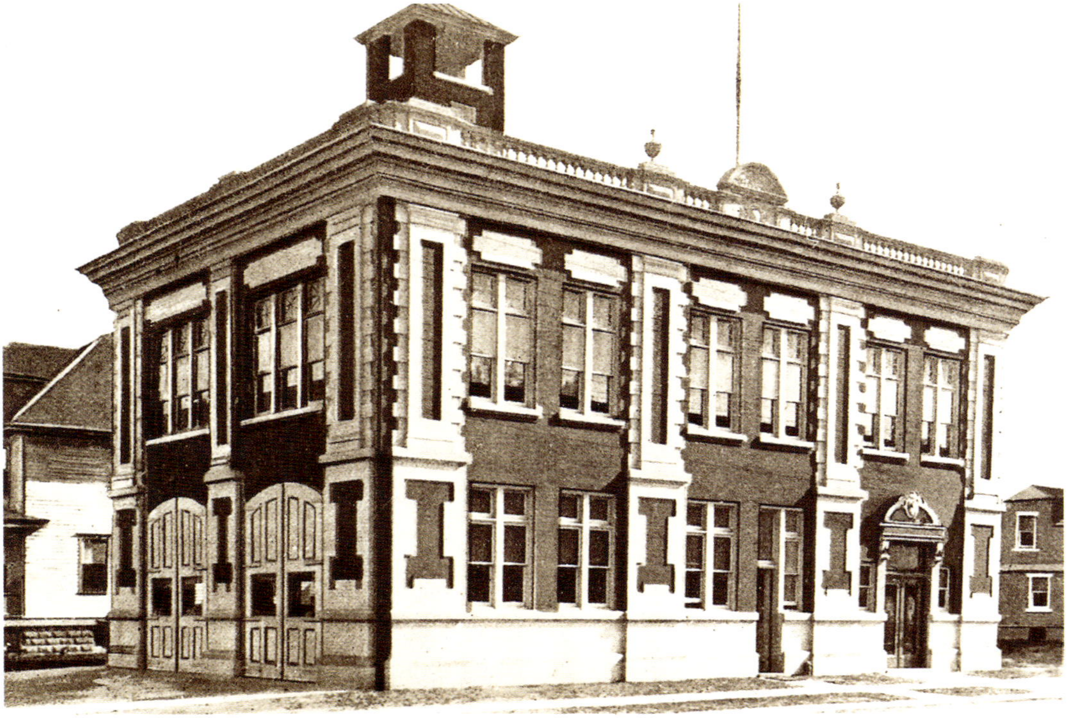

THE UNION FIRE HOUSE: The fire house was built in 1911 at the corner of 9th Avenue and E Street in Belmar. Pictured shortly after its construction, the notable changes include an addition along E Street and the removal of the lookout tower.

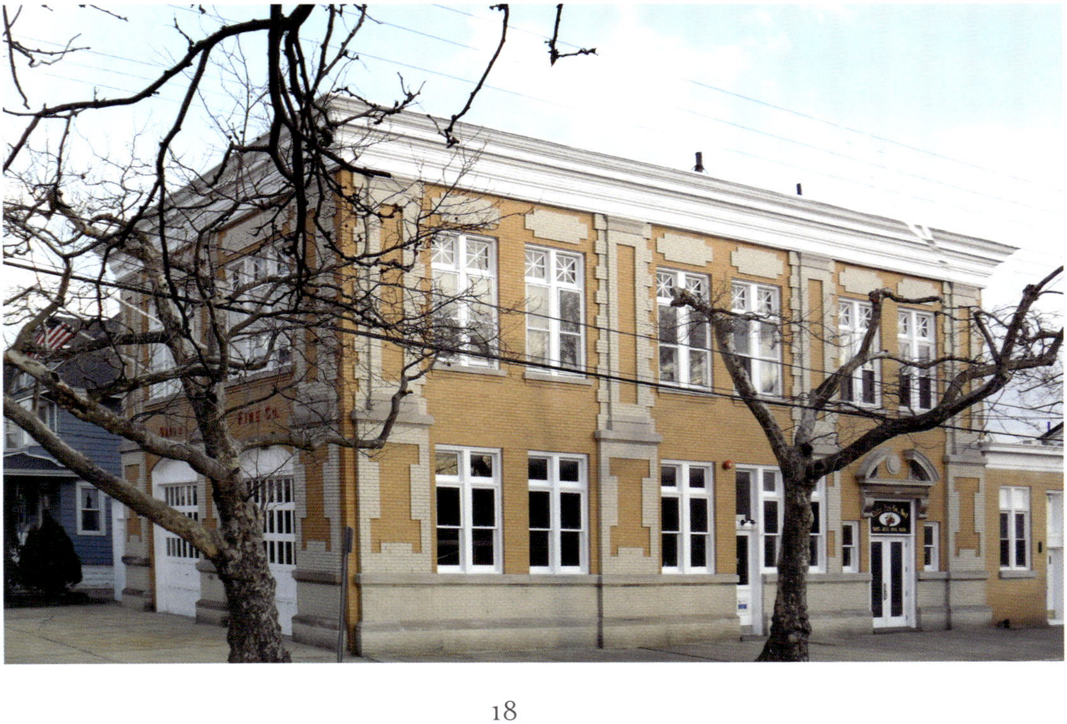

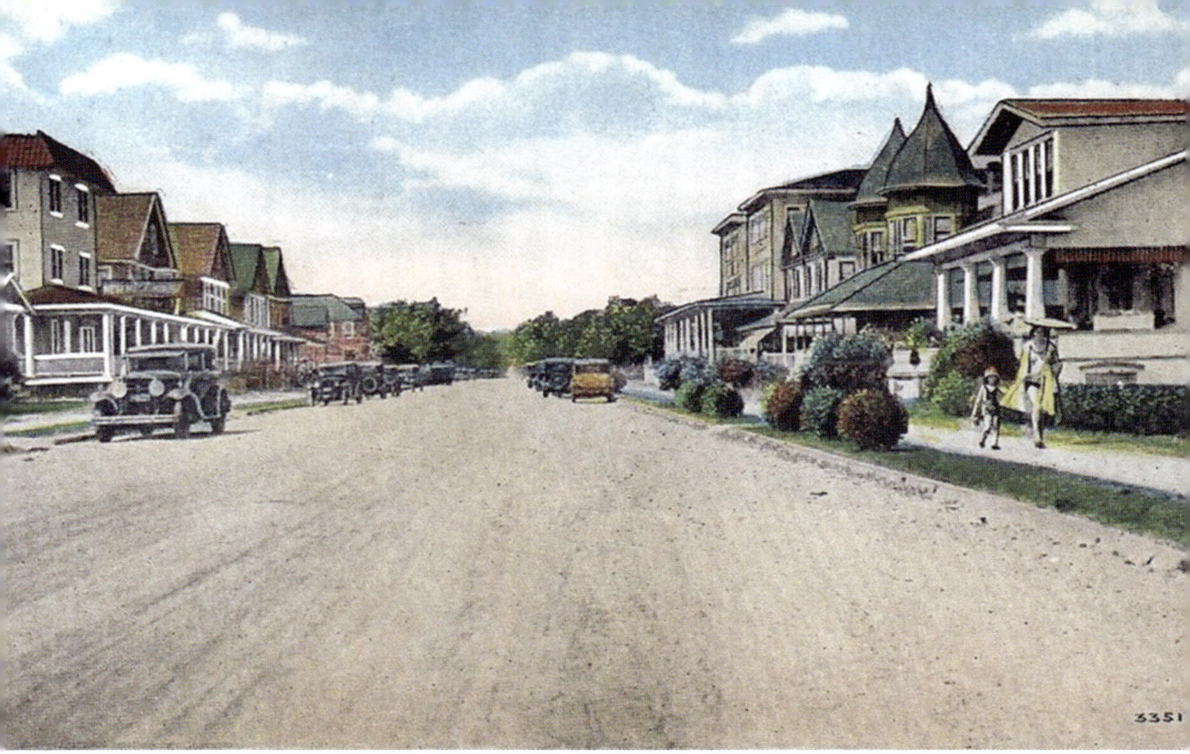

TWELFTH AVENUE: This 1920s postcard view of Twelth Avenue looking west from Ocean Avenue in Belmar shows that the block has remained remarkably intact, despite the many poundings that Mother Nature has dealt to the Belmar oceanfront. Unlike neighboring Spring Lake, Belmar still has many operational hotels in their oceanfront sector which trace their origins to nearly a century ago.

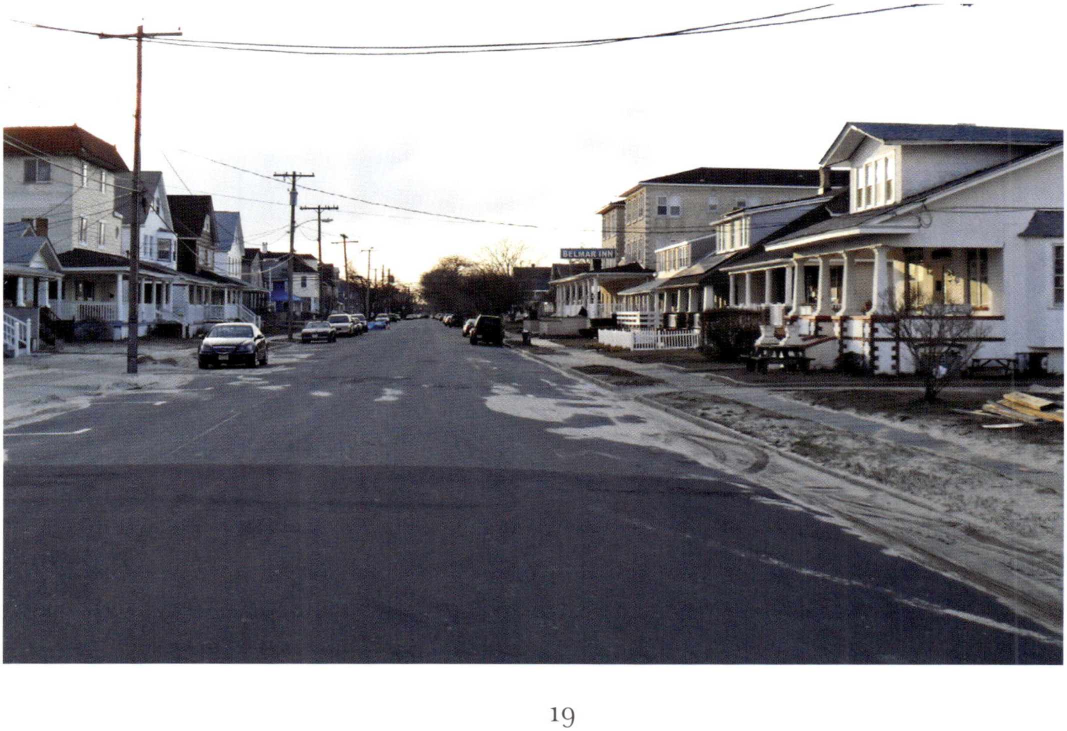

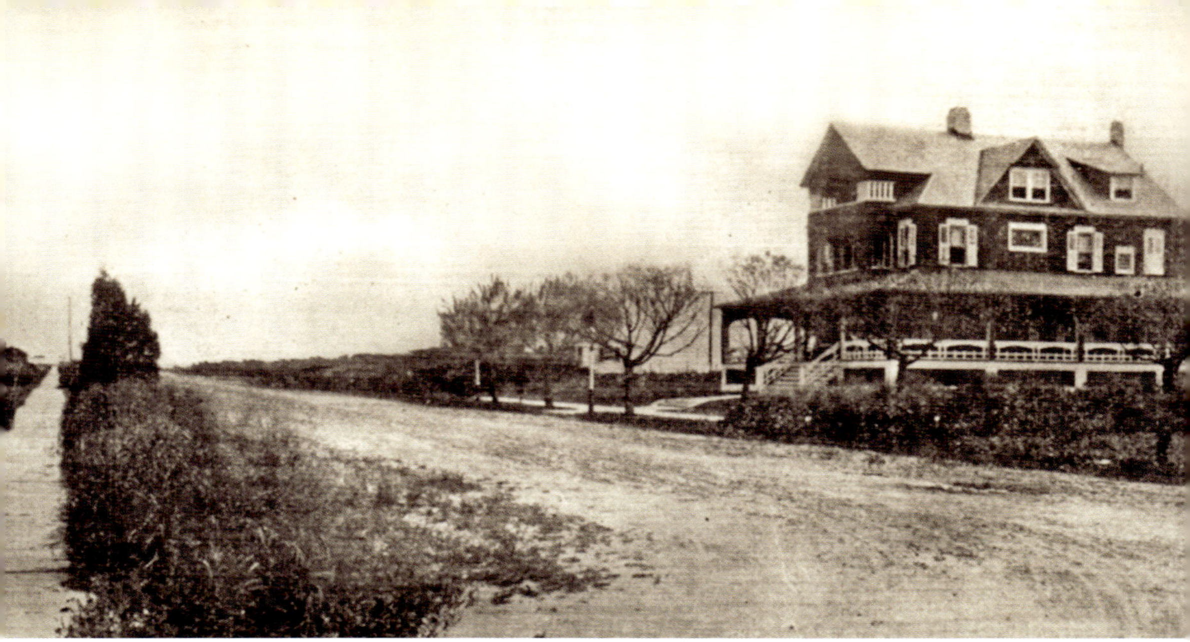

AVON-BY-THE-SEA: One can truly appreciate the development of Avon-by-the-Sea when studying this photo comparison from 1900, the year of the town's founding. The view is the intersection of Garfield and Second Avenue, looking east toward the ocean. Today's reader may find it hard to fathom that there are no buildings on the Garfield 100 block, the prime real estate nearest to the beach.

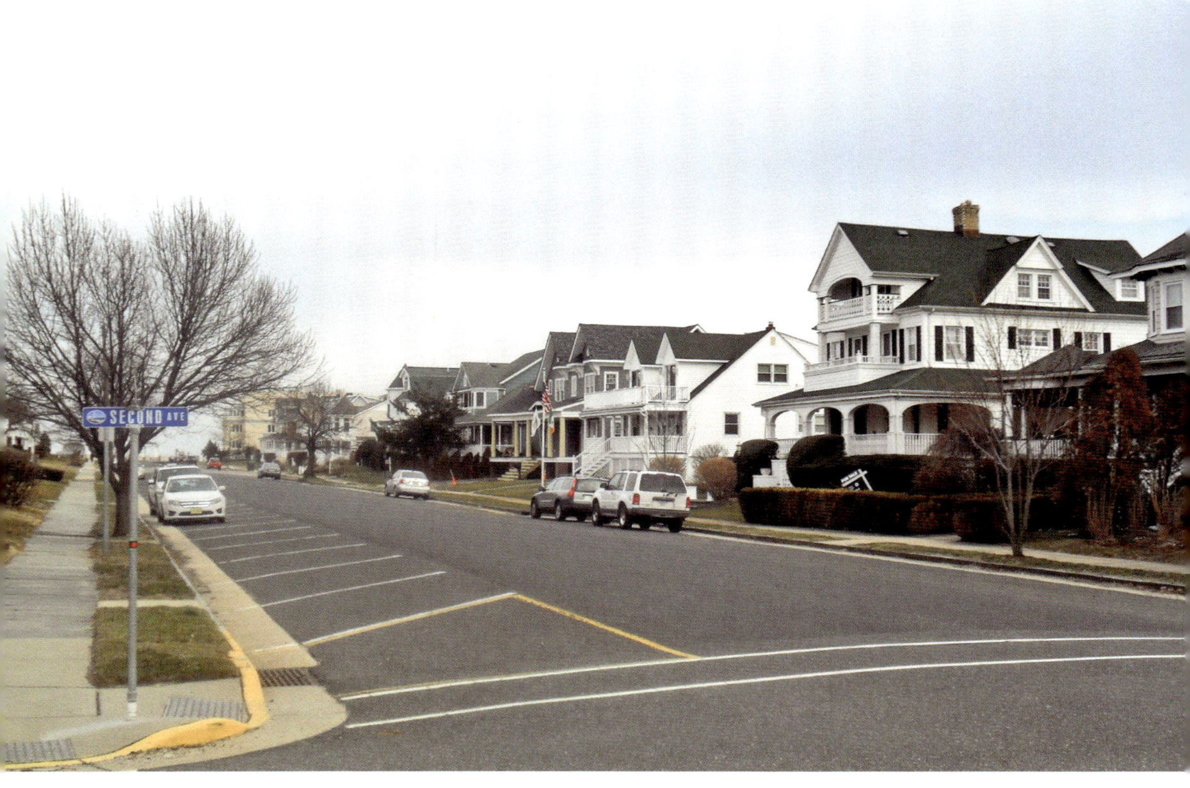

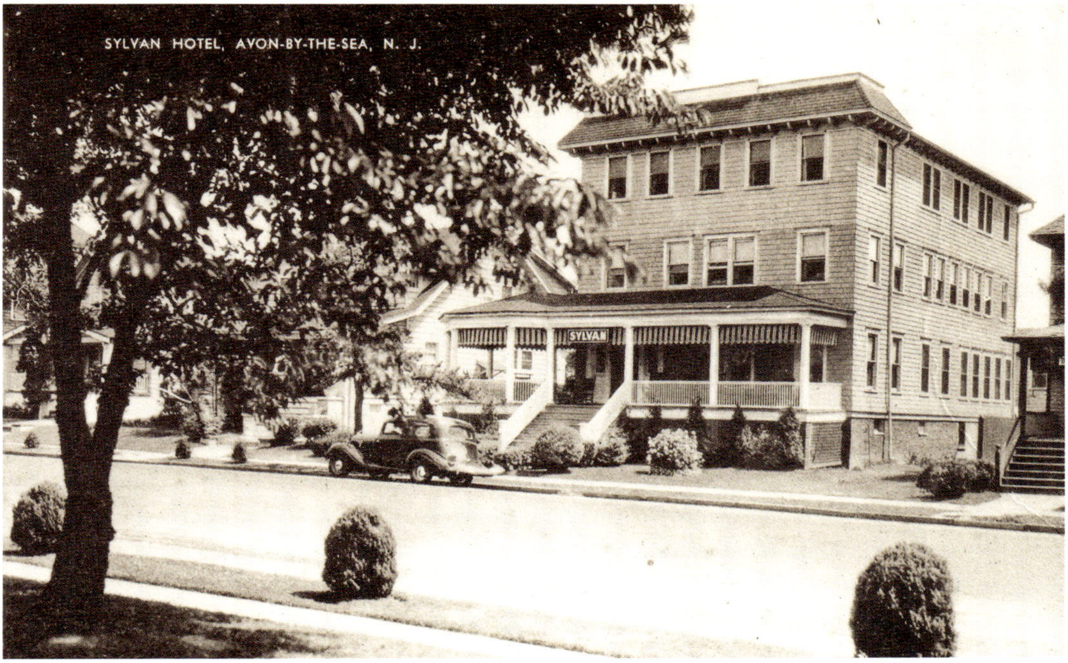

THE SYLVAN HOTEL: The former Sylvan Hotel in Avon is still somewhat recognizable, despite extensive alterations to the building's front wall, on its namesake Sylvania Avenue. This 1930s view captures the quiet residential sector which still endures and has been the retention factor for families living in Avon for many generations.

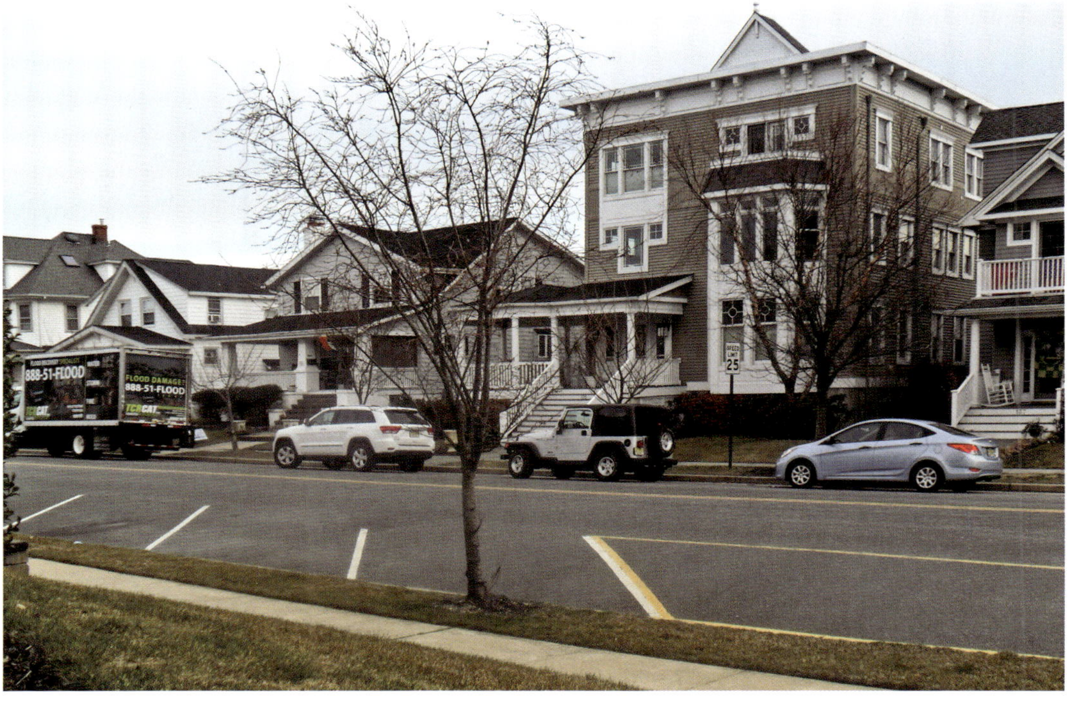

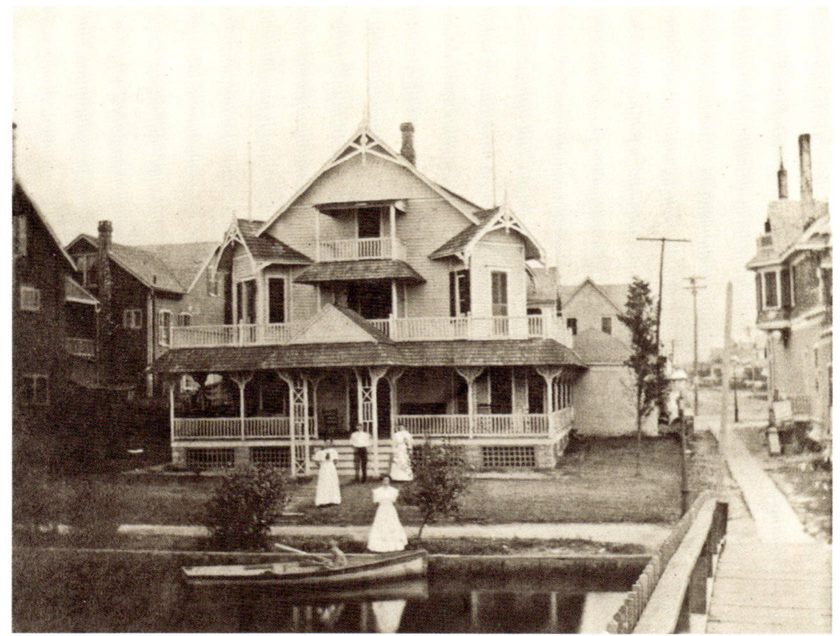

BRADLEY BEACH: This interesting image of a Bradley Beach residence is from a private mailing card from early in the twentieth century. Even more interesting is the documentation of Lake Terrace when it existed only as a narrow footpath. During the late 1950s, the borough of Bradley Beach embarked on a project to add fill to Fletcher Lake to carve out an important automotive route along its northern border.

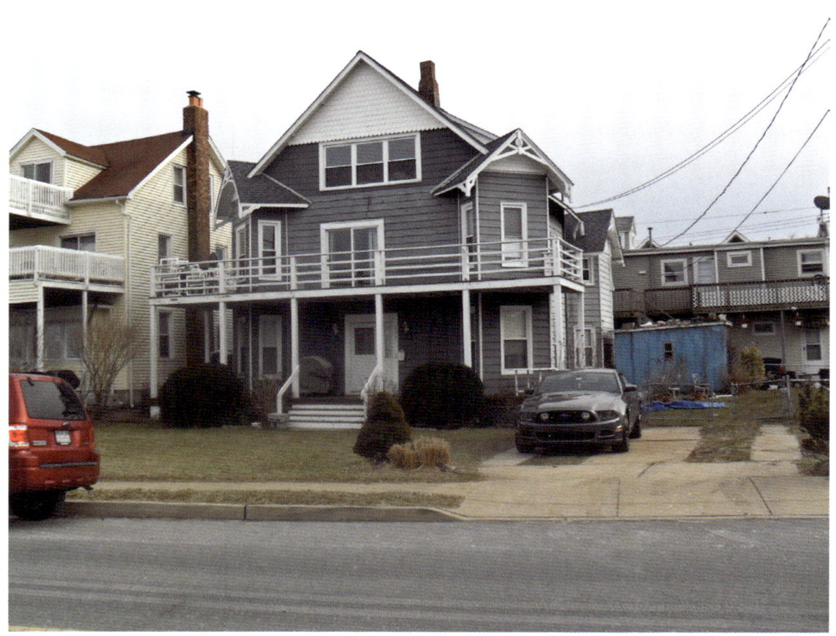

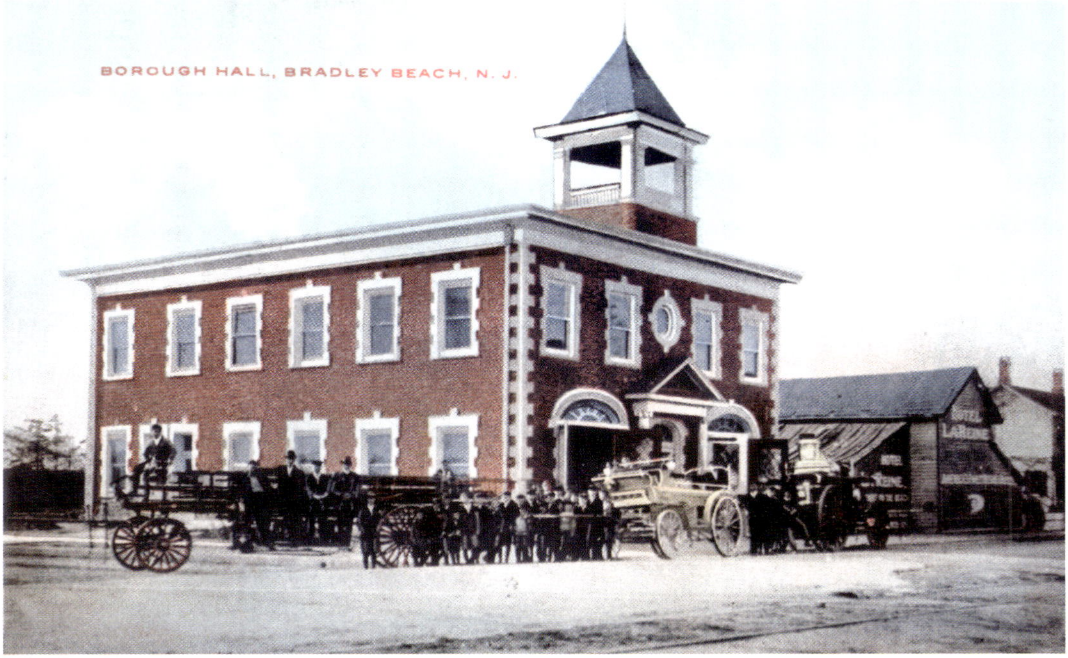

BRADLEY BEACH BOROUGH HALL: The Hall is pictured shortly after its completion in 1900. The LaReine Hotel, which for many years operated at the intersection of Ocean and LaReine Avenues ran a small annex building on the lot next to the borough hall. This was eventually torn down when the municipal body purchased the adjoining lots for expansion of their operations.

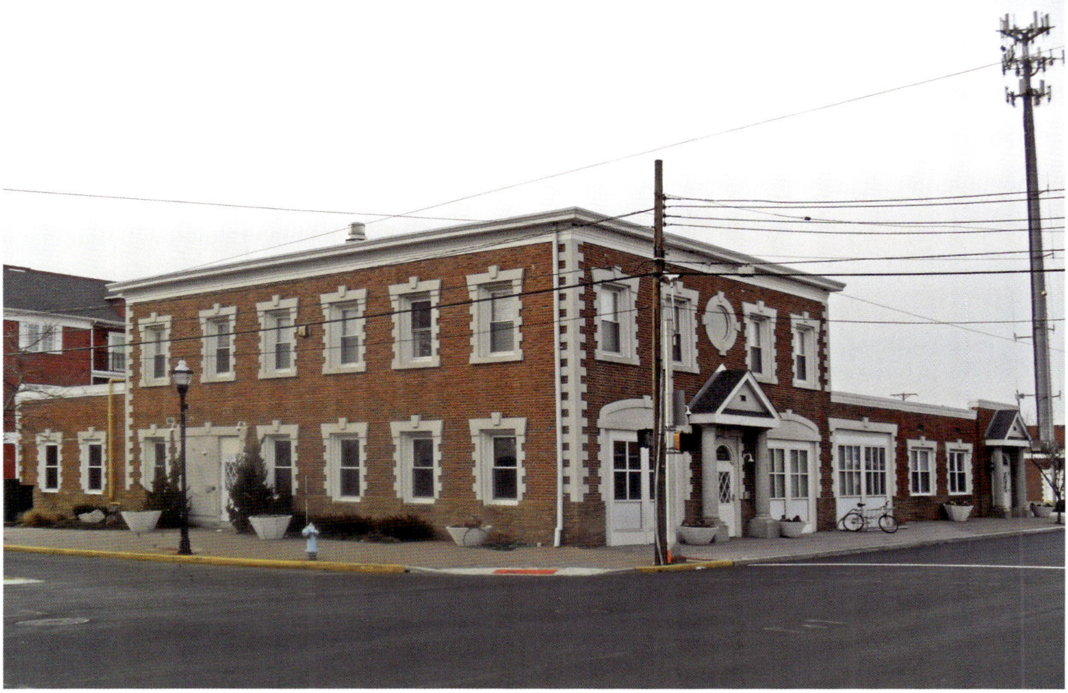

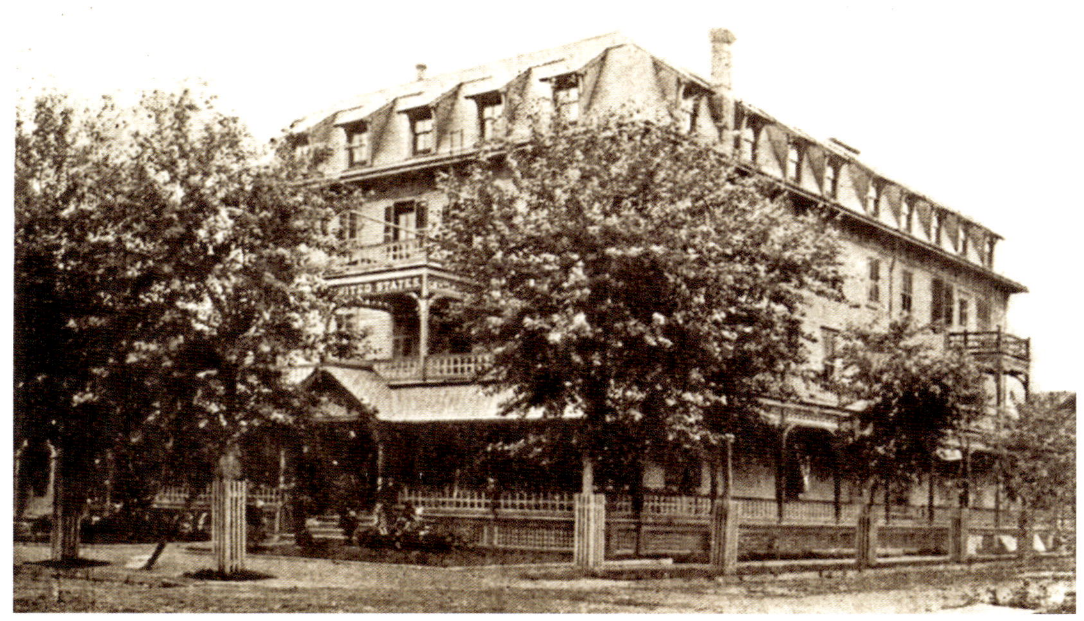

OCEAN GROVE: This is the site for many years of the Grand Atlantic Hotel in Ocean Grove which is pictured here in the 1890s in its original incarnation as the United States Hotel. During the depression, the hotel continued to thrive, thanks in part to the opening of a very reasonable cafeteria on the first floor. For decades after the depression, the Grand Atlantic cafeteria continued to be a destination for those locals 'in-the-know' seeking to chow down on excellent food at extremely reasonable prices.

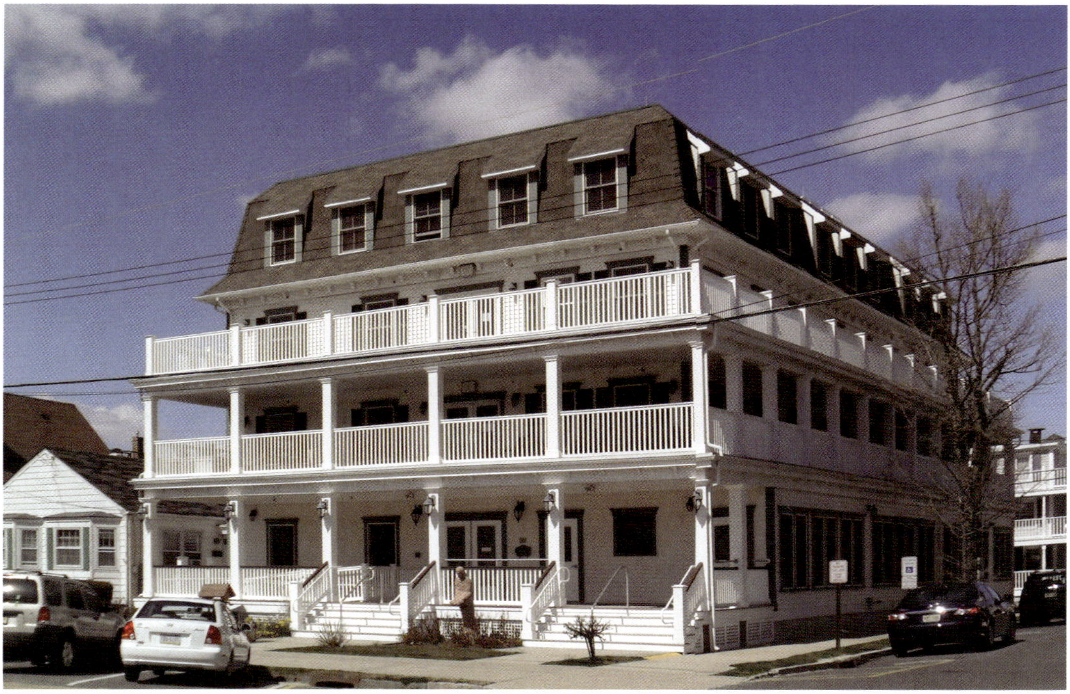

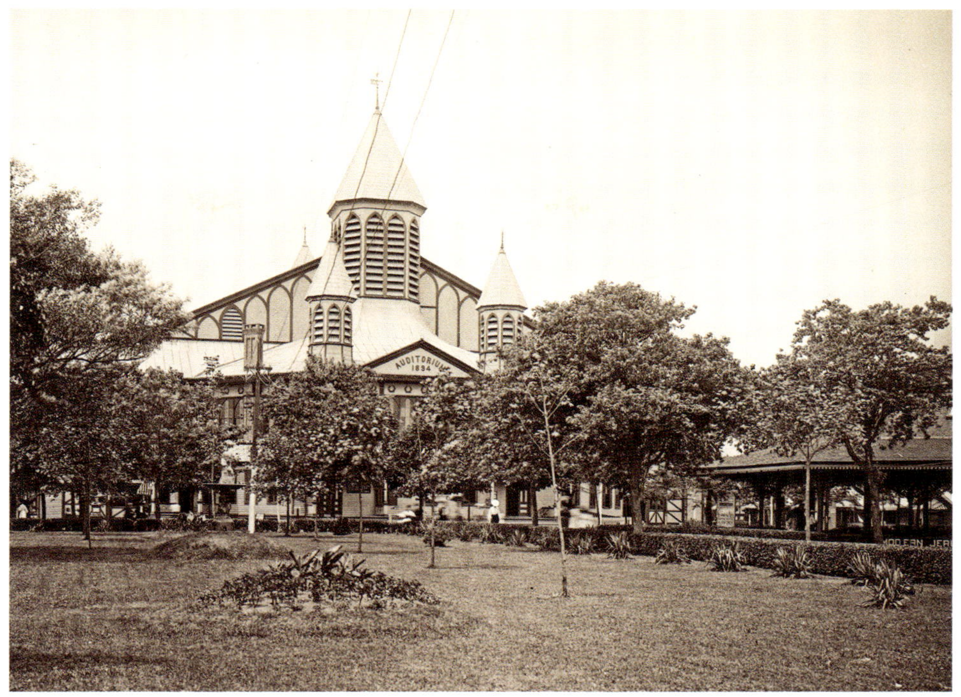

THE GREAT AUDITORIUM IN OCEAN GROVE: The Auditorium is a remarkable wooden structure which has survived and endured in a beachfront community for well over a century. Constructed in 1894 as the centerpiece of the Camp Meeting Association, the auditorium continues to be a popular venue for both traditional religious functions presented by the Association and non-religious concerts and entertainment presentations alike.

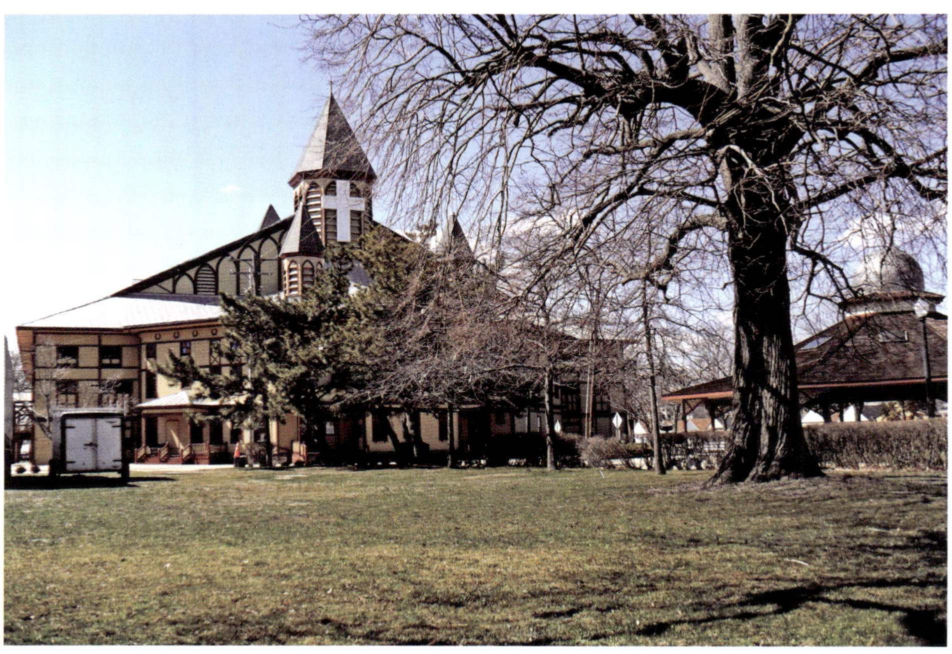

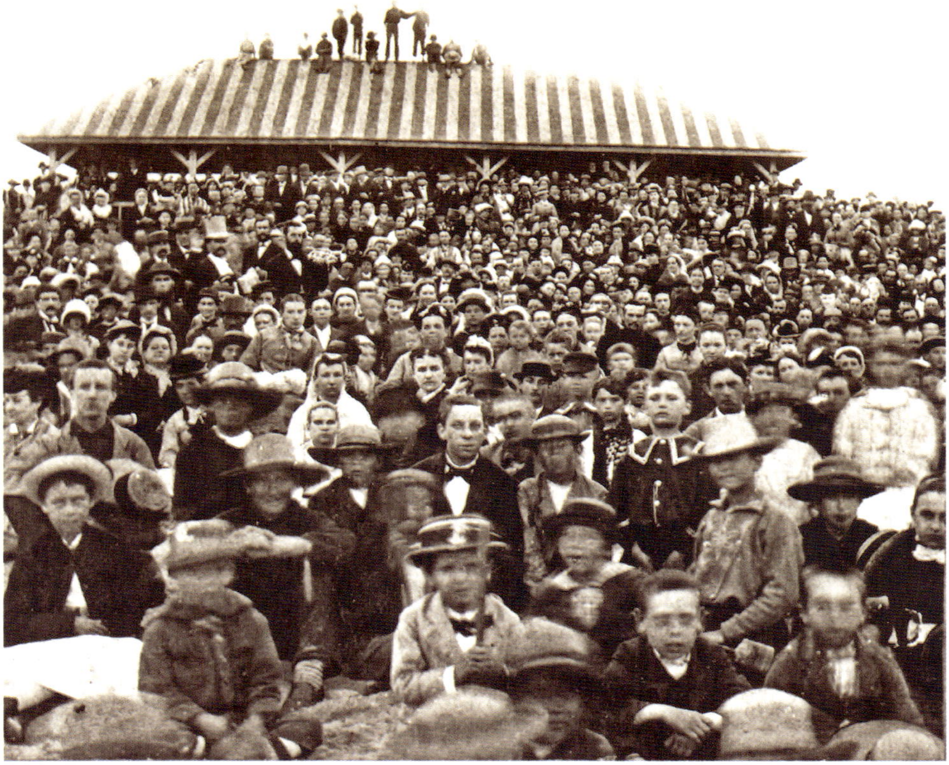

THE SUMMER WEEKLY SURF PRAYER MEETINGS: The meetings were held on Sunday afternoons in the open-air pavilion on the beach at the foot of Ocean Pathway in Ocean Grove were known for many years to draw huge crowds. Pictured here during the early years of Ocean Grove in the mid 1870s, the pavilion has been rebuilt a number of times, but remains essentially the same. Beach lockers currently occupy the space immediately in front of the pavilion, but it remains a perfect spot for a Sunday picnic, regardless.

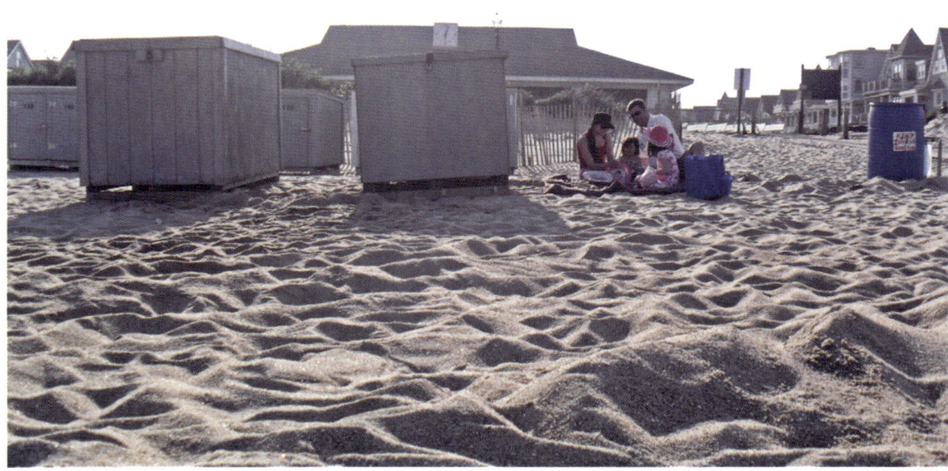

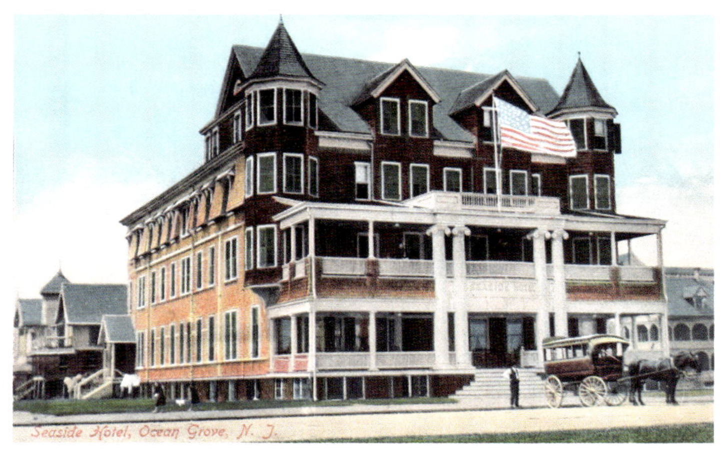

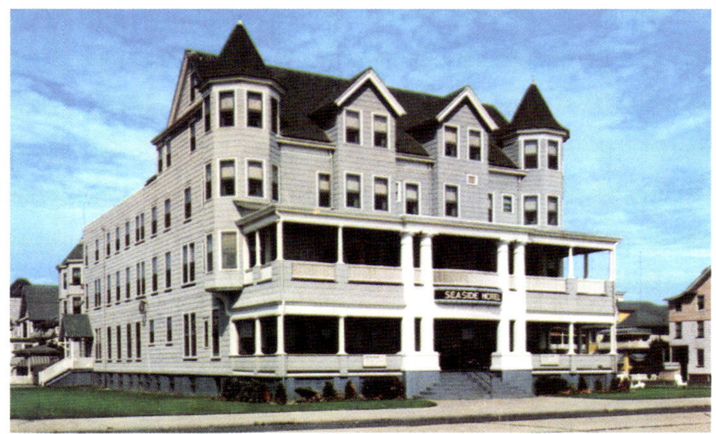

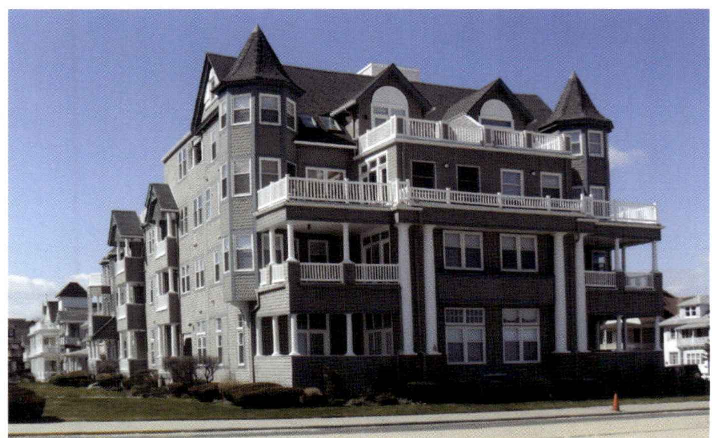

THE SEASIDE HOTEL: The hotel was constructed in the 1890s at the corner of Seaview and Ocean Avenues. Seen here in the 1900s, 1950s, and 2013 the structure remains remarkably intact. It has been converted into condominium units, a stroke of fate which has saved many of the grand hotels of Monmouth County.

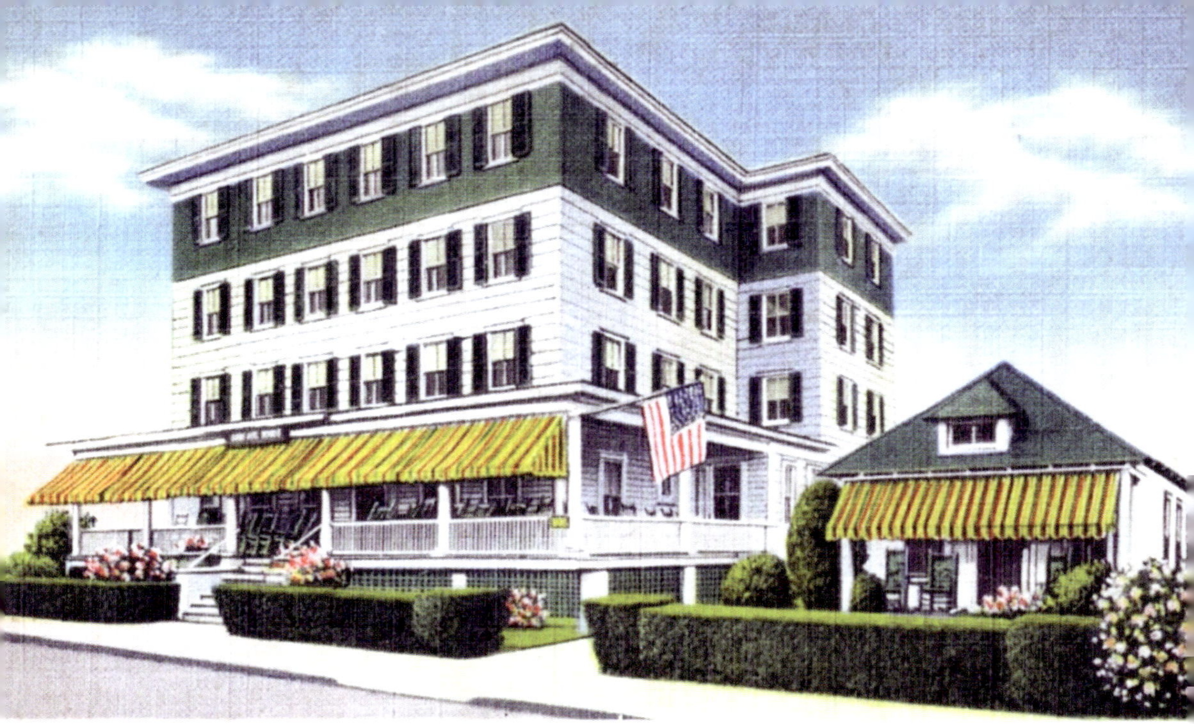

SURF AVENUE HOUSE: 'Going retro' seems to be the redevelopment trend in Ocean Grove. The former Surf Avenue House is given its final touches on its 2013 Victorian retrograde. Perhaps in a few years, nobody will remember the building as depicted on this 1940s postcard – in the form in which it was built and existed for over a century. The restaurant building has been conservationally spared, however.

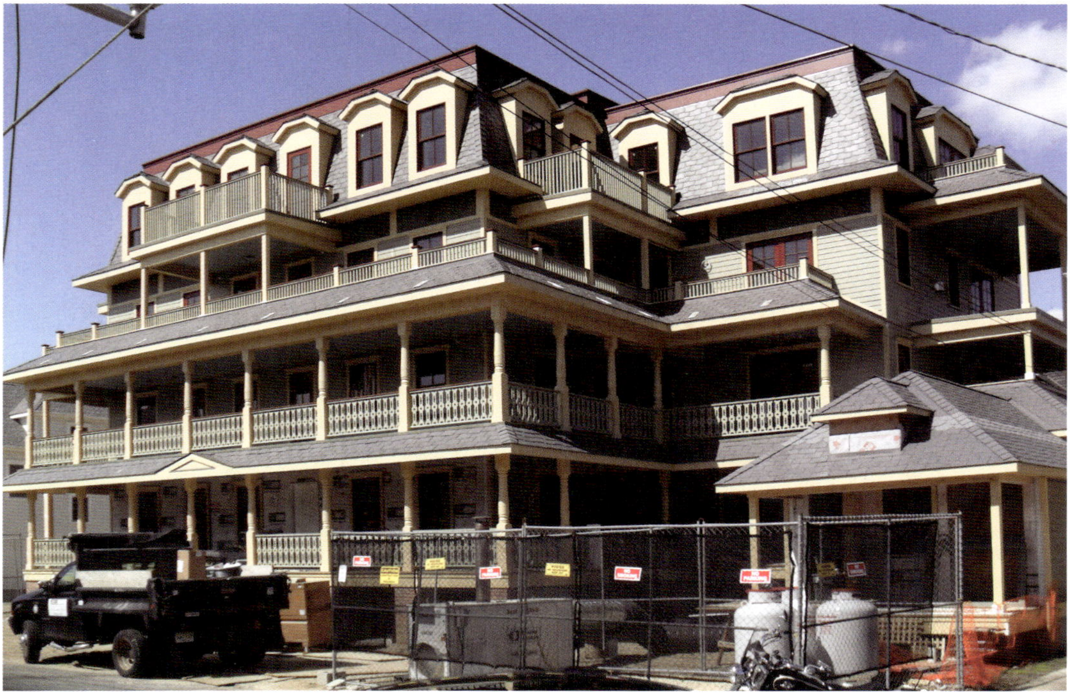

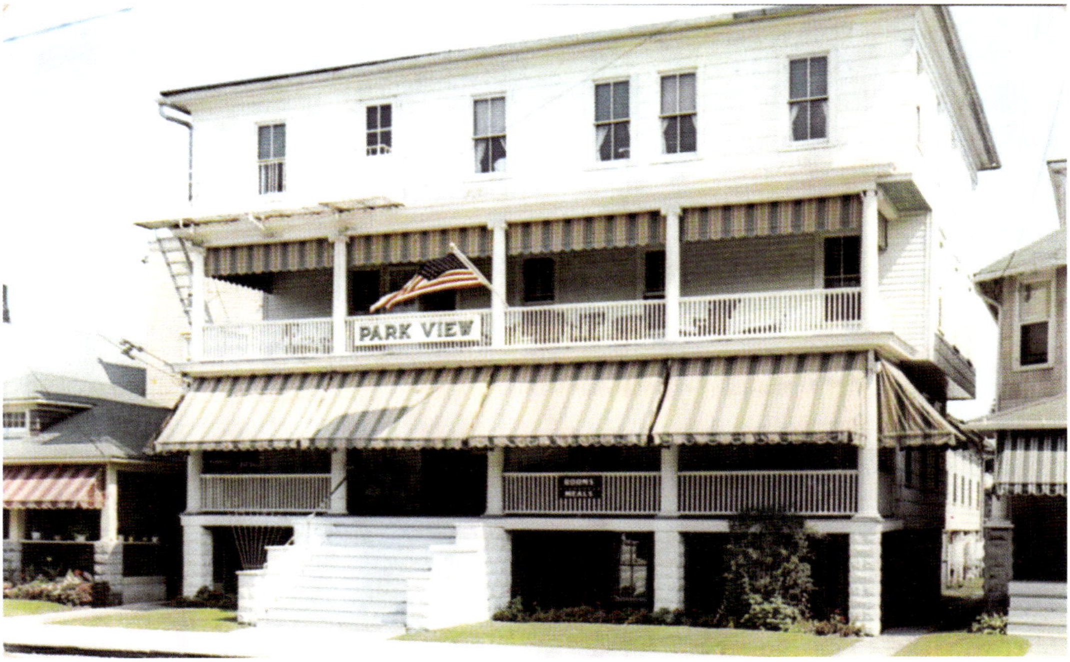

PARK VIEW INN: Not every old building in Ocean Grove is as lucky as the Surf Avenue House. Pictured in the 1950s, the sadly abandoned Park View Inn wearily awaits her fate. Built as two boarding houses in 1885, the structures were combined to form the present configuration in 1895. Closed in 2006, the Seaview Avenue structure's state of disrepair has since been a oft-spoken local concern.

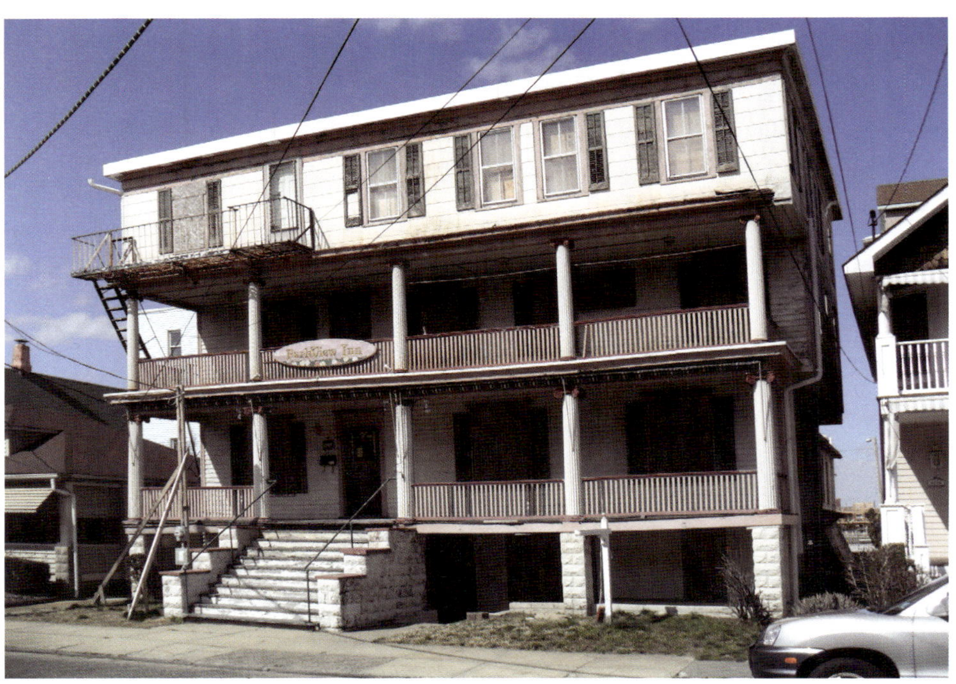

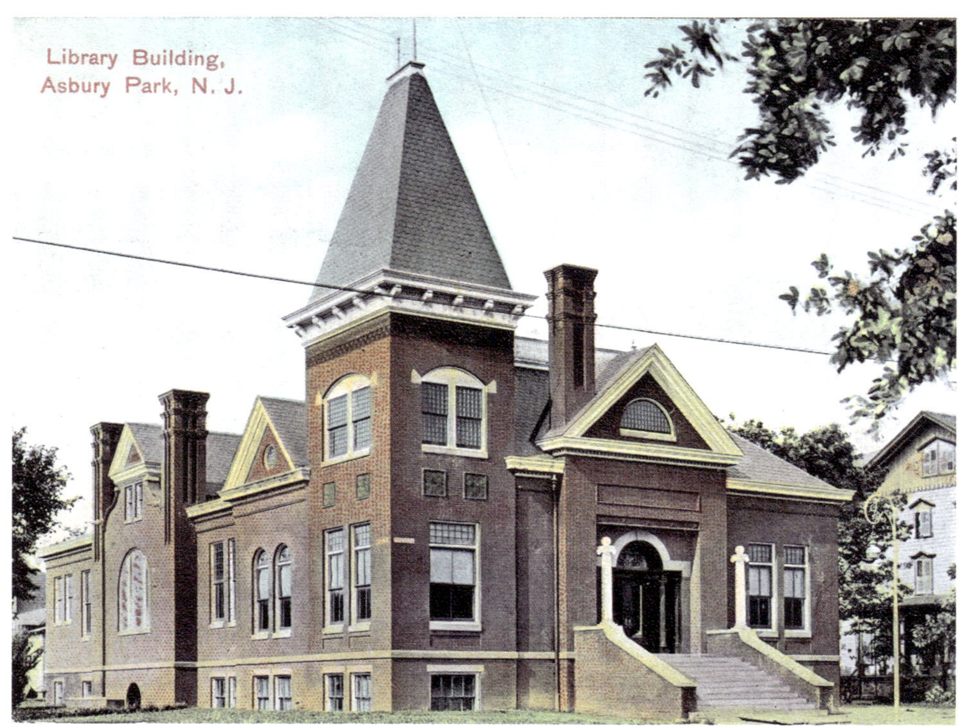

ASBURY PARK PUBLIC LIBRARY: Helen Bradley, the wife of the founder of Asbury Park, James Bradley, made the success of the Asbury Park Public Library her personal passion. Construction began in 1881, and the library still boasts beautiful stained-glass Tiffany windows. In 1930 the building's front gable and tower were removed. The library has an unparalleled collection of historic local newspapers available on microfilm.

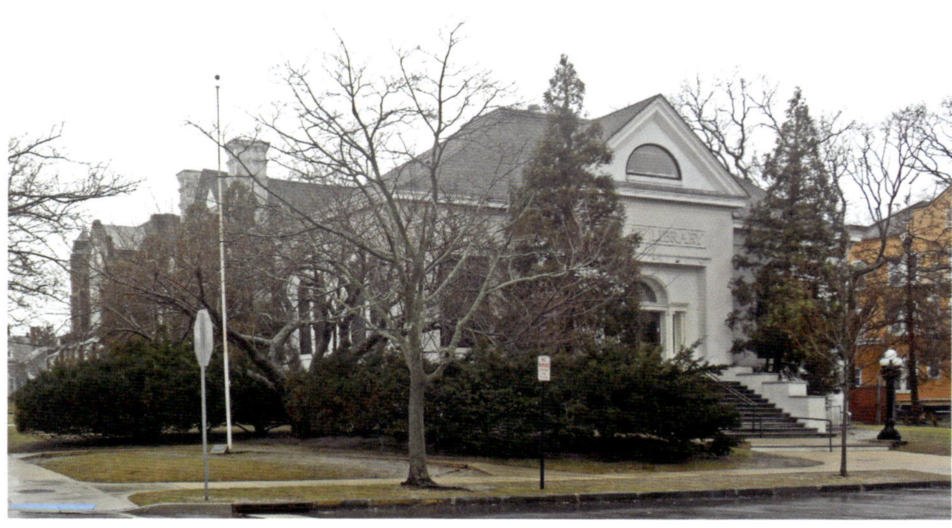

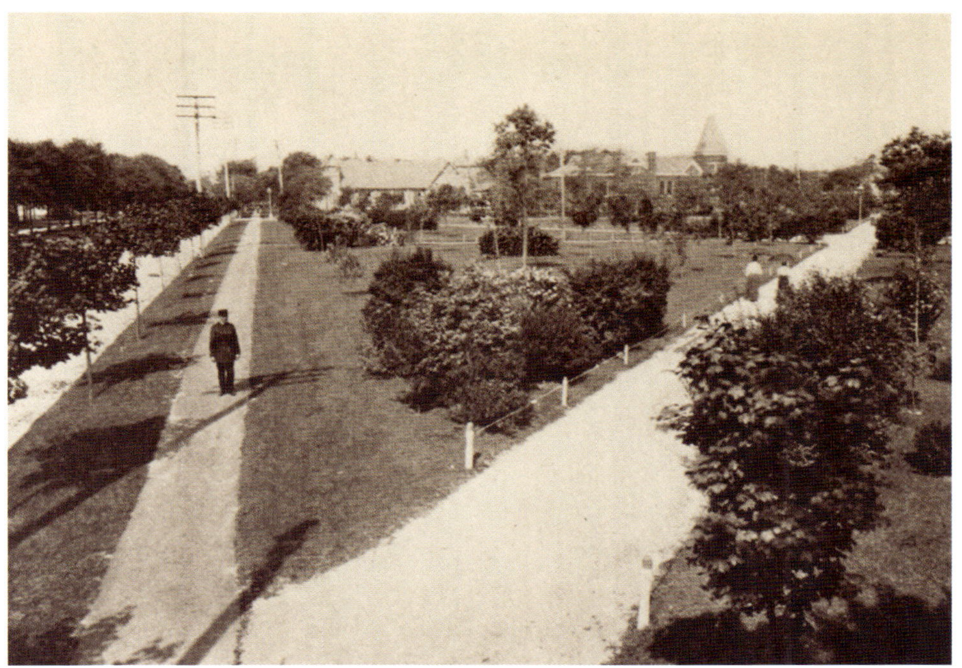

LIBRARY SQUARE PARK IN ASBURY PARK: The park was laid out by James Bradley as a surprise anniversary gift to his wife, following the groundbreaking of the library in 1881. Because of the perpetual terms set by Bradley, this small tract of nature in an otherwise built up city will remain a welcome promenade for generations to come. The picture here dates from about 1910.

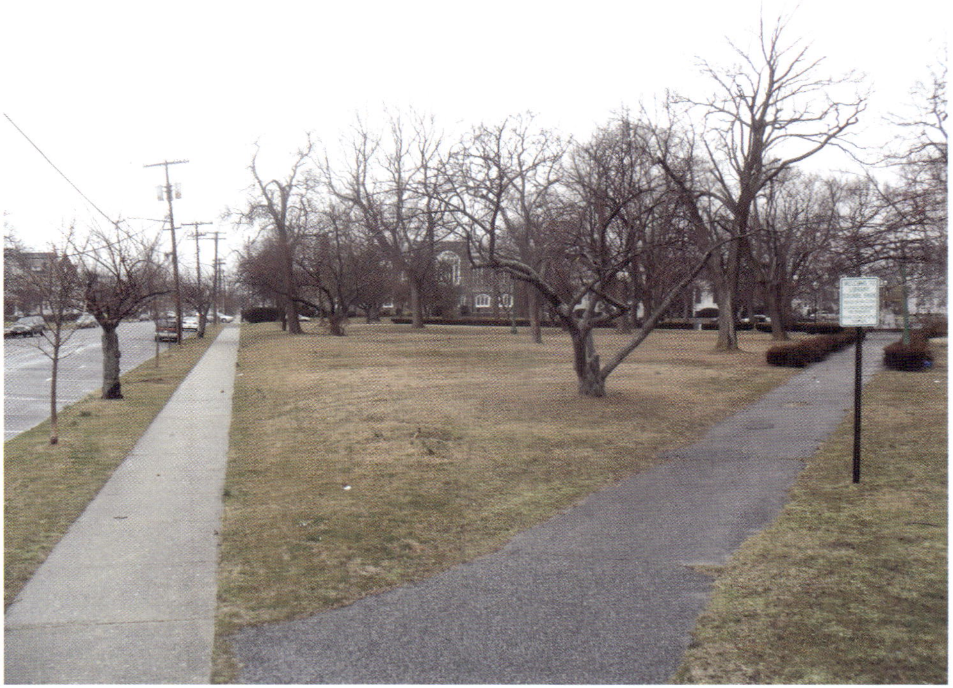

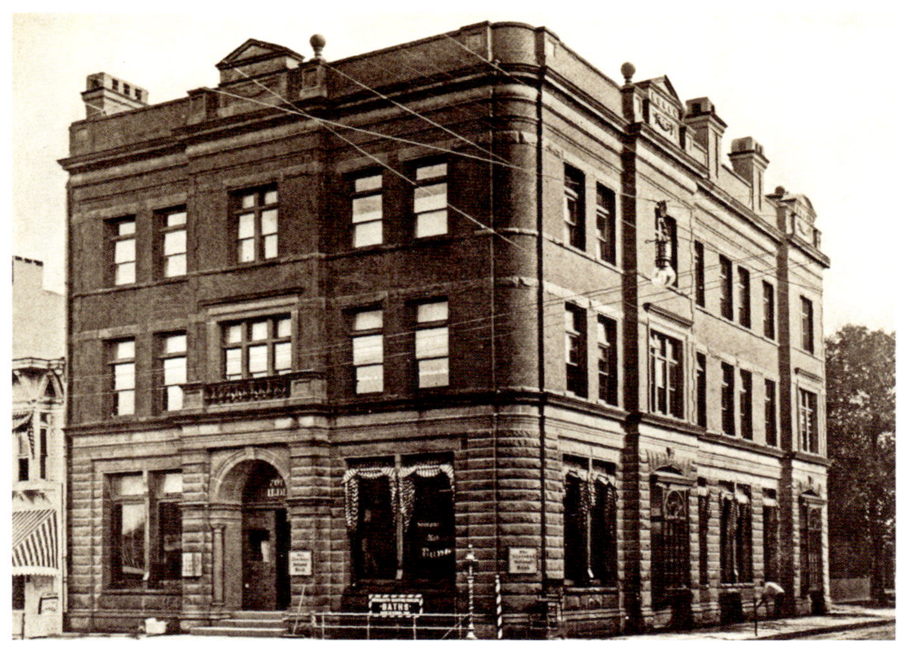

THE SEACOAST NATIONAL BANK OF ASBURY PARK: The Bank is pictured here in 1905. The building was constructed in the late 1870s, and was one of the three national banks located in Asbury Park. National currency bank notes issued by the bank from 1882 through 1903 are considered extremely rare, and are highly sought out by collectors. The building is currently home to offices and community outreach organizations.

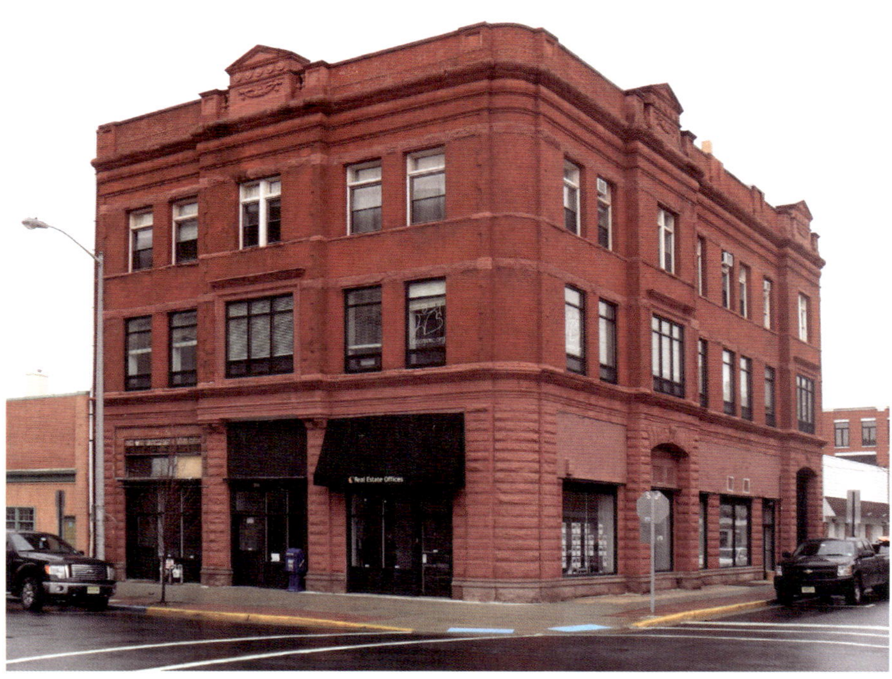

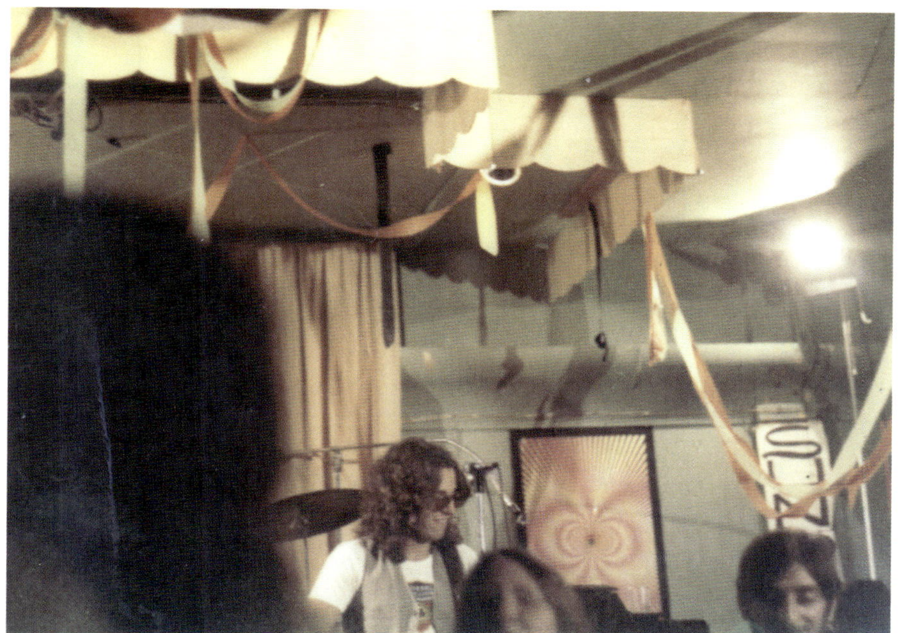

BRUCE SPRINGSTEEN: A rare color snapshot from the collection of Vini Lopez taken at the Student Prince on Kingsley Avenue. The gentleman pictured is the bandleader and namesake of the Bruce Springsteen Band. The Student Prince was a popular hangout for Monmouth College students in the late 1960s/early 1970s. The building was constructed about 1914. Bruce Springsteen met Clarence Clemons at this club for the first time within a few days of this photo, during the fall of 1971. The former stage area is currently a bar in the 2013 incarnation, the Porta restaurant/lounge.

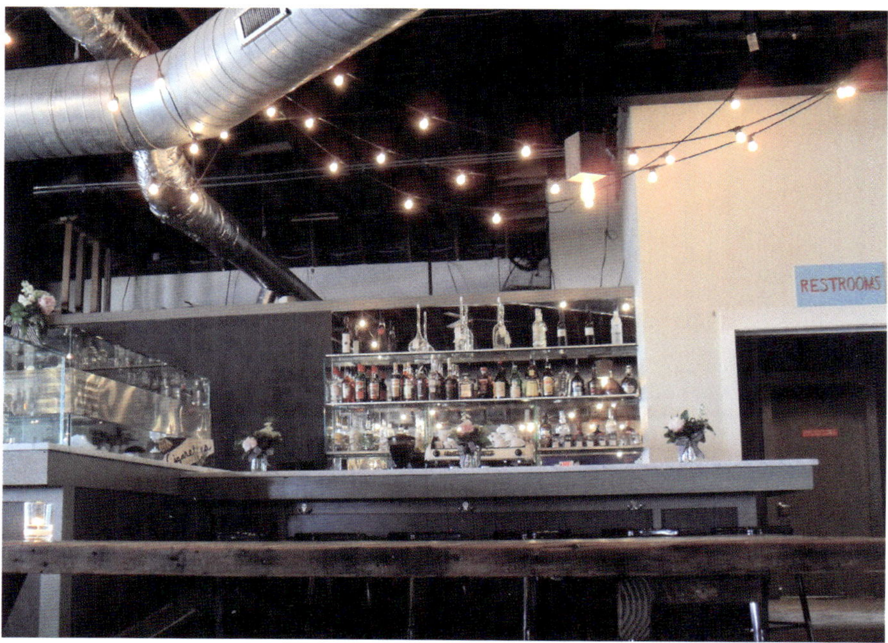

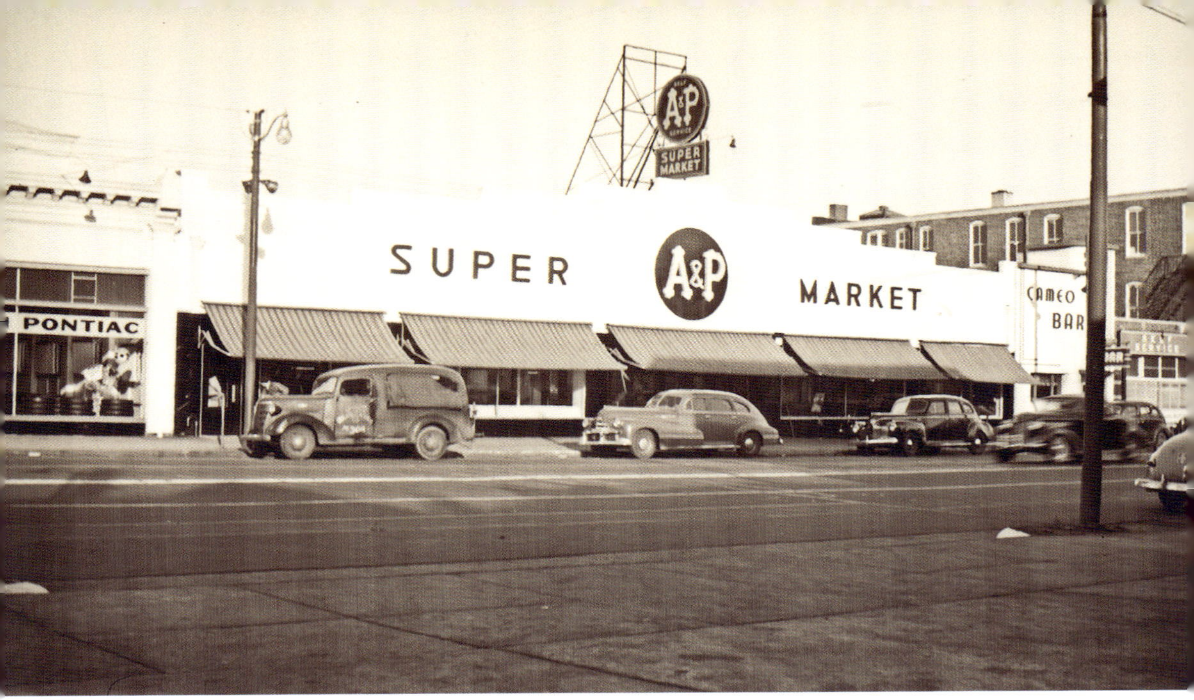

THE GREAT ATLANTIC & PACIFIC TEA COMPANY: Established in 1859, the Company was the first organization to develop the true concept of a modern supermarket in the 1920s and began to open locations coast-to-coast. Previous to this, you had to visit several different stores to obtain the basic food essentials. How revolutionary! The Asbury Park location on Main Street was an early example. The store moved to Neptune City in 1957. Pictured here in the 1930s, the Cameo Bar is still going strong.

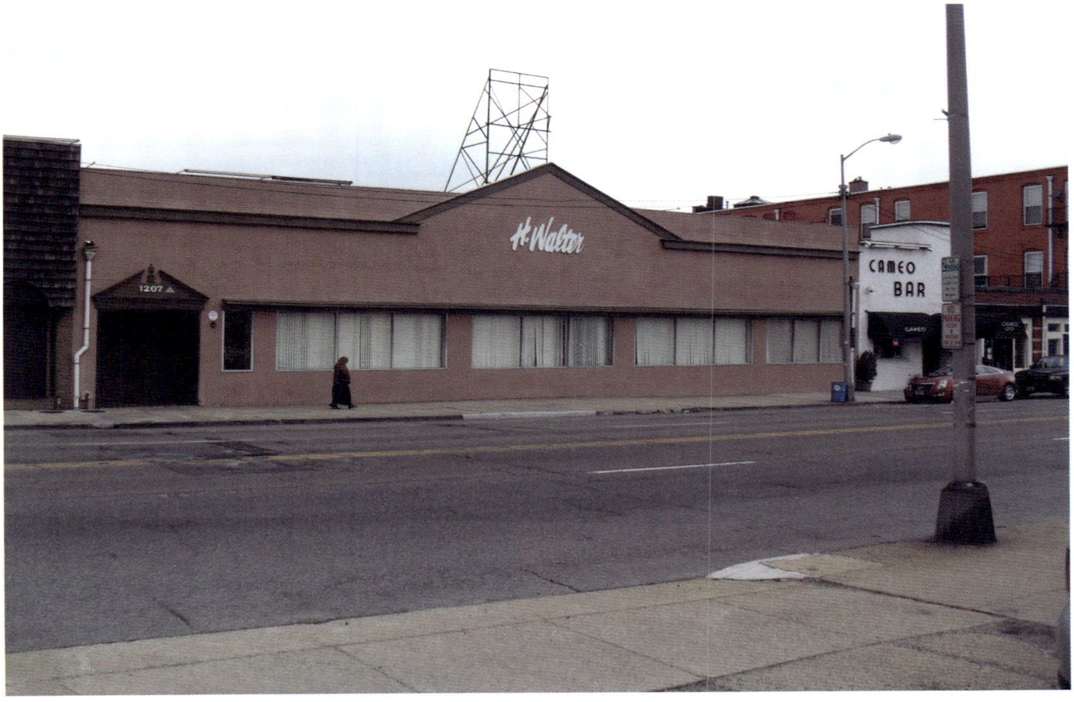

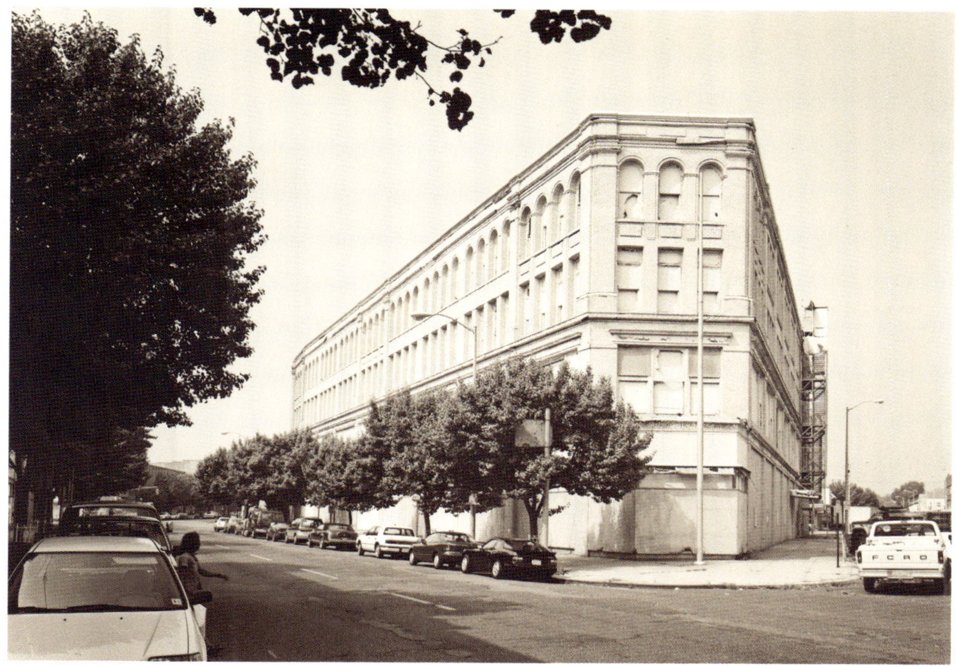

COOKMAN AVENUE: The amazing rebirth which transpired on Cookman Avenue during the first decade of the twenty-first century is very clear when comparing 2013's vibrant present with the dreary scene pictured in the 1990s. The former Steinbach department store currently serves as retail and condo space. The recent renaissance of the downtown district and the beachfront is a welcome return to fine form for the grand old city of Asbury Park.

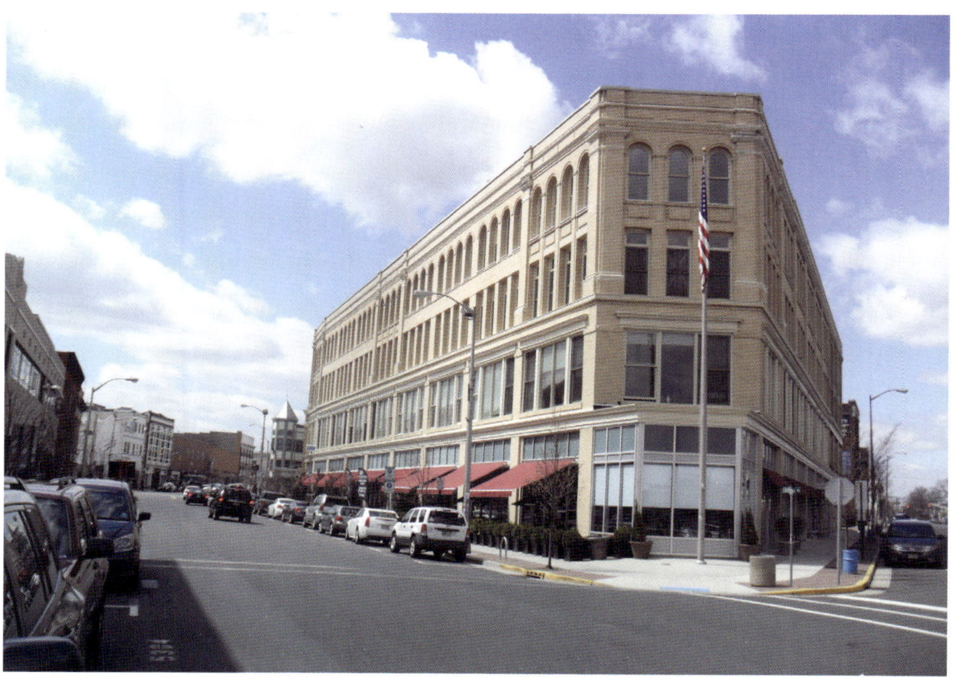

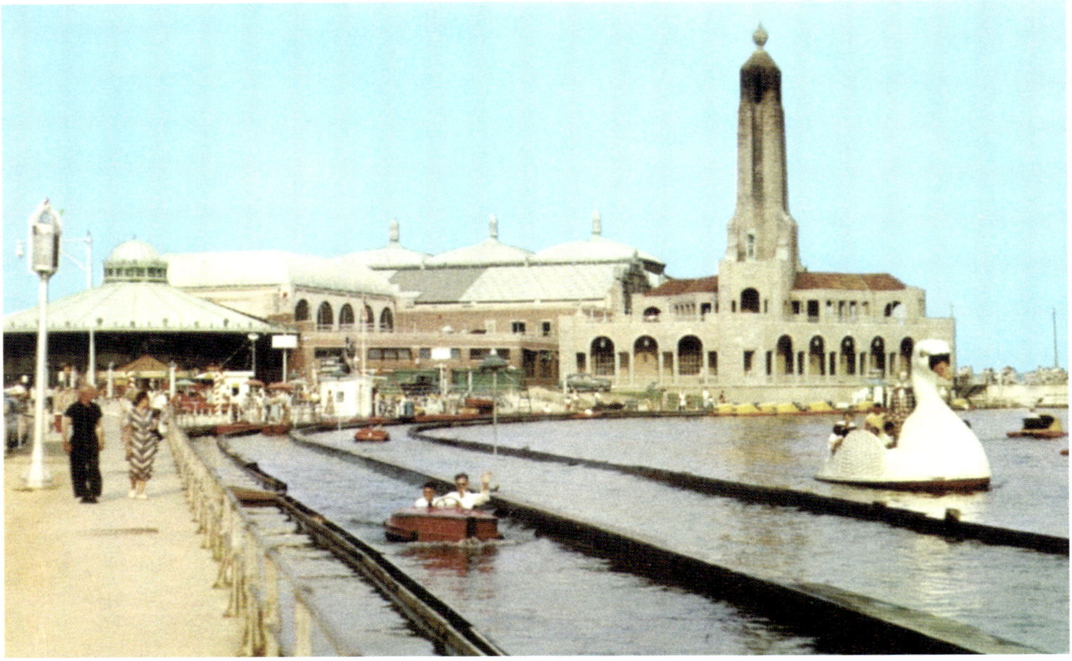

THE CASINO BUILDING AT THE FOOT OF WESLEY LAKE: The casino and the adjoining heating plant have long been fixtures marking the entrance into Asbury Park from Ocean Grove. Built in 1929, the complex has been under renovations since 2008. In 2011, the famous swan paddleboat rentals returned to Wesley Lake. Pictured here is a postcard view from the 1960s.

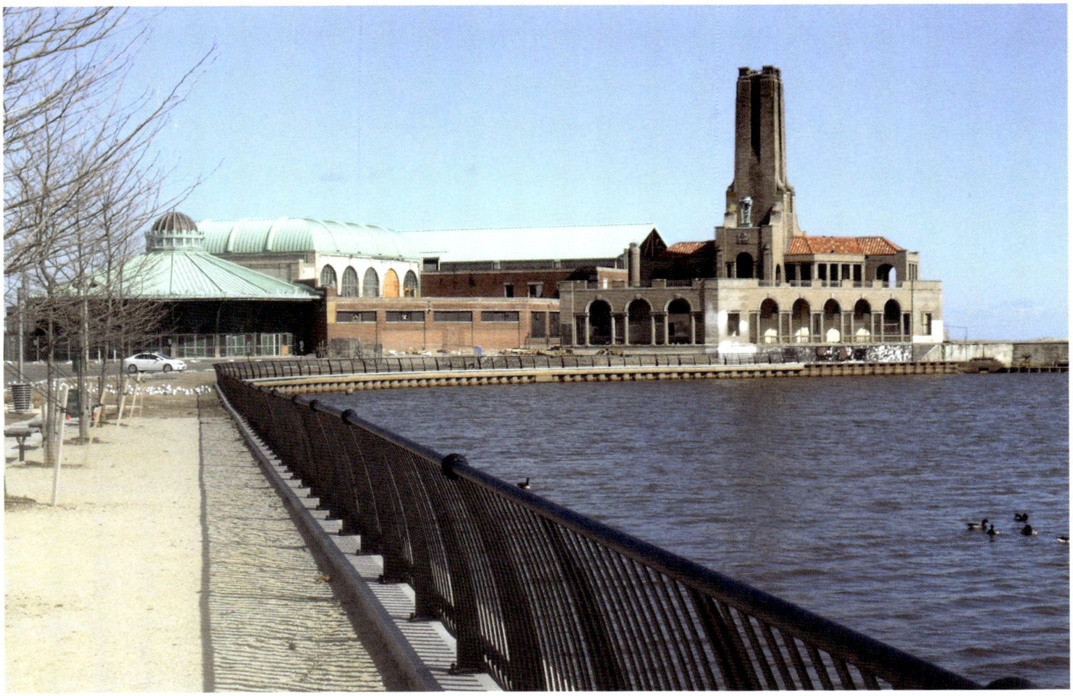

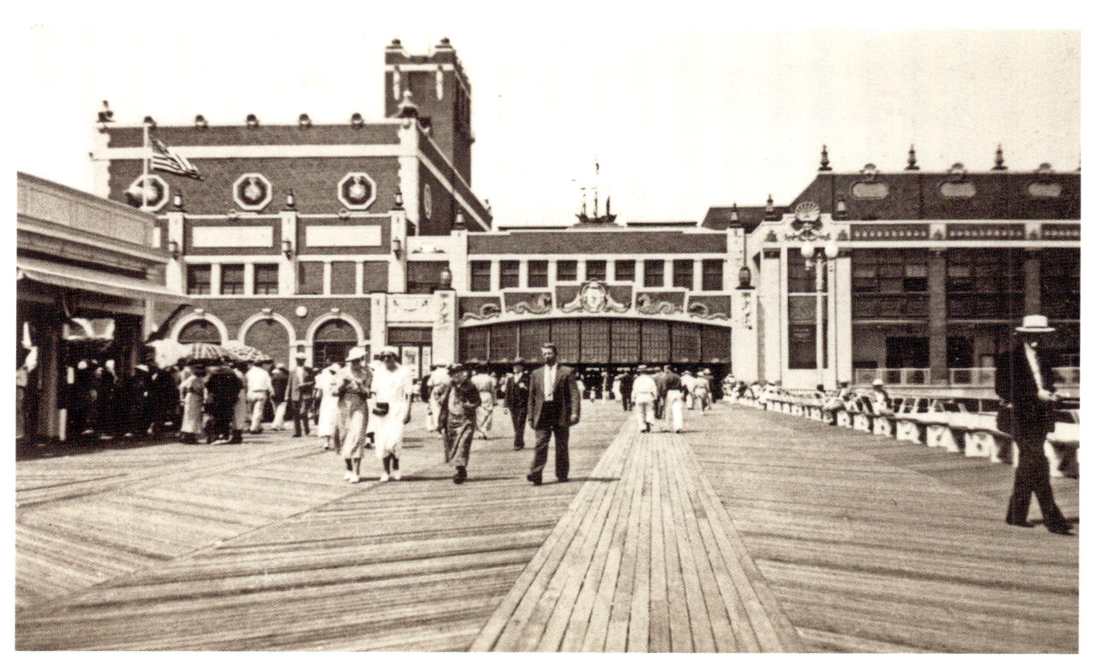

CONVENTION HALL: Convention Hall is pictured shortly after its completion in 1930. The reader may attribute the boards on the doors of the 2013 image as outstanding damage from Hurricane Sandy, when in fact the facility is being readied for President Barack Obama's May 2013 visit. The extremely mangled boardwalk railing was, however, Sandy's handiwork.

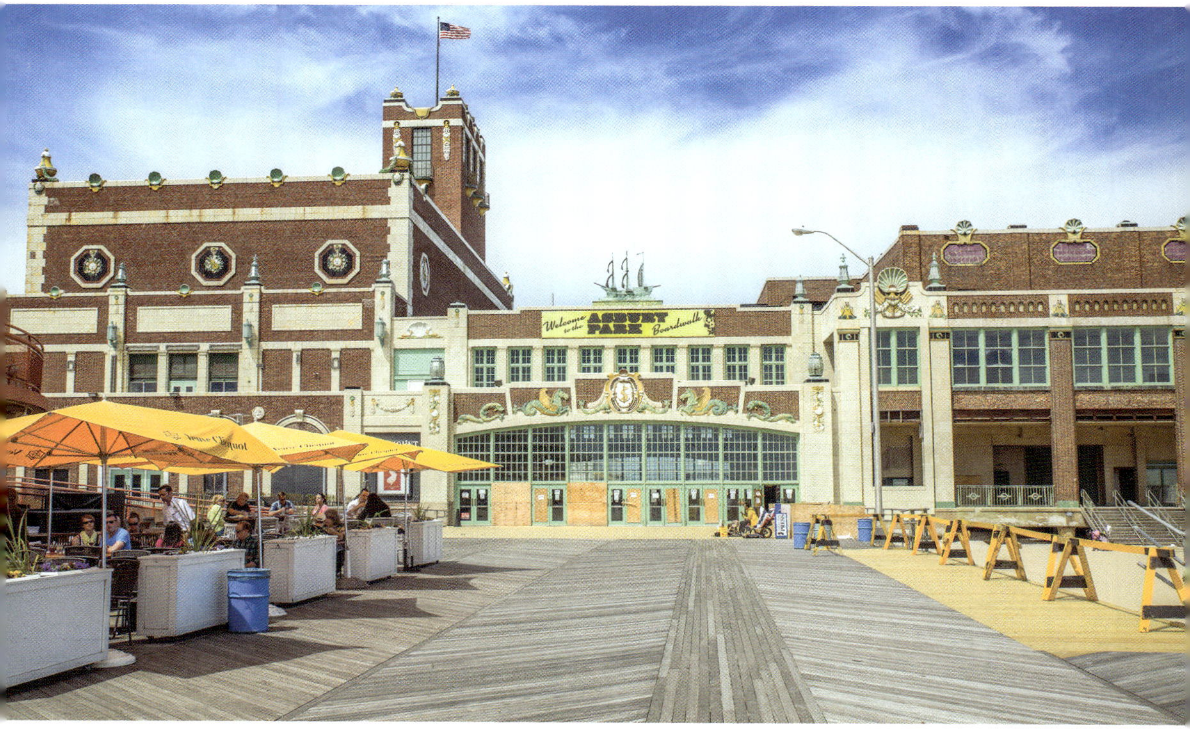

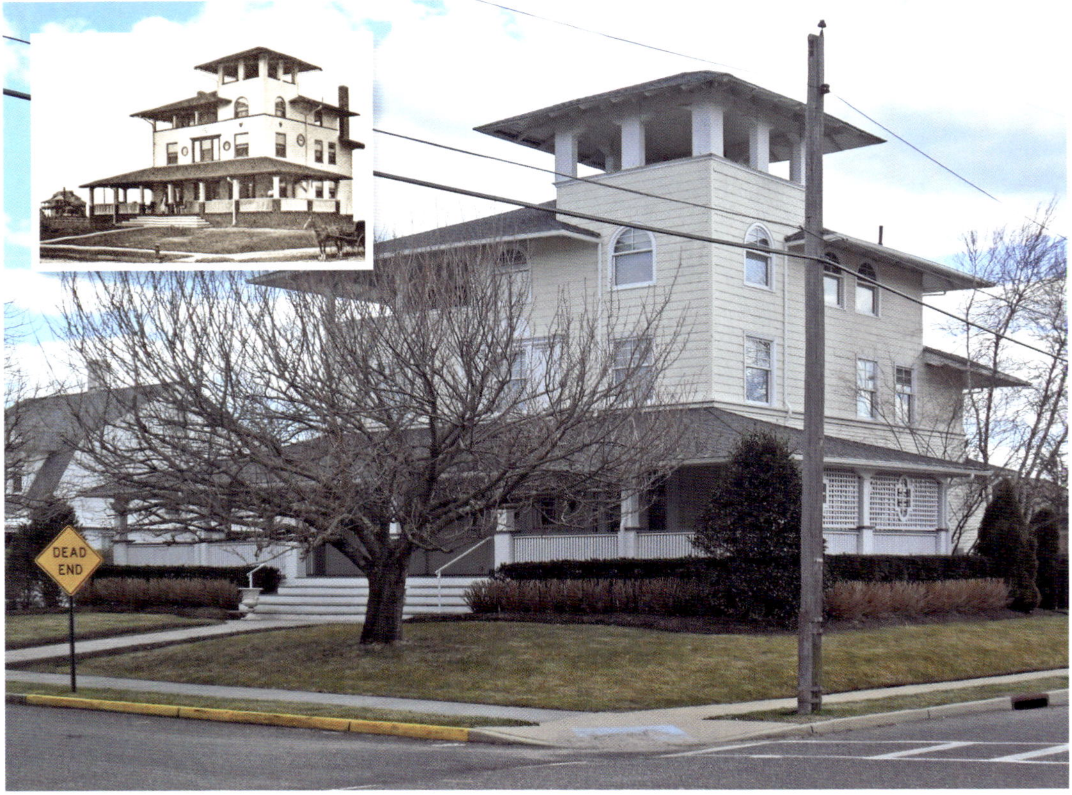

THE BEAUTIFUL SUMMER COTTAGES OF ALLENHURST:

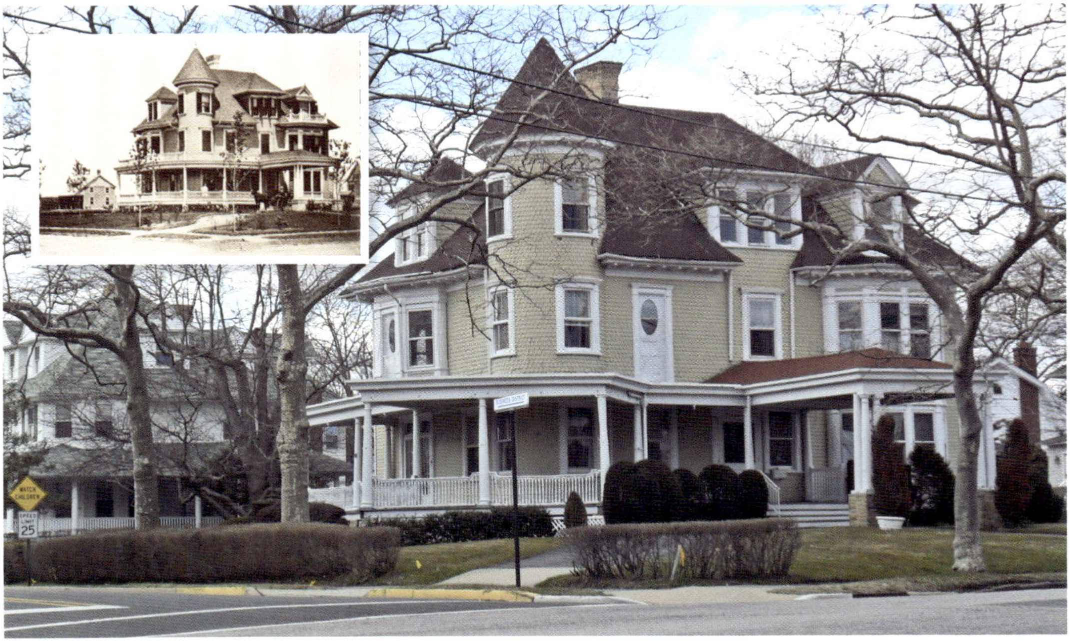

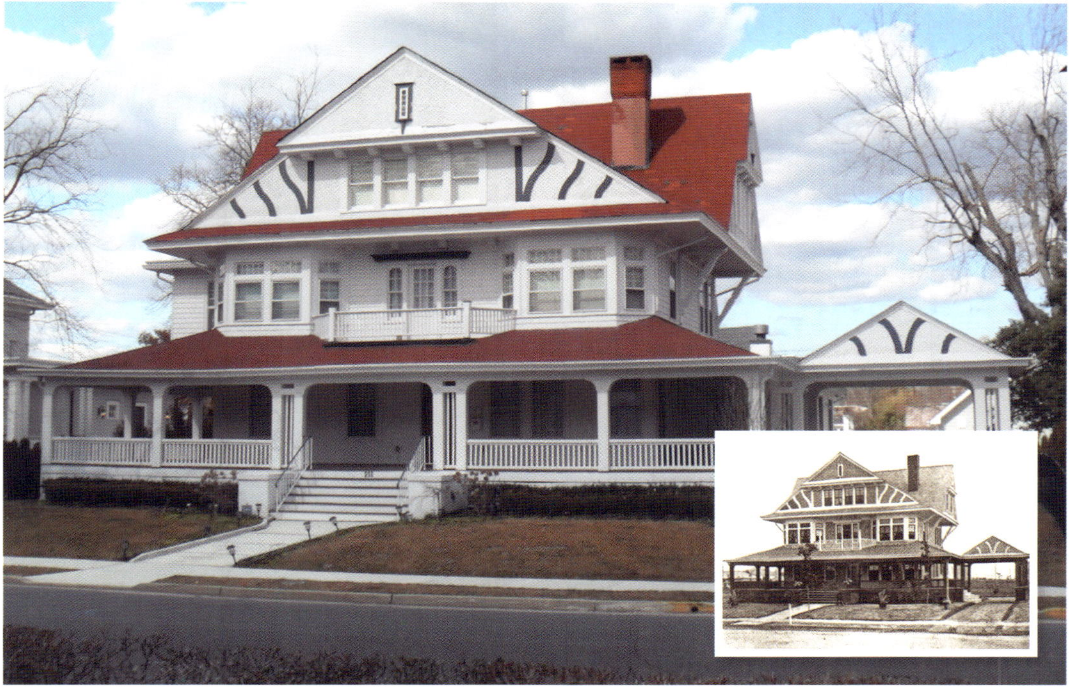

THE COAST LAND IMPROVEMENT COMPANY: The Company bought the 120-acre Allen homestead farm in Allenhurst in 1895, and a decade later produced a marketing booklet detailing the progress and improvements made to date, which is the source of these vintage photographs on this pair of pages. Allenhurst became a year-round residential area for some of the more successful entrepreneurs from Asbury Park, as well as hosting the wealthy seasonal residents in the summer months.

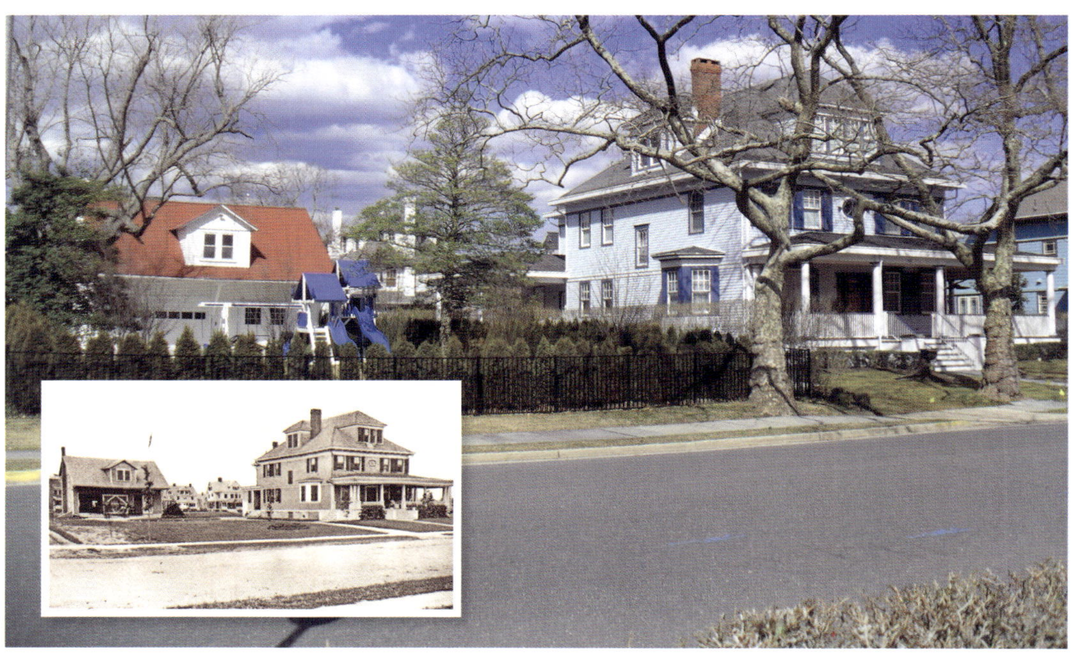

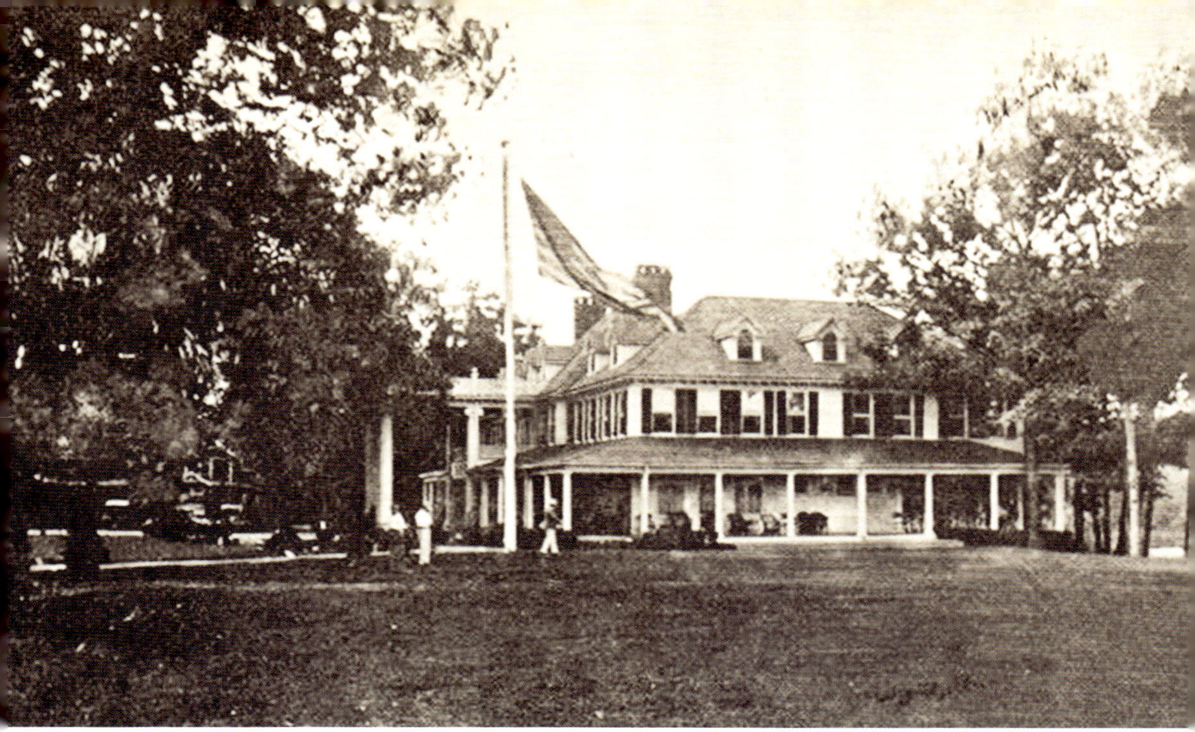

THE DEAL GOLF AND COUNTRY CLUB: The Club was organized in the late 1890s. George Washington Young laid out a nine-hole course which was the earliest golf course on the Jersey Shore. In 1898, the clubhouse was completed, which was expanded and updated in the 1920s, and again in the late 1950s. Many golf legends have played these holes, as the Deal Invitational tournament was regionally renown for many years.

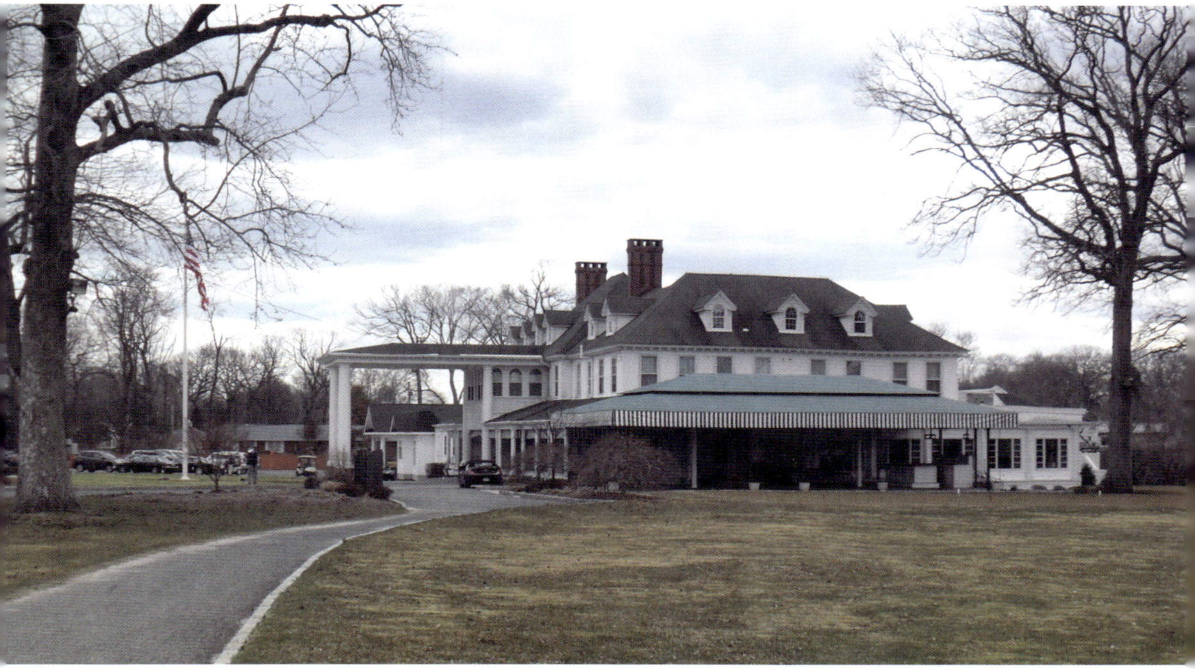

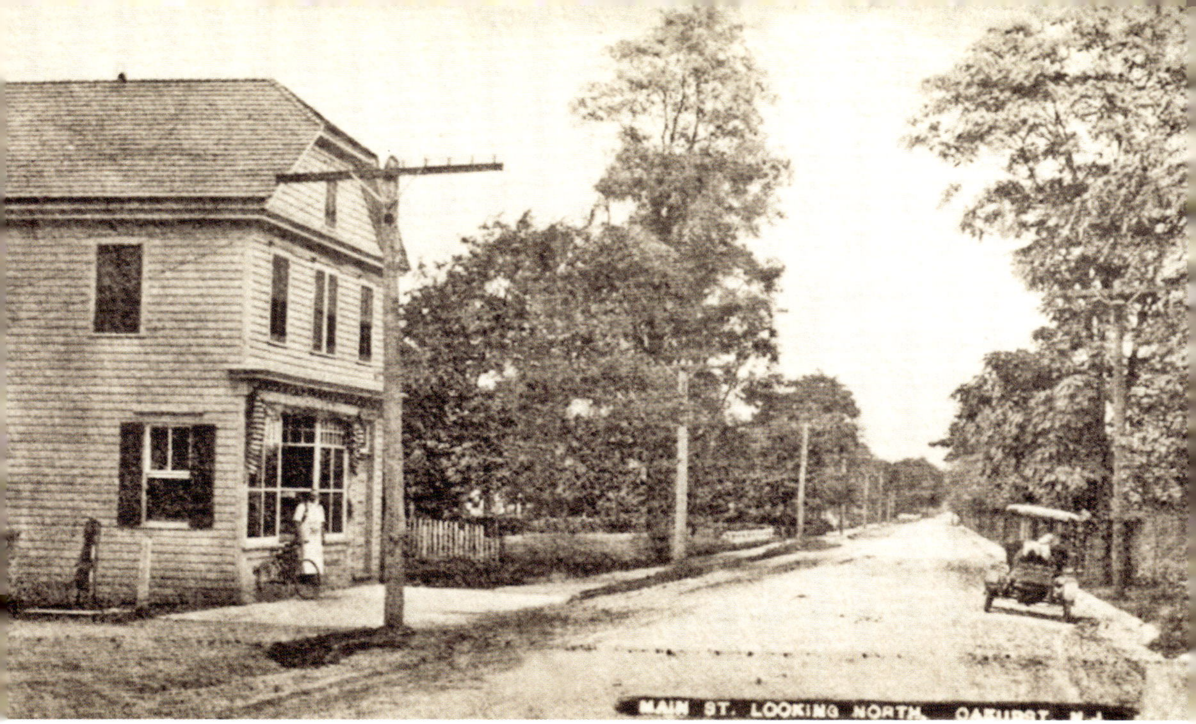

MONMOUTH ROAD: The principal features looking north on Monmouth Road have essentially remained the same since this 1900s postcard view was captured. The Oakhurst section of Ocean Township has managed to retain a good deal of its original rustic charm. The Monmouth Road corridor serves as an essential 'back-road shortcut' for savvy locals trying to avoid seasonal traffic on the main thoroughfares.

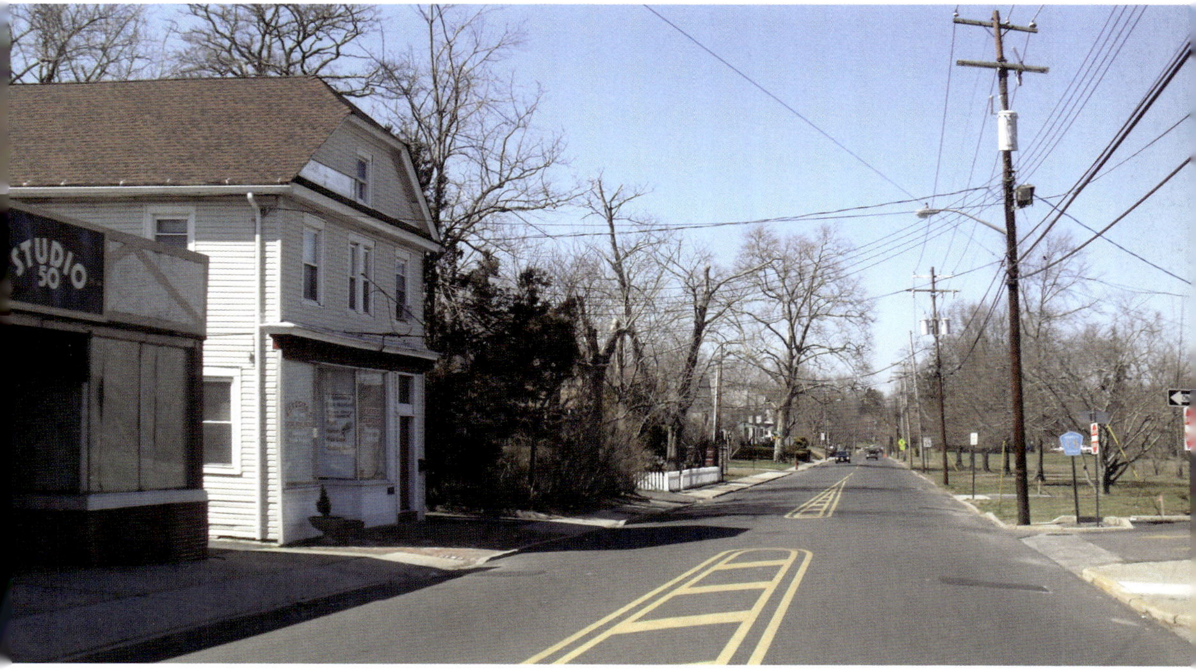

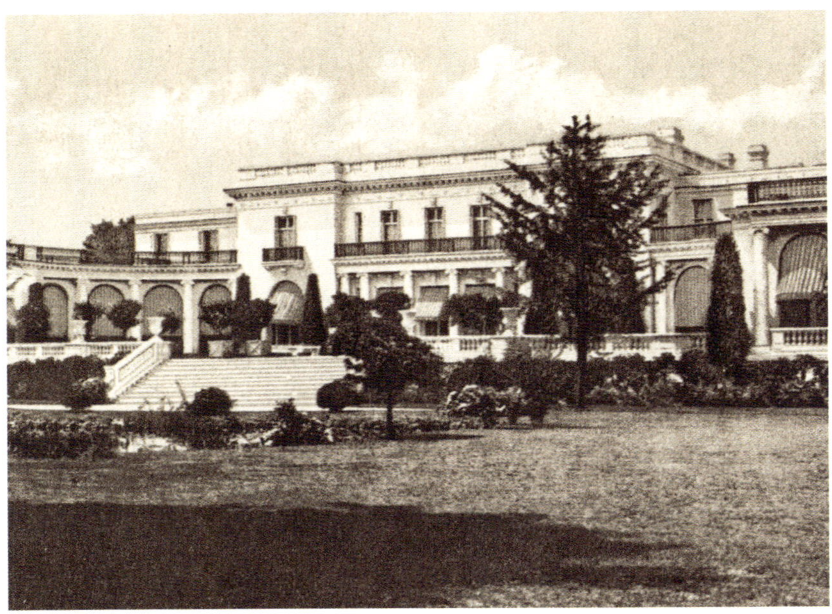

THE GUGGENHEIM FAMILY: The Guggenheims immigrated to the United States from Switzerland in 1848, and many of the siblings of which carved out mogul status in various sectors of business during the progressive era. Murry Guggenheim initially studied the family lace and embroidery trade, but ultimately found his niche in smelting operations. He built this summer cottage on Cedar Avenue in West Long Branch in 1905, shown *c.* 1910. After his widow died in the late 1950s, the Guggenheim foundation conveyed the estate to Monmouth College where it has since served as the library.

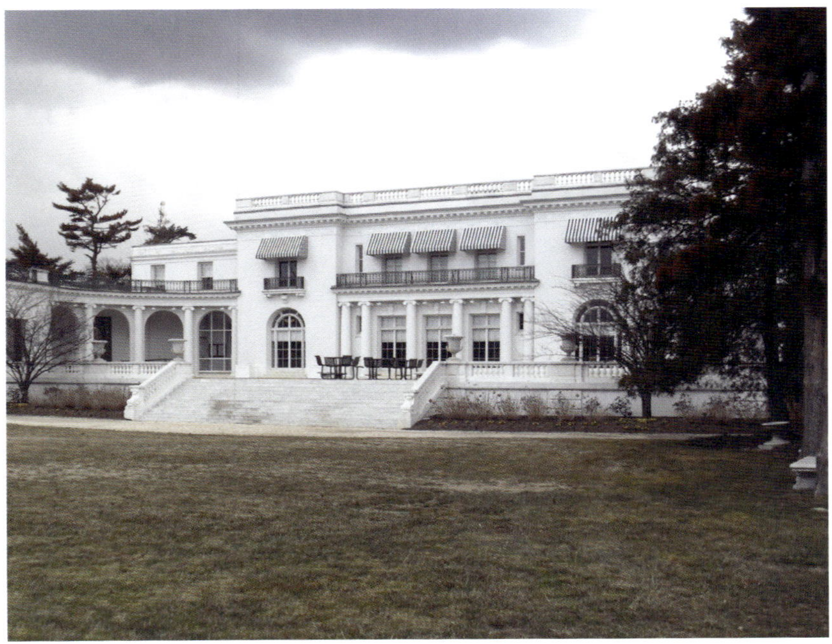

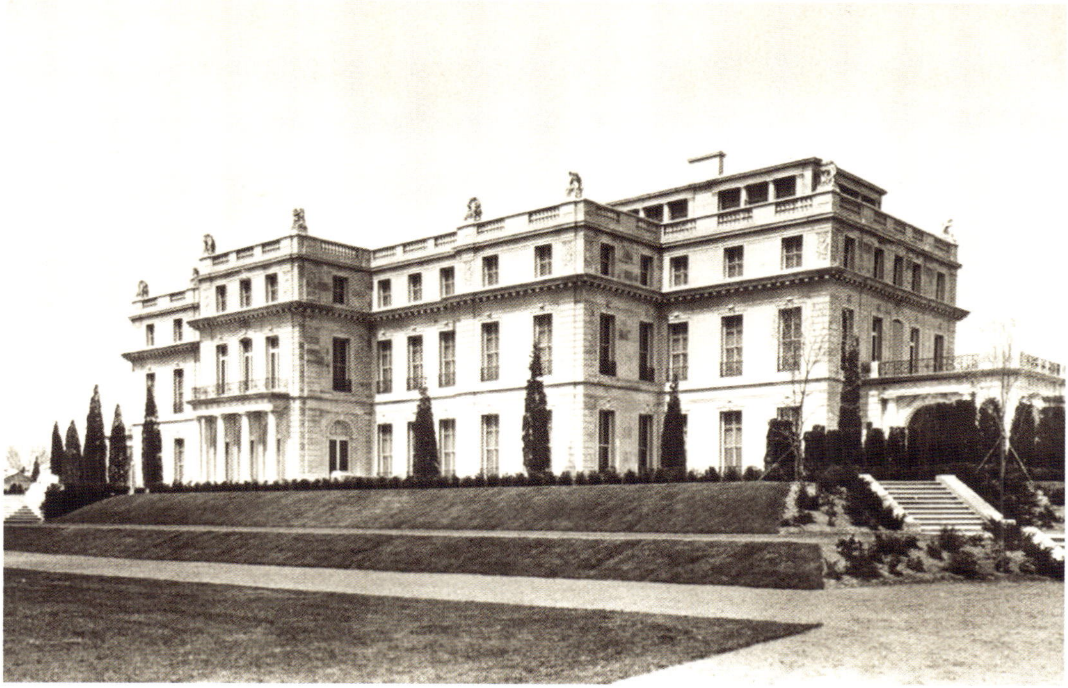

MONMOUTH UNIVERSITY: Hubert Parson, former president of F. W. Woolworth set out to build the most opulent house ever imagined at the Jersey Shore in 1929. He did not expect to lose all of his money during the Great Depression, and shortly after the completion of the building (pictured here) it was seized by the municipality of West Long Branch. Highland Manor Junior College, a private girls' school, utilized the campus until Monmouth College (University in 1995) was reorganized in 1956 as a four-year institution.

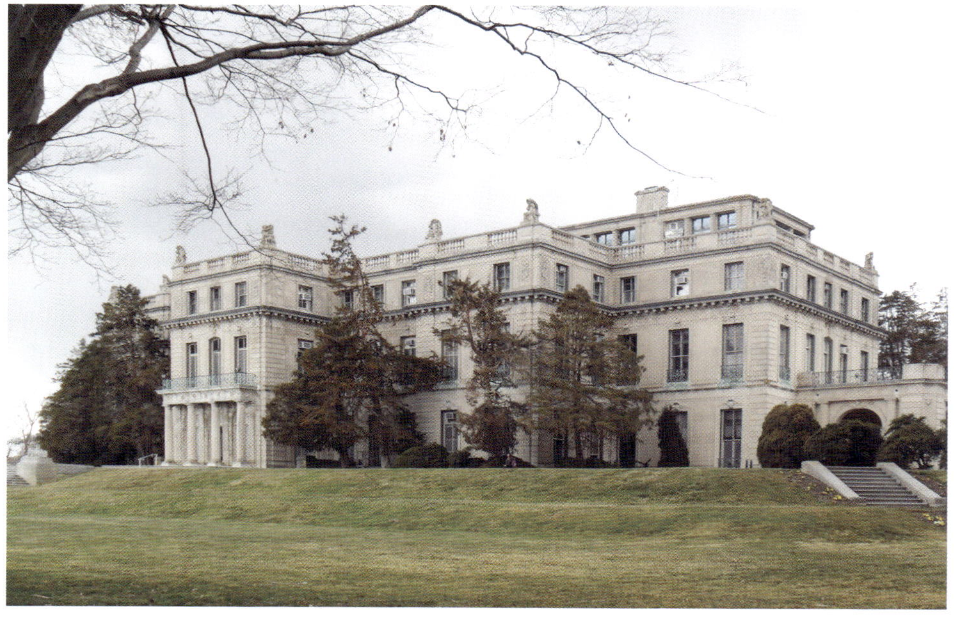

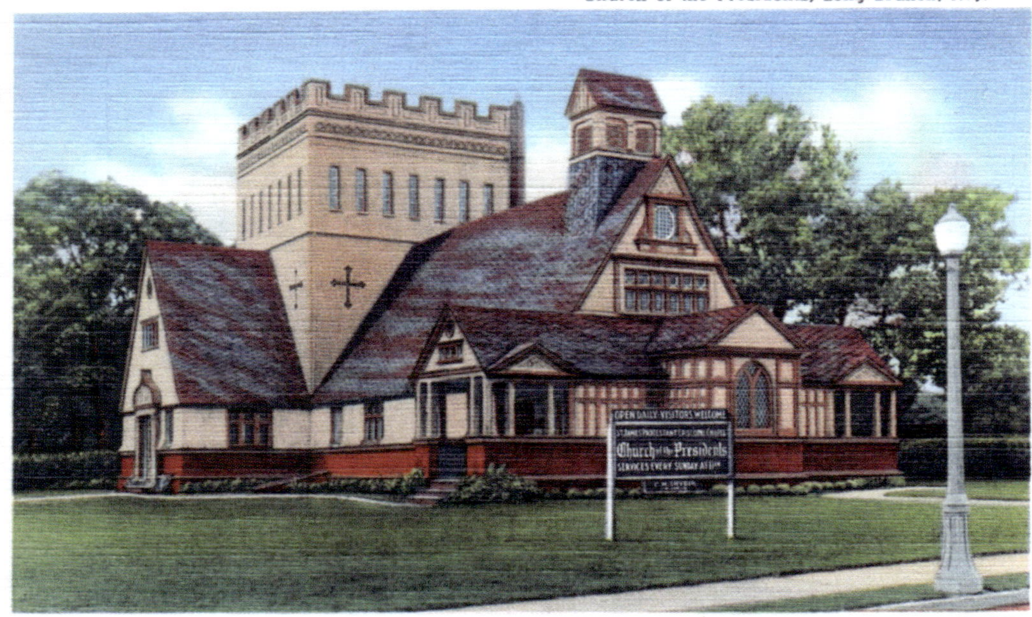

ST JAMES' CHAPEL: The Chapel was built in 1879 when Long Branch was the premier summer resort in the United States. St James was attended by presidents Grant, Hays, Garfield, Arthur and Wilson. James Garfield passed away in a mansion across the street after he had been shot by a deranged preacher. As Long Branch's resort popularity waned, attendance fell and the church was deconsecrated in the 1950s. It served for nearly fifty years as a museum, but was closed in 1999. As of 2013, it is slowly being restored.

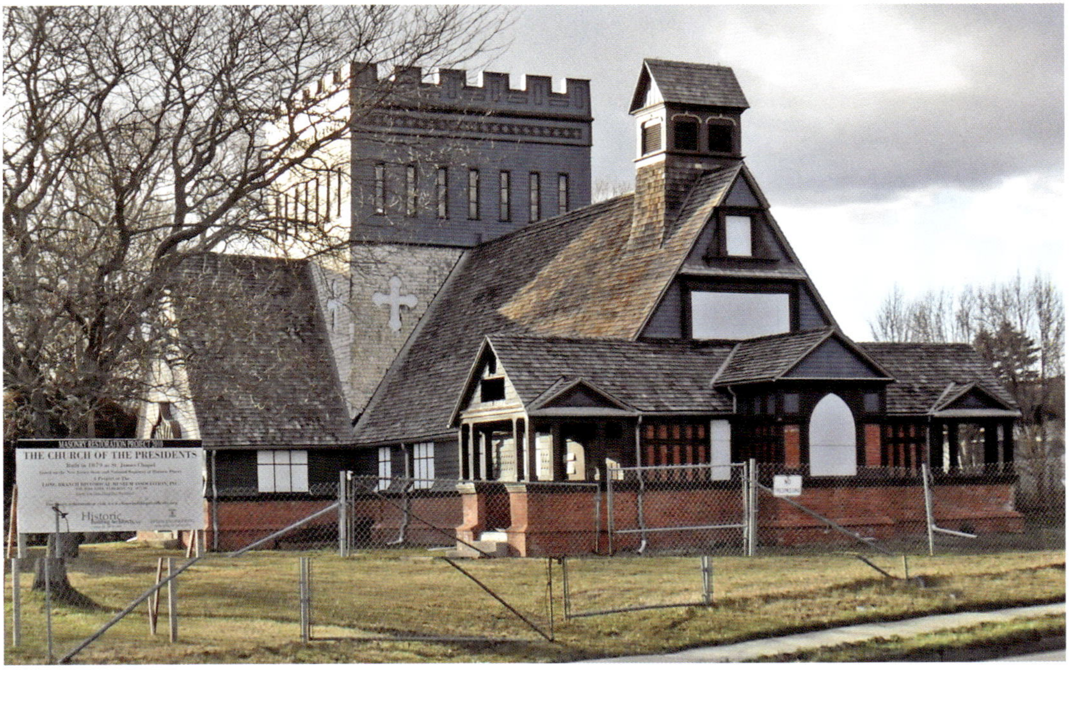

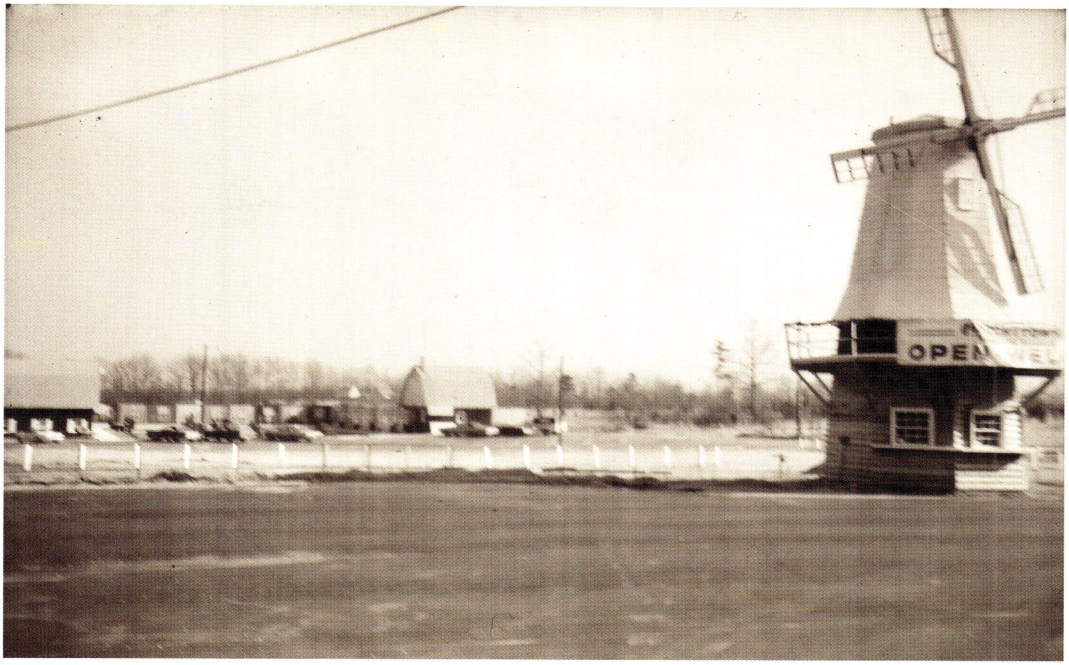

THE WINDMILL HOTDOG STAND: This is an extremely rare snapshot of the fabled Windmill hotdog stand in its original incarnation, shortly after opening in 1964. A banner emblazoned with the likeness of the giant frankfurter which has now gained legendary status on the Jersey Shore proclaims the institution open for business. The building was significantly redesigned in the late 1960s when it was enclosed. Measures were also made in the redesign to detract seagulls from congregating on the roof, as they had also proven to be big fans of Windmill fare as well.

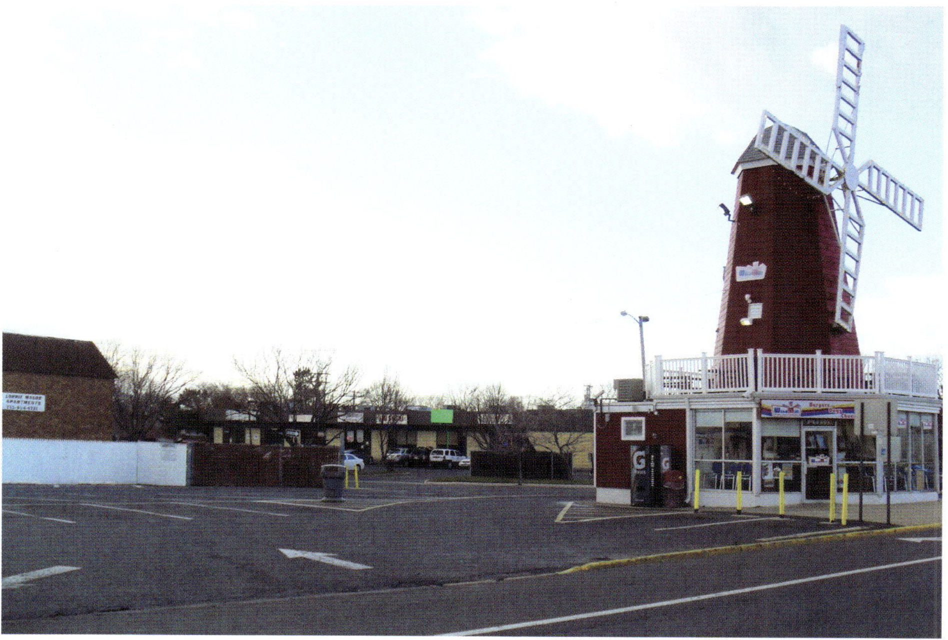

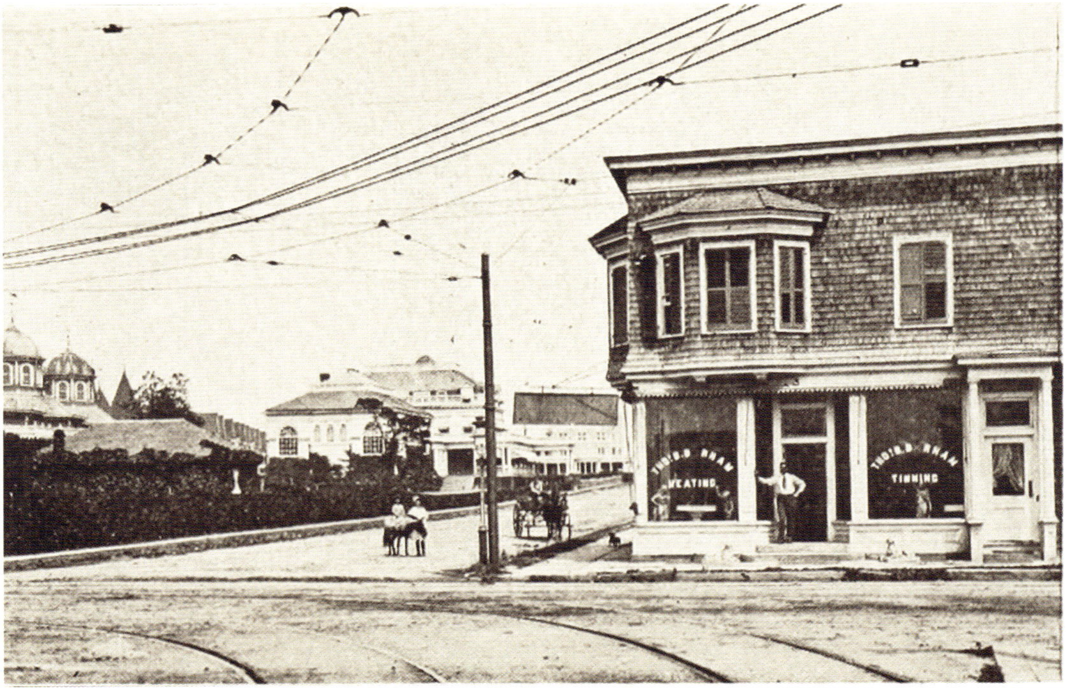

WEST END, LONG BRANCH: Thomas Barham proudly stands in the doorway of his heating and tinning establishment located on Second Avenue in the West End section of Long Branch. The image dates from around 1905. The building is one of the few recognizable features in the area that has survived from Long Branch's heyday.

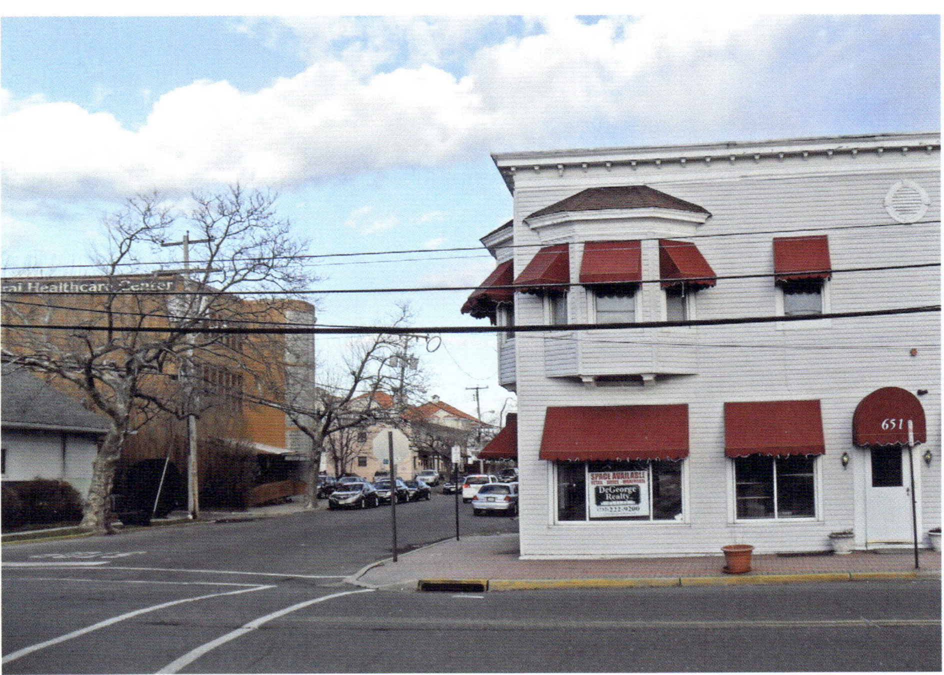

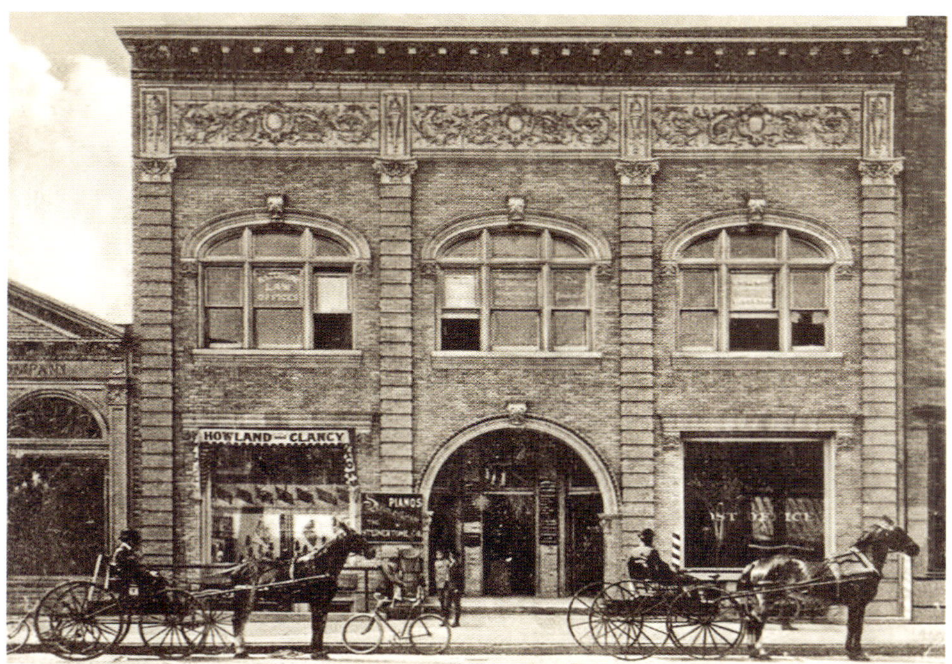

THE POST OFFICE, BROADWAY: Before the grand post office was constructed on Third Avenue this location filled the vital role on Broadway. Like many early post offices, the building also served other purposes, as a real estate business and law offices are also tenants in this 1890s view. Beautifully maintained and preserved, the building currently serves as a supermarket and hub of the Long Branch Latino community.

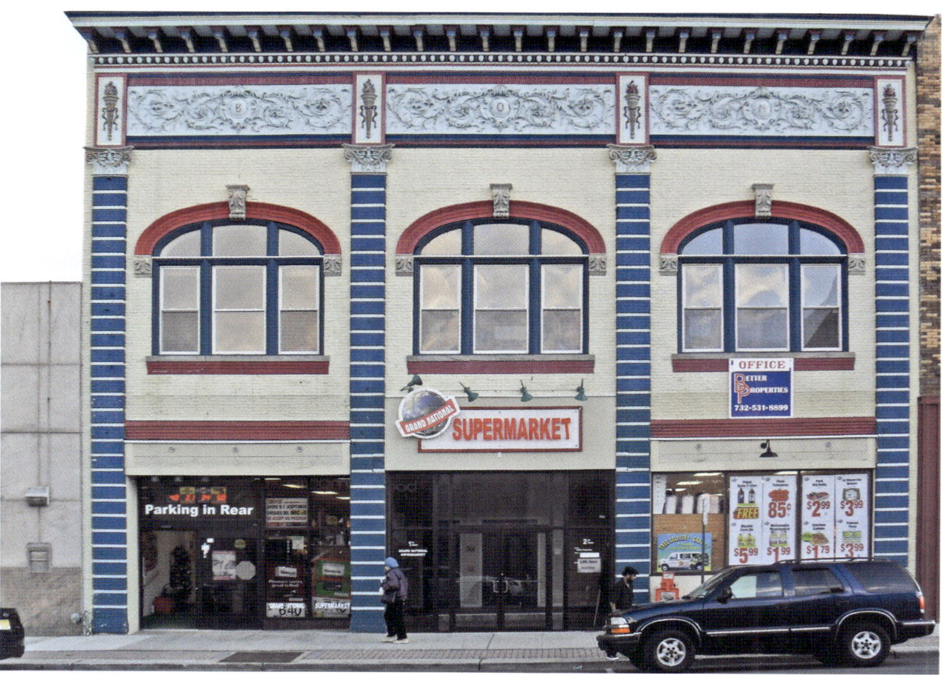

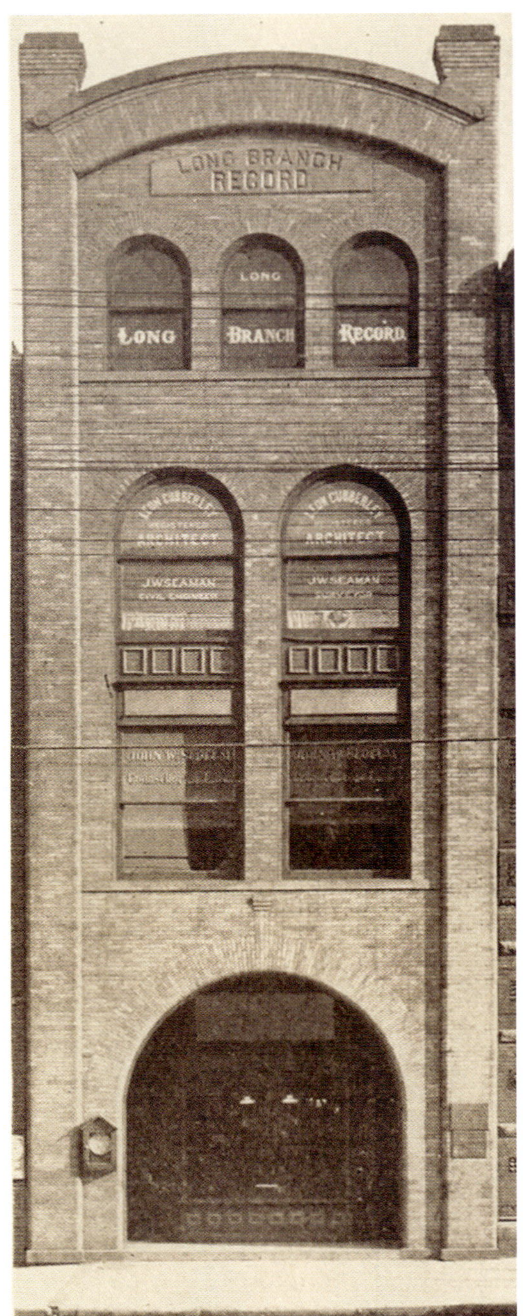

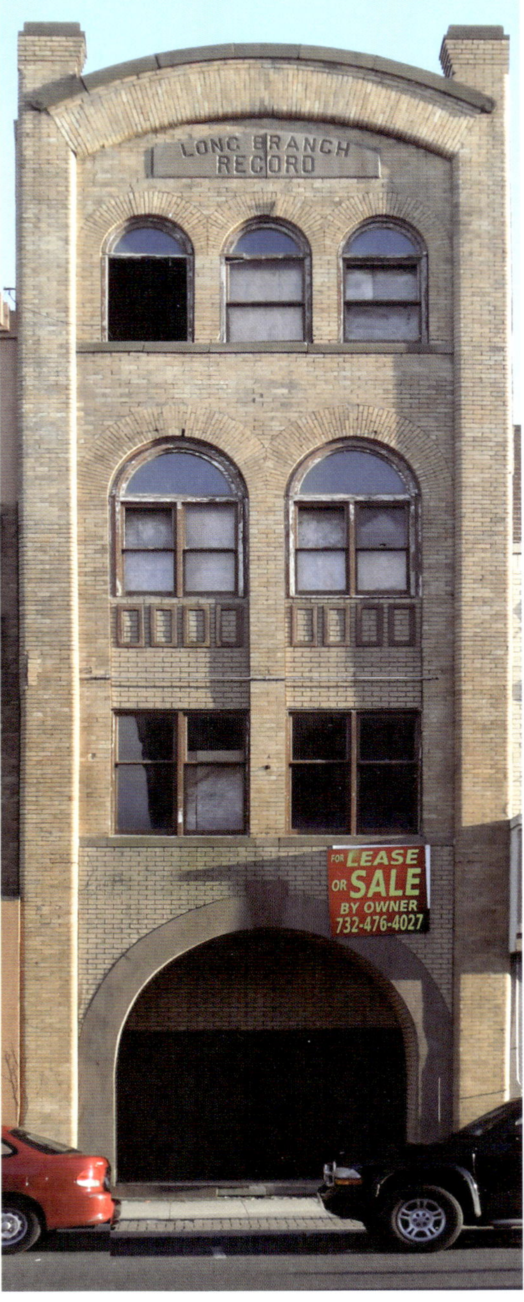

THE *LONG BRANCH RECORD* HEADQUARTERS: The former headquarters of the long-defunct *Long Branch Record* is pictured in its prime in 1910. Built in the 1890s, the *Long Branch Record* ceased publication in 1973. Offices and various business ventures have long occupied the building, but as of 2013, the building is waiting for a potential savior to breathe some life back into this Broadway landmark.

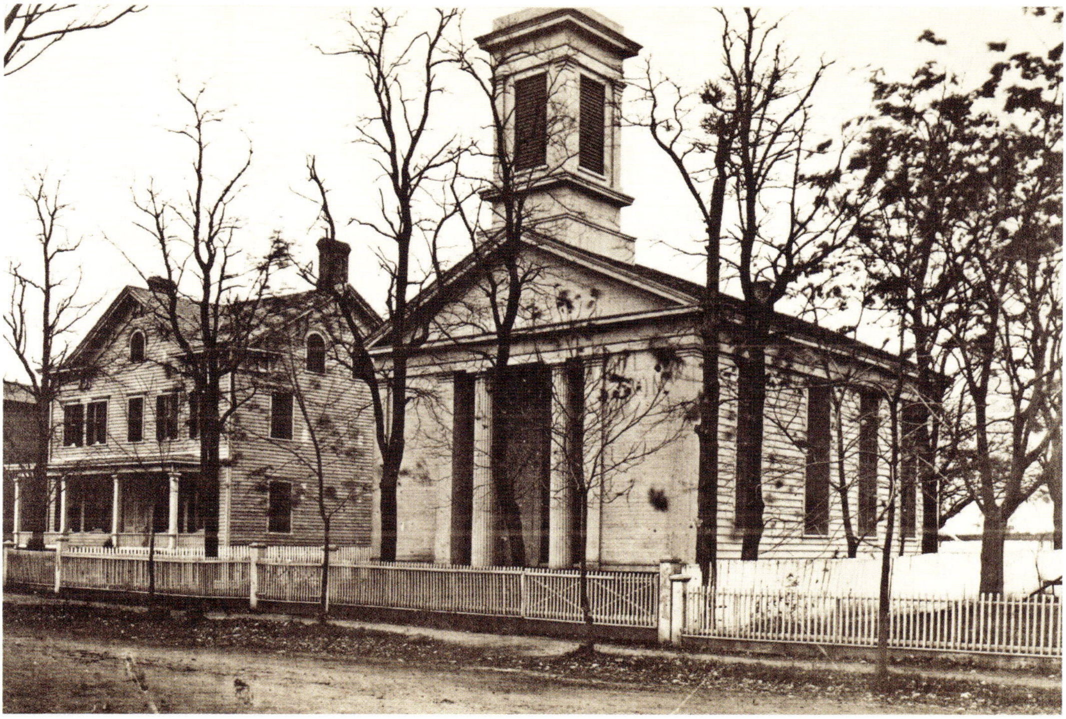

The First Reformed Church of Long Branch: The Church and parsonage on Broadway at the intersection of Grove Street is pictured in 1869. The congregation was established in 1857, and the original church edifice and parsonage were completed shortly thereafter. The church building was radically enlarged in 1902, but the original structure exists within the current configuration to some degree.

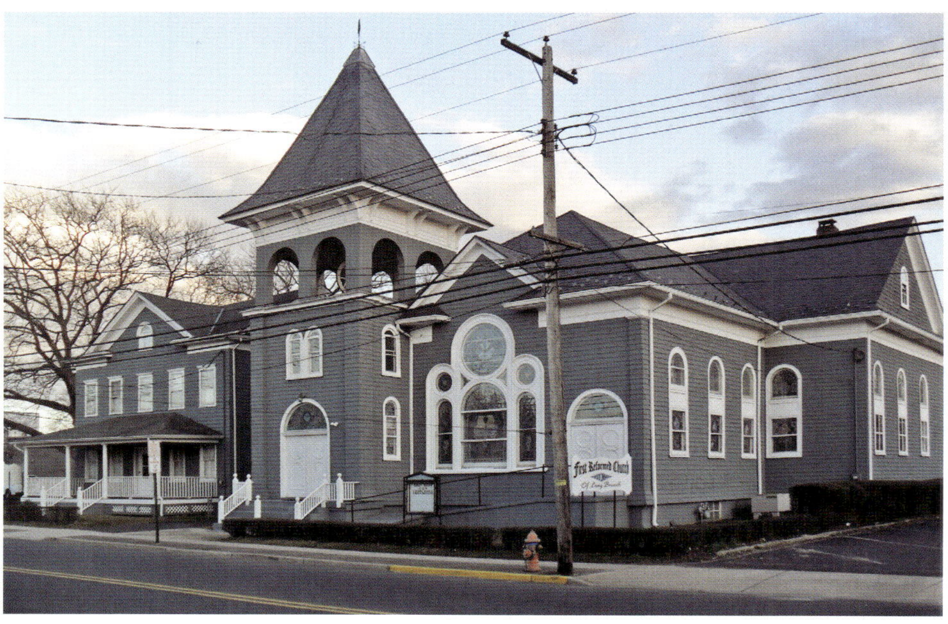

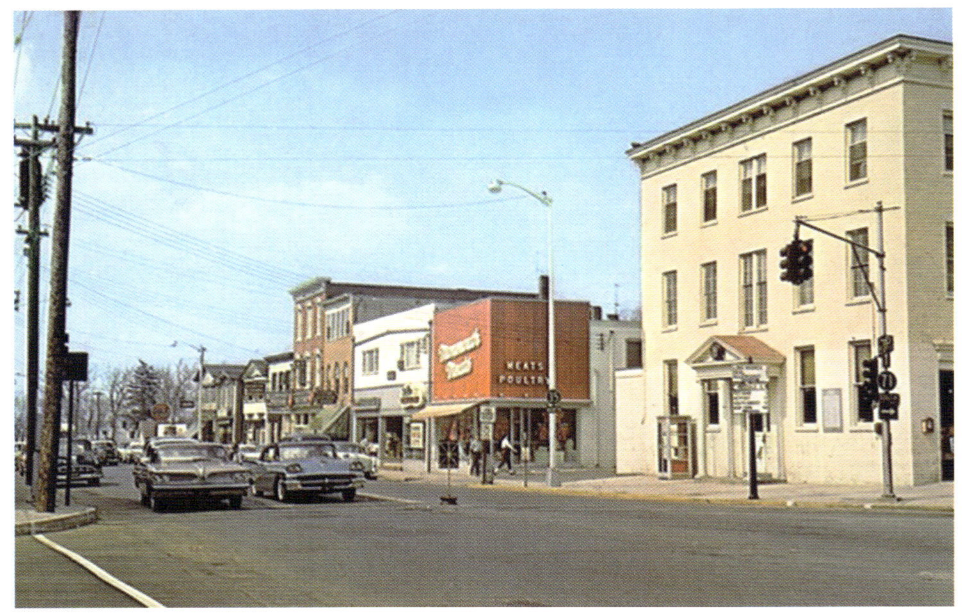

EATONTOWN: A mid-1950s postcard view of the Miracle Mile section of Main Street in Eatontown. With the exception of the enormous building constructed in 1969 at right, the core principle buildings pictured have existed with little outward change in appearance for the past century.

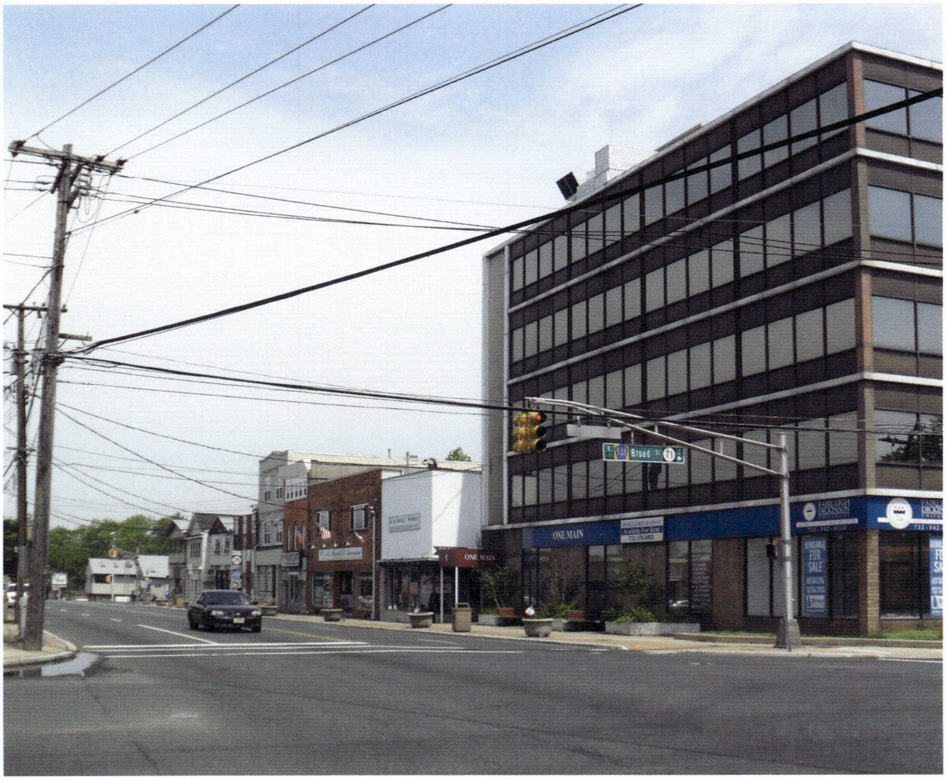

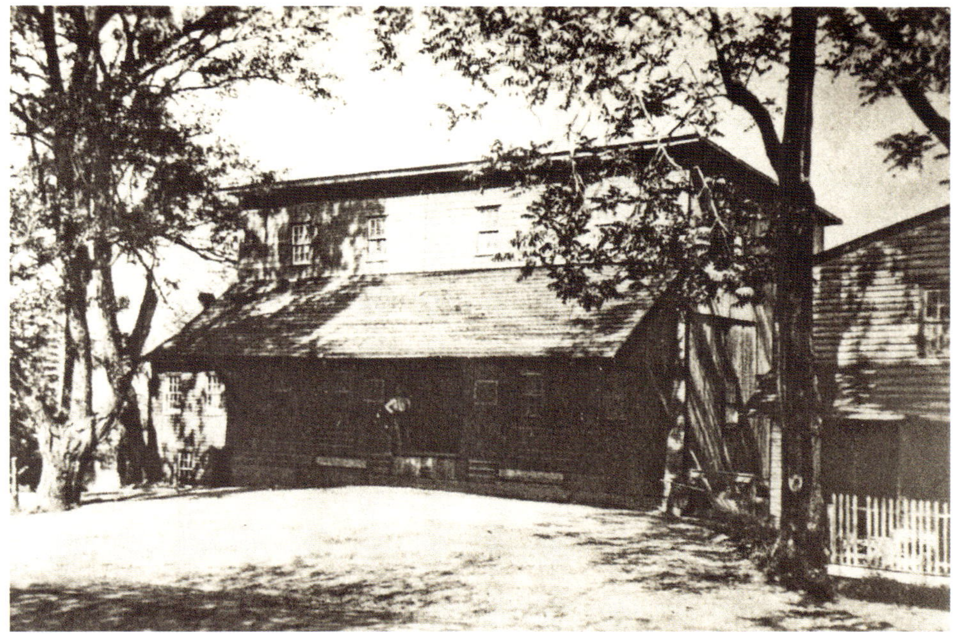

THE OLD GRISTMILL: The Old Gristmill on Pine Brook in Tinton Falls is pictured during the first decade of the twentieth century. The original mill was built in the second half of the seventeenth century, and the current remodeled version likely dates to the first half of the nineteenth century. Milling operations ceased at this location in the early 1920s, and it has subsequently functioned as an art studio, dinner theater and has for many years served as a restaurant, its current incarnation.

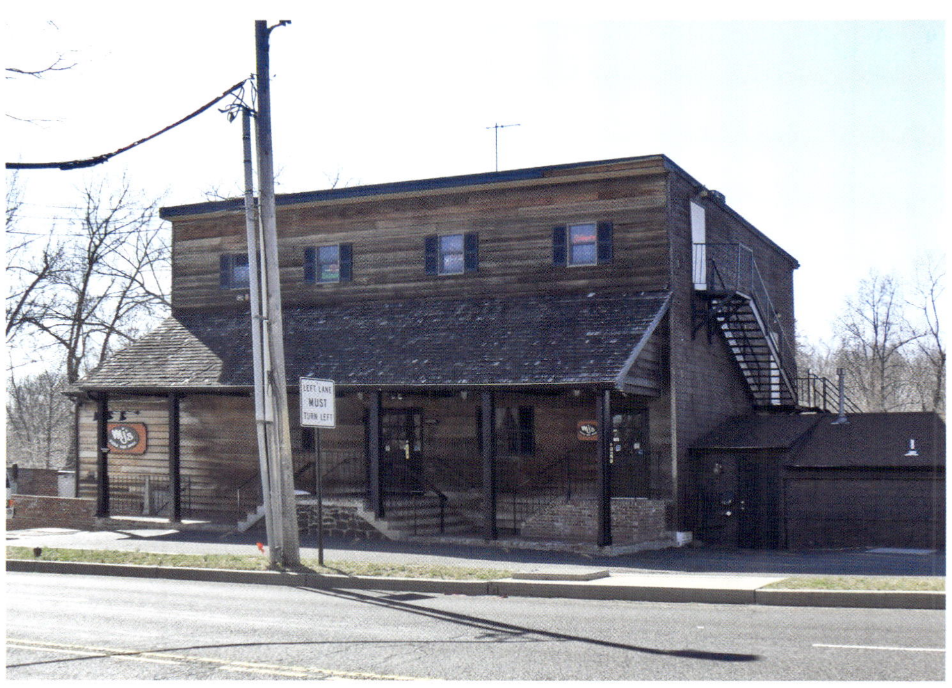

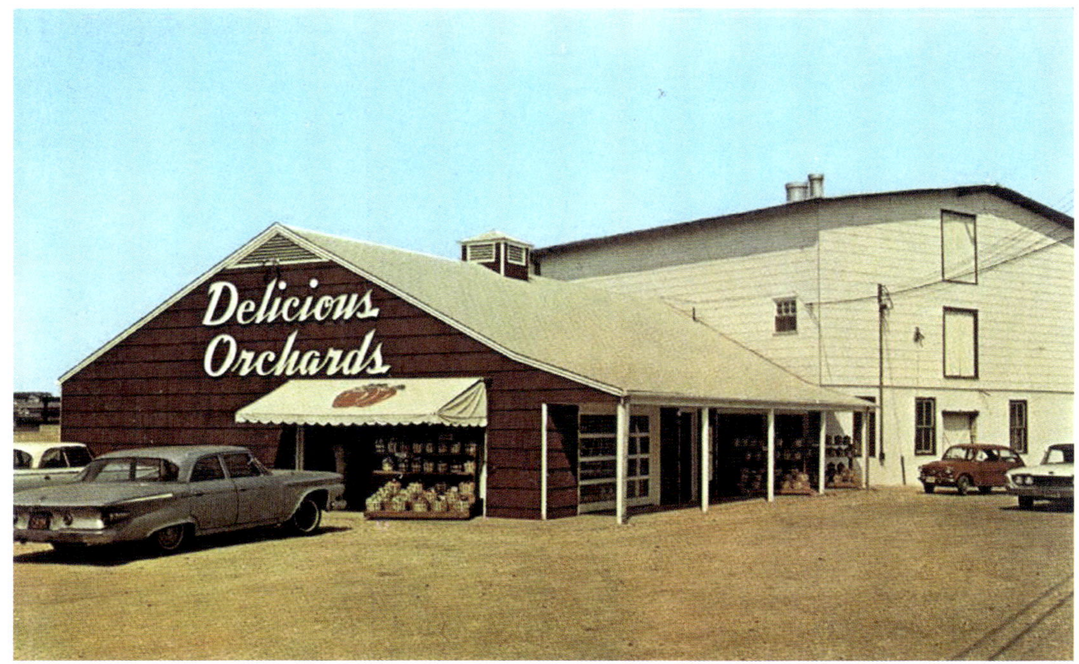

DELICIOUS ORCHARDS IN COLTS NECK: Delicious Orchards started as a roadside stand among the celebrated apple orchards which have lined Route 537 for over two centuries. In 1960 the first permanent stand, as pictured here, was constructed. By the end of the 1960s the retail business was moved to the current location on nearby Route 34. Although the original stand was demolished, the processing is still conducted in the large building pictured on the right, located at the foot of the orchard.

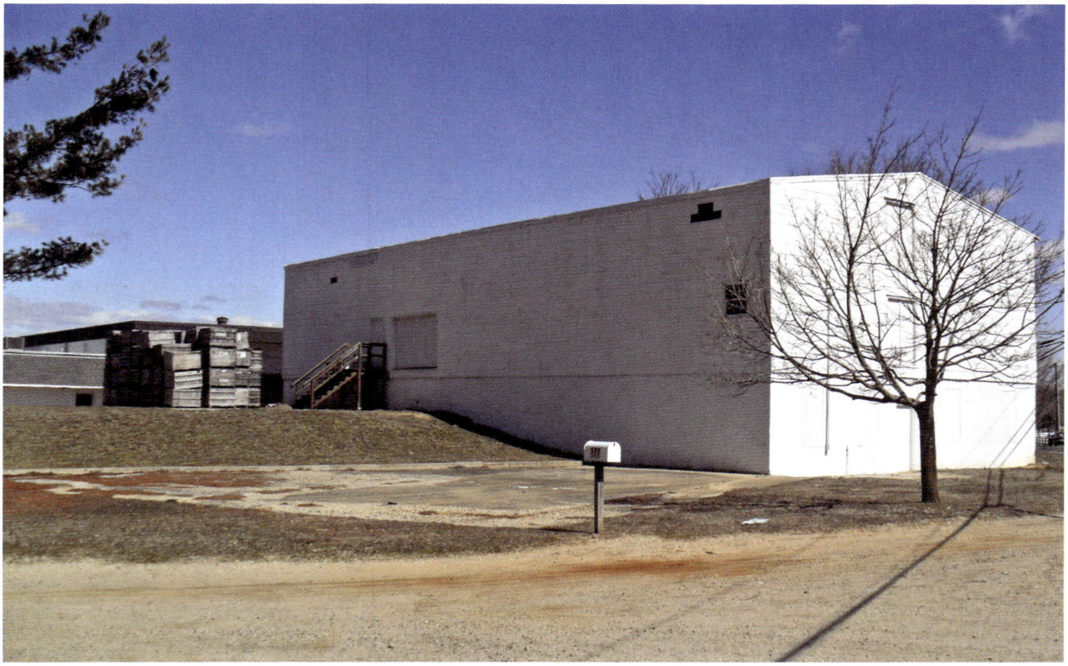

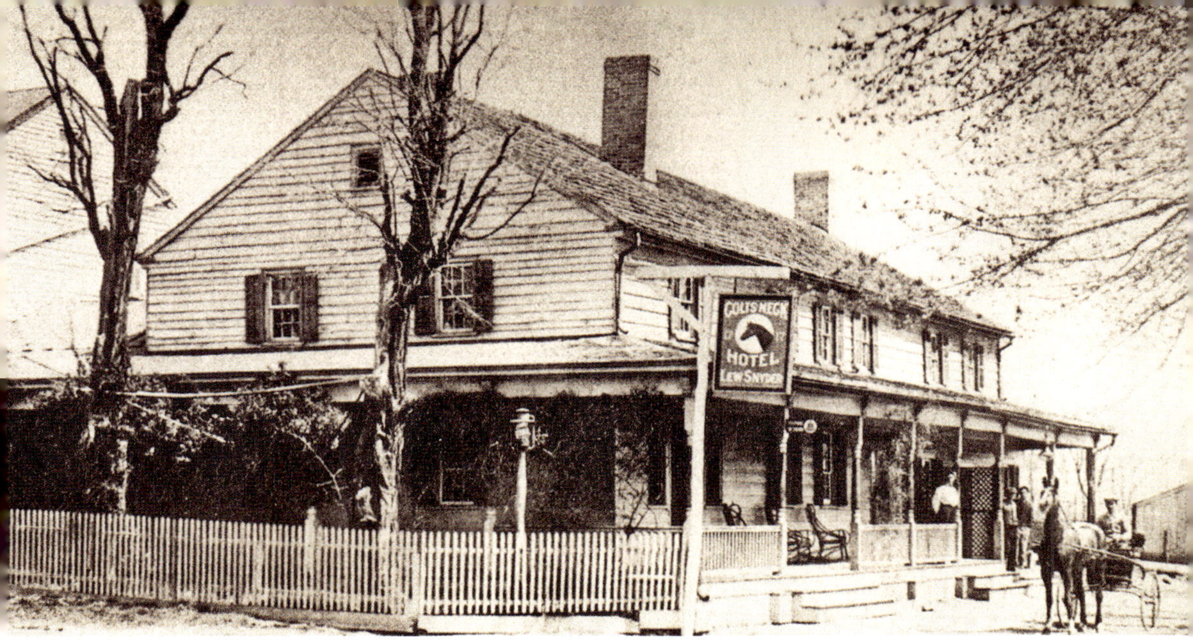

THE COLTS NECK INN: The Inn was built by the Laird family in 1717 and long served as a tavern and stage stop. Robert Laird began to distill applejack using the acres of apples from the family orchards located nearby. Laird befriended George Washington, who after sharing a toast with Laird, immediately requested the recipe, which he in turn began to distill at his home plantation at Mount Vernon. The Laird family eventually sold the inn, pictured on a 1900s postcard, but continues to operate the oldest distillery in New Jersey.

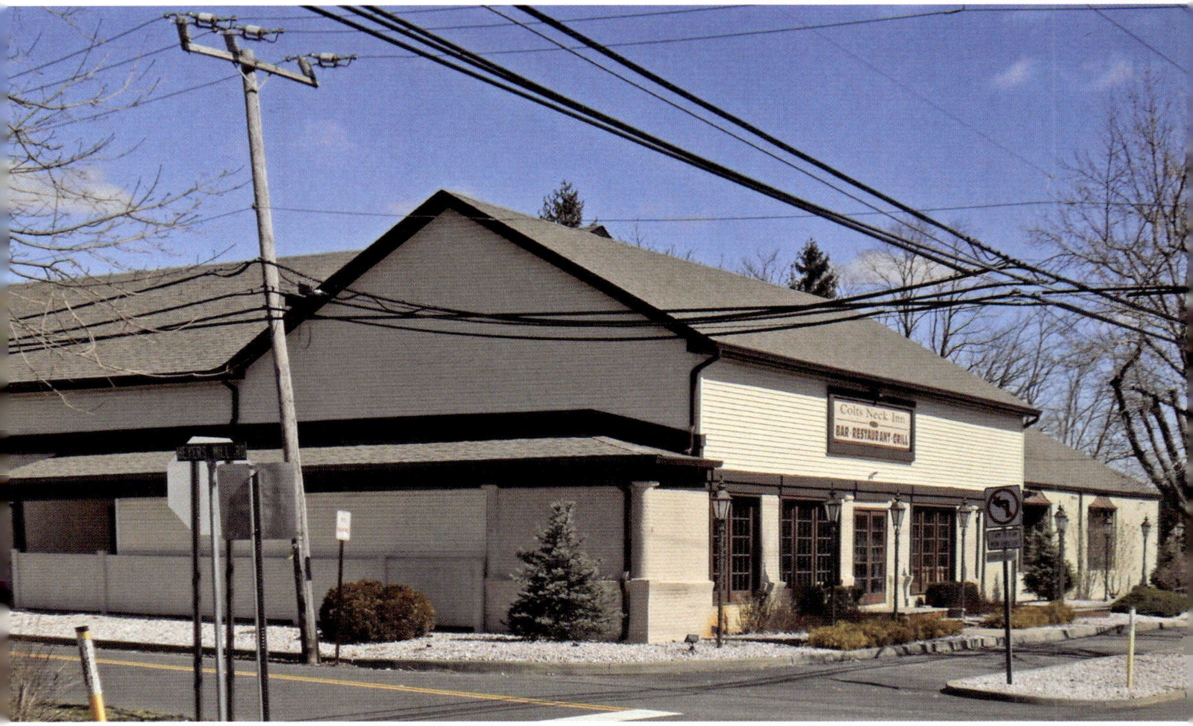

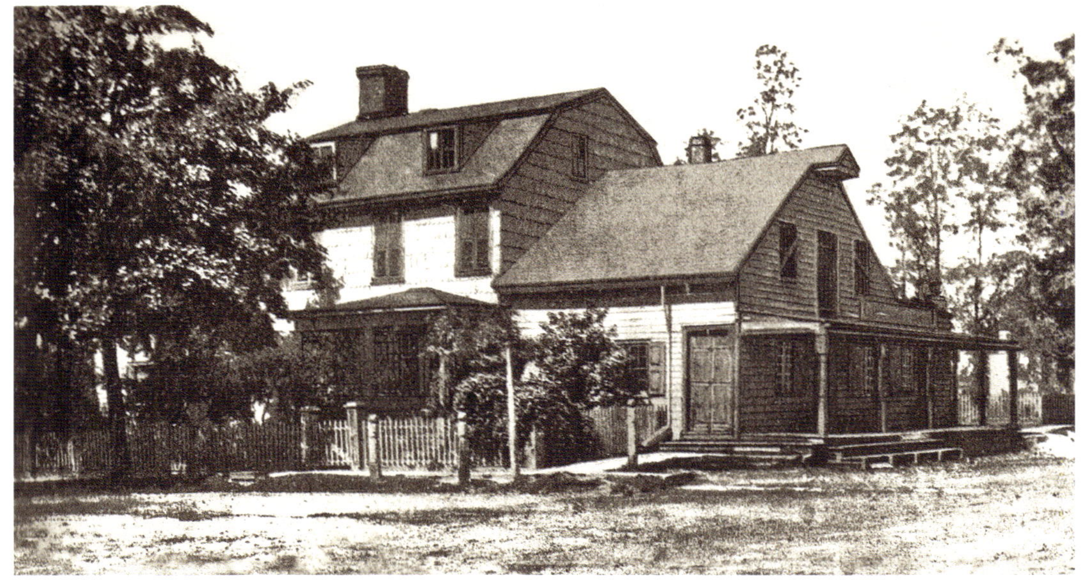

THE ALLEN HOUSE: New York City merchant Richard Stillwell built the core of what is known as the Allen house at the corner of Sycamore and Route 35 in about 1740 as his summer home. He died shortly thereafter, and Josiah Halstead bought the property and operated the Blue Ball Tavern for many years, expanding the building several times. The Allen family purchased the business in 1814, and ran a pharmacy, and later a general store on the premises. The complex is pictured shortly before a devastating fire in 1914 claimed the general store section.

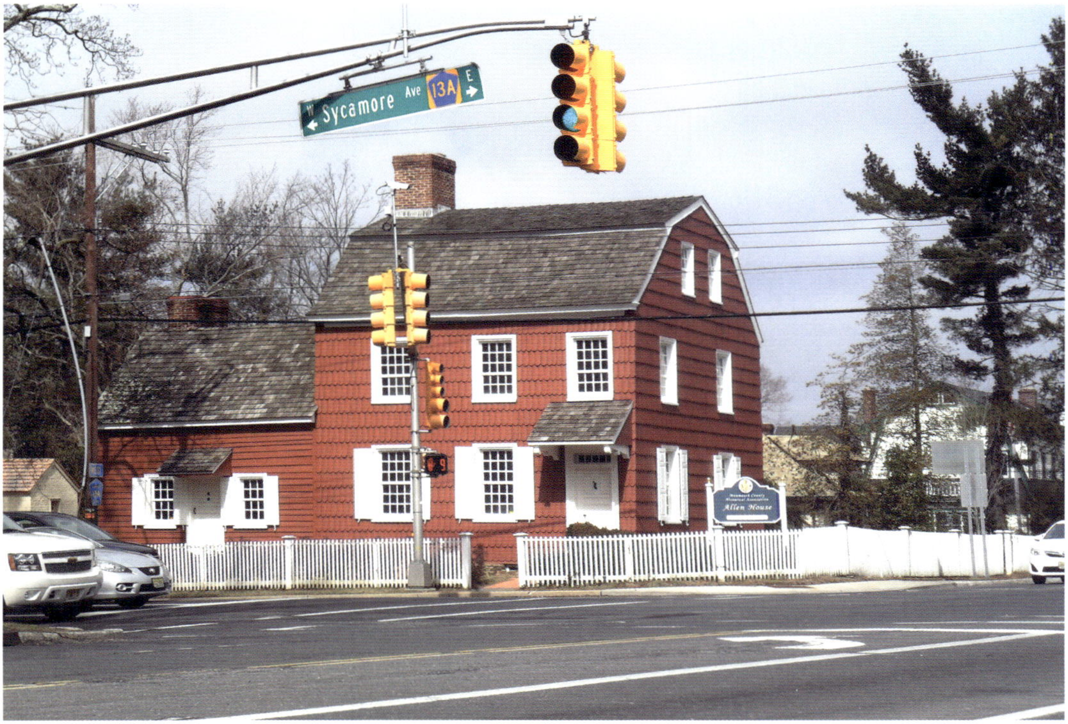

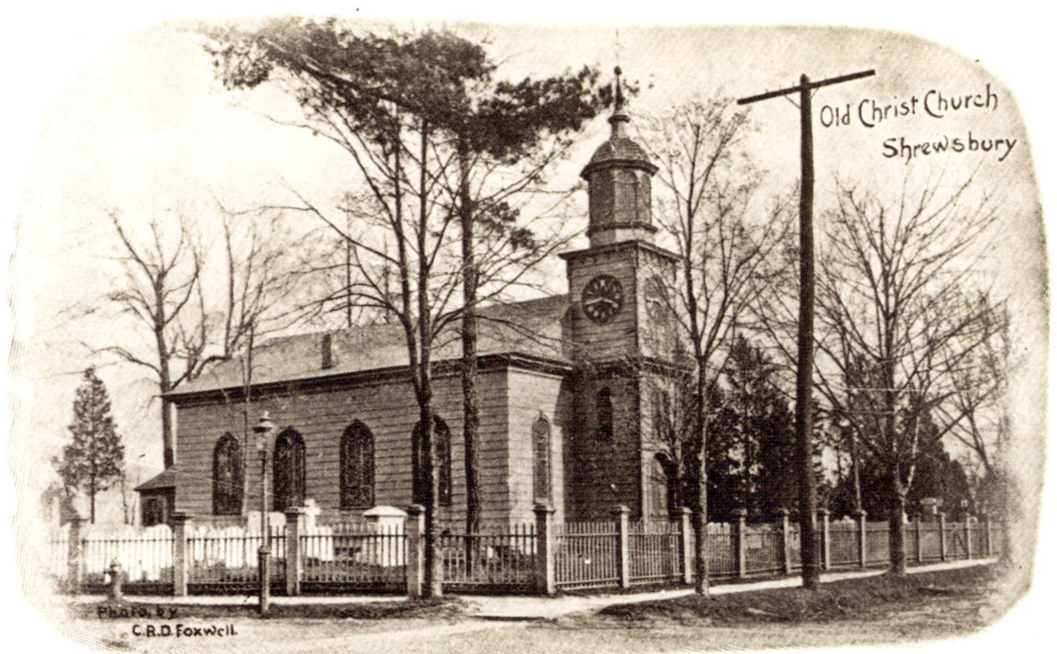

THE CHRIST CHURCH OF SHREWSBURY: Diagonally facing the Allen House, the Church, pictured in 1900, was constructed from 1769-74. The clock tower was added one hundred years later. The church was used as a barracks for patriot soldiers during the Revolutionary War, who shot musket balls through the pulpit and steeple as a sign of disrespect to the British Crown. Ironically, these musket-damaged artifacts were never repaired, and now are proud relics of the still active Episcopal congregation.

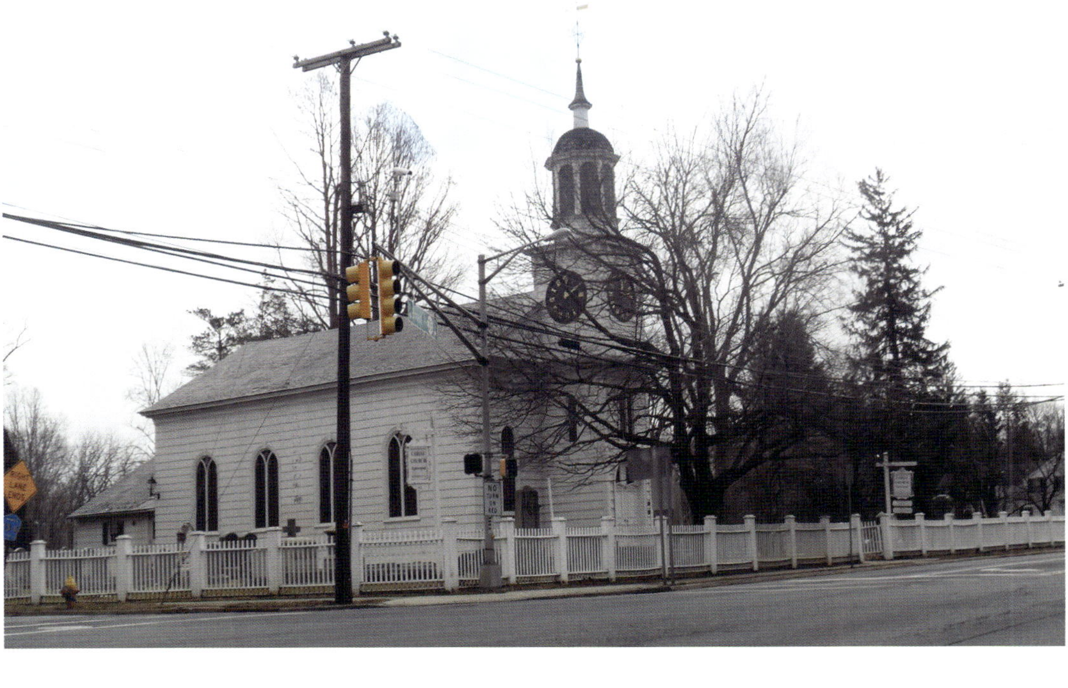

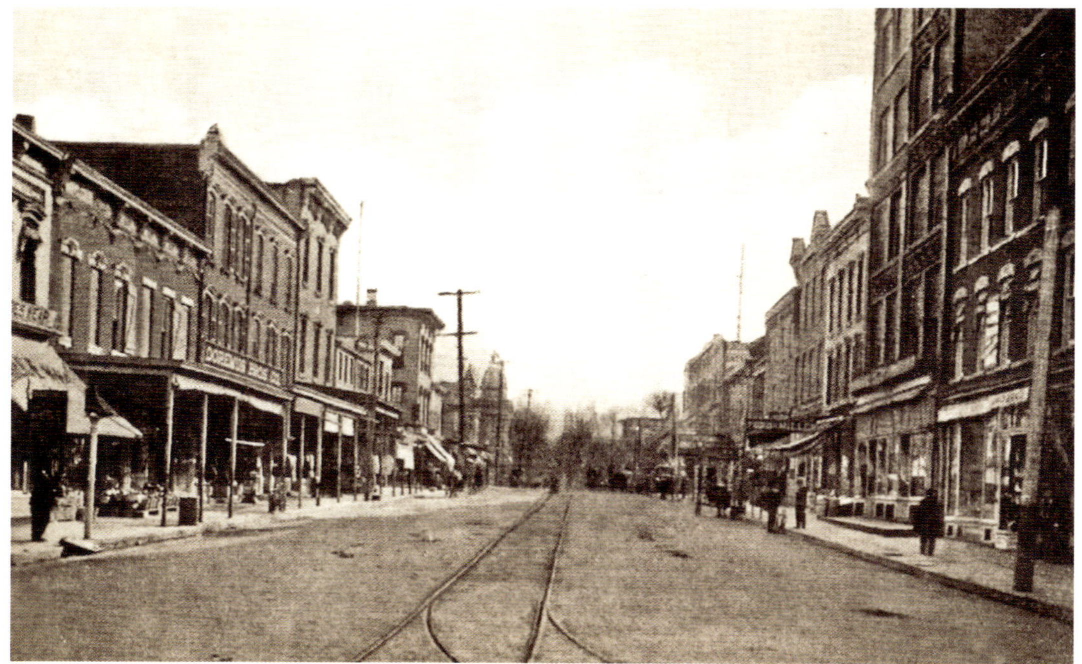

BROAD STREET: Looking south on Broad Street from Front Street in Red Bank one can truly appreciate the integrity of the neighborhood in 2013 when studying an image from the 1890s. Much like the current rebirth of Asbury Park, Red Bank was similarly revitalized when the Eisner apparel factory was redeveloped into retail space the 1990s and became an attraction for the successful and the chic.

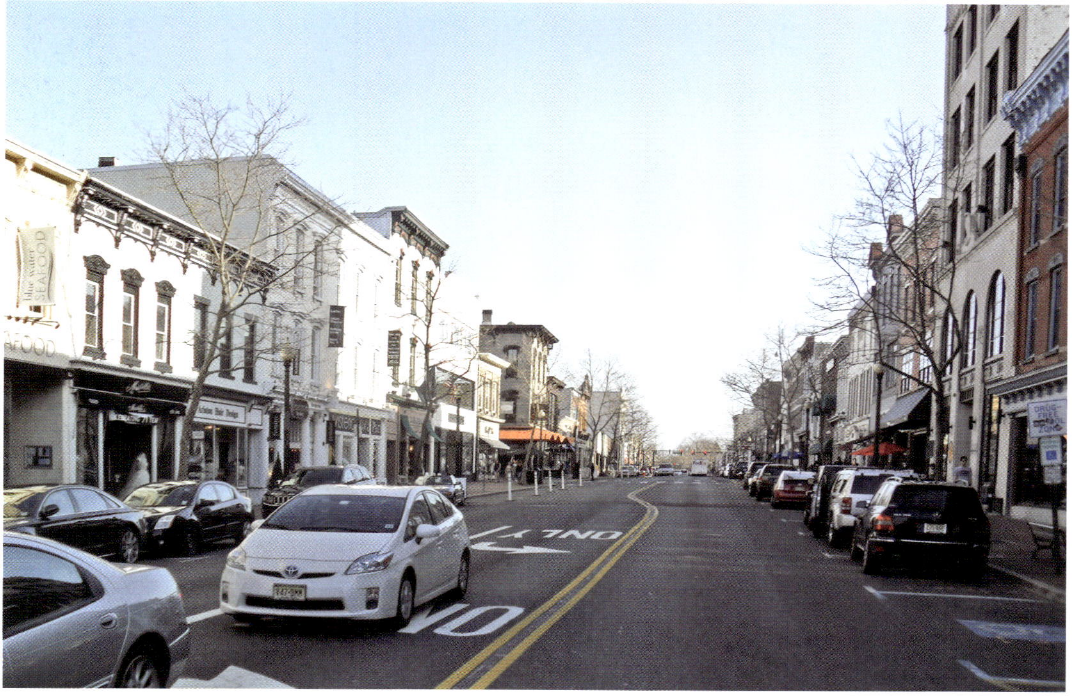

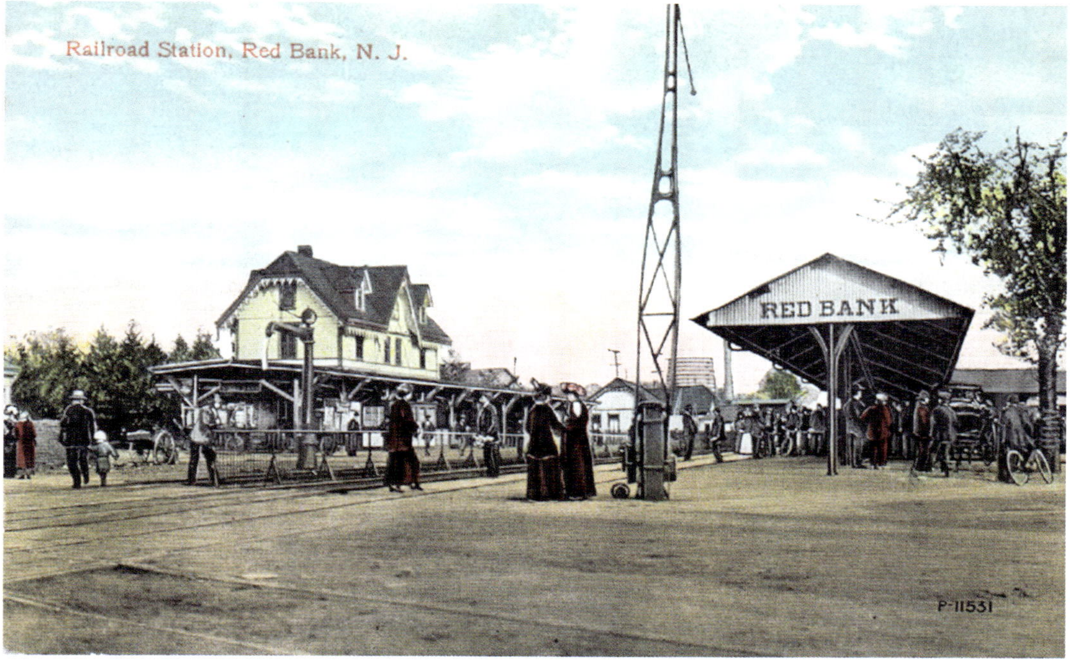

RED BANK TRAIN STATION: The station was completed in 1875. Pictured in 1905, these nearly identical 'stick style' buildings, were used extensively by the Central Jersey Railroad throughout the 1870s. Today only three still exist. Two are located in Monmouth County: Red Bank and Matawan (see page 75). The third existing station building is located in Fanwood.

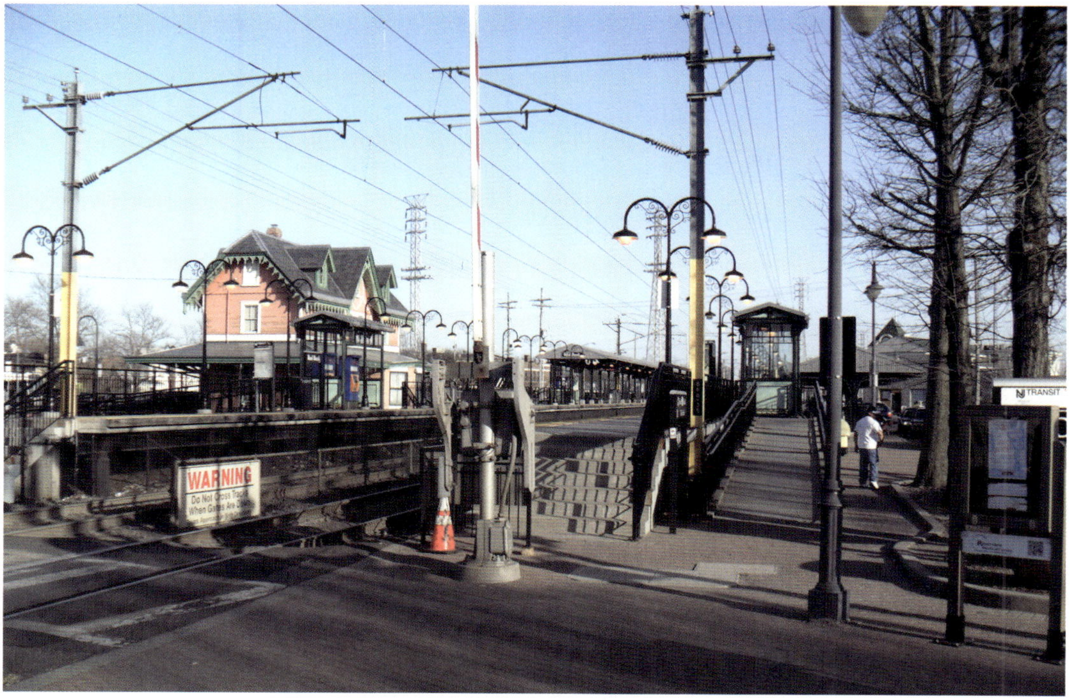

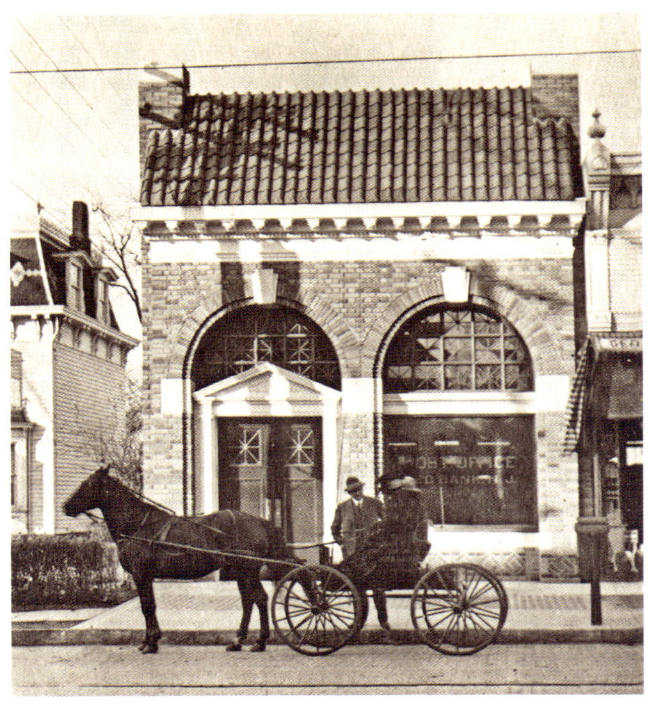

RED BANK POST OFFICE: The original location of the Red Bank post office on Monmouth Street is pictured in 1906. The vintage image captures the Robert Allen House (which today houses the Dublin House restaurant) at extreme left shortly after its move from Broad Street. The post office building has housed the popular Monmouth Music store since 1987.

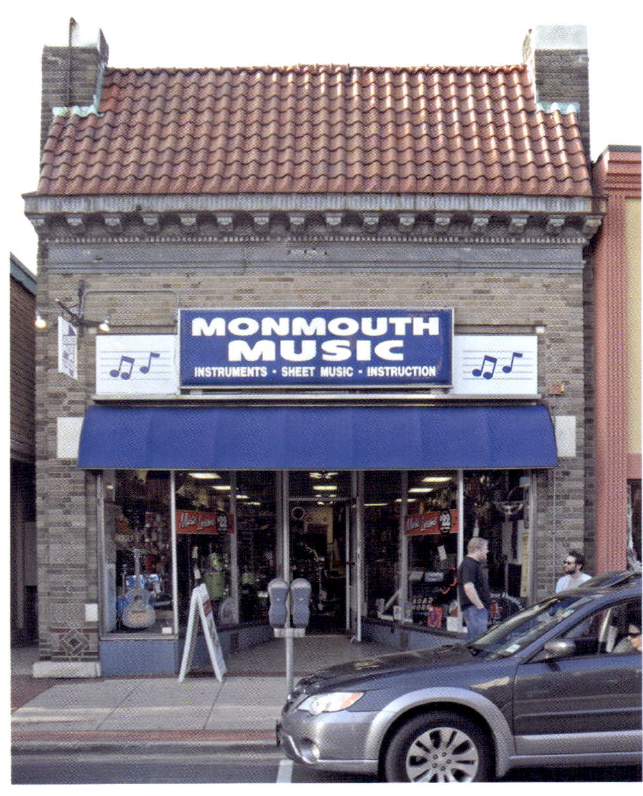

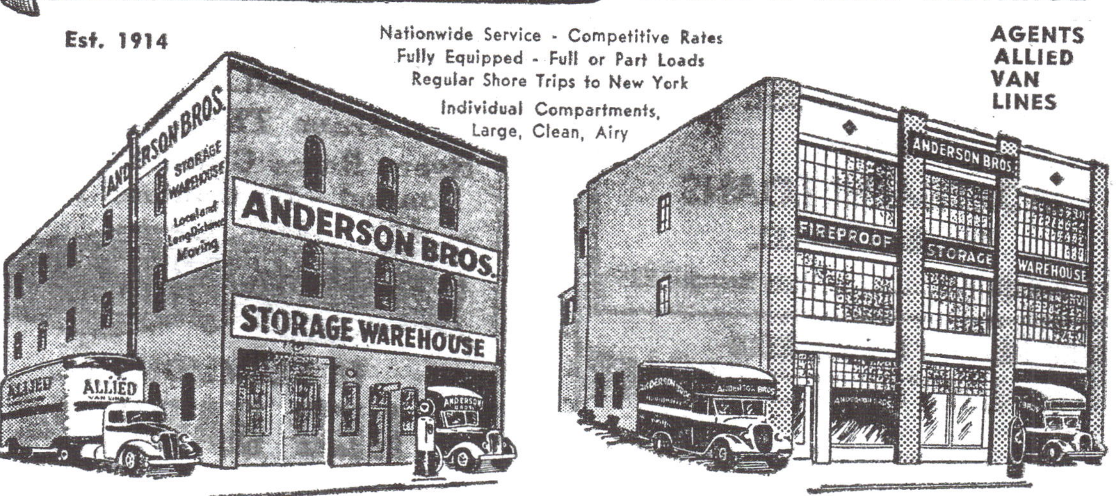

ANDERSON BROTHERS: Reprinted here is an early 1940s advertisement for Anderson Brother Moving & Storage. The company started off in the Mechanic Street building in Red Bank pictured here. Shortly afterward they expanded, building a large warehouse in Bradley Beach. Both original locations are still intact, as illustrated. In the early 1950s, Anderson Brothers moved their operations to another existing building, diagonally across from the Red Bank train station.

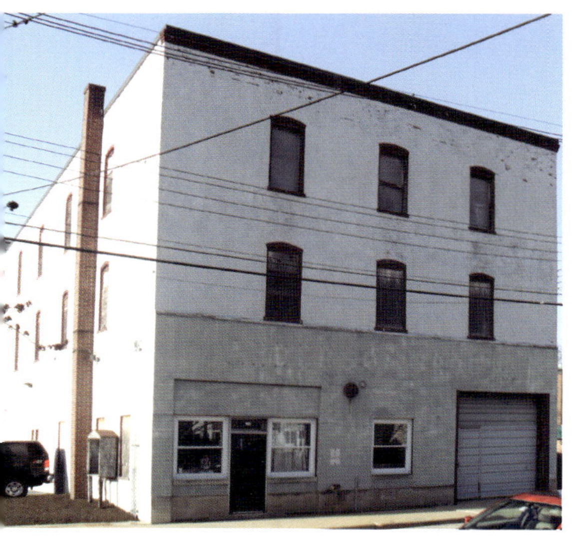

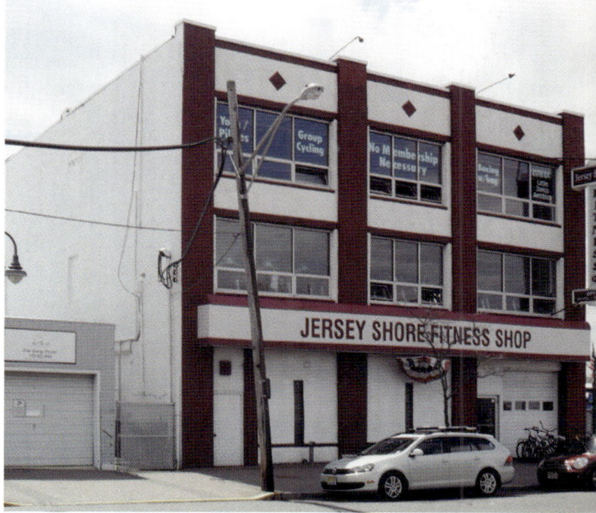

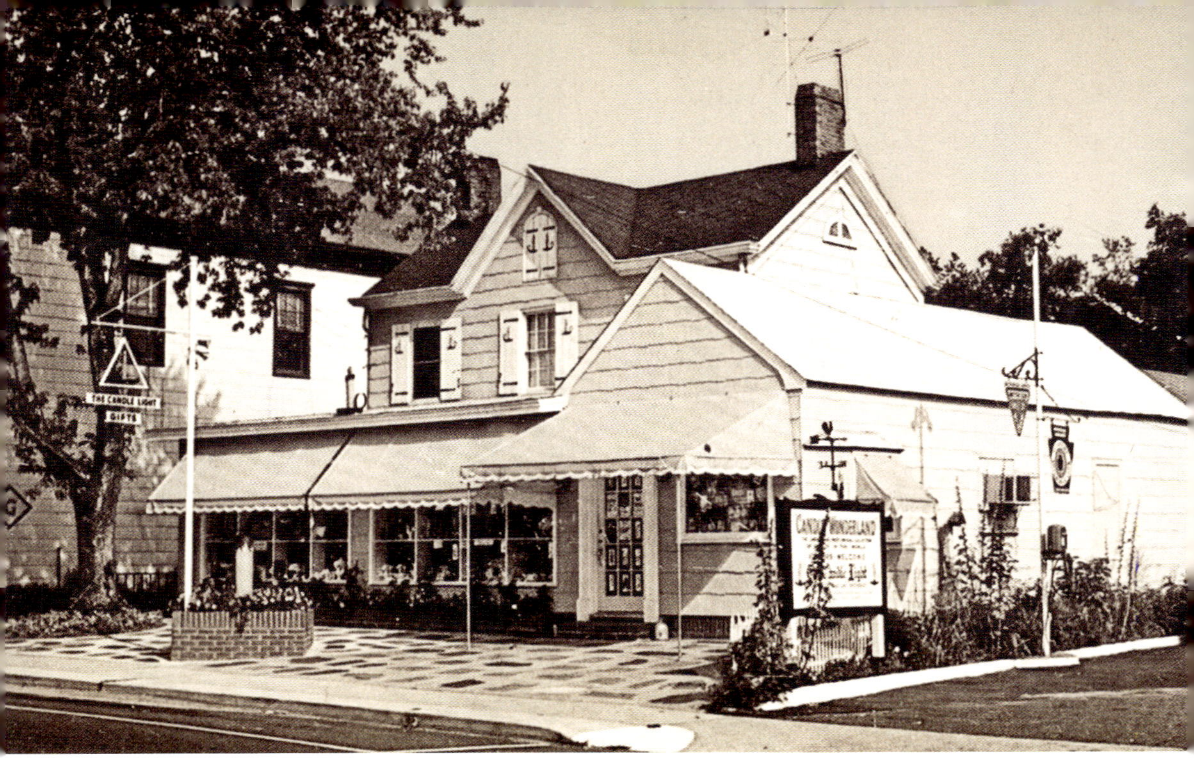

THE CANDLE LIGHT GIFT SHOP: The Shop on River Road is pictured in the 1950s. The unusual complex is actually a combination of two separate small buildings which were moved from their original locations in Fair Haven to the current location in 1947. The building has housed a deli for the past few decades.

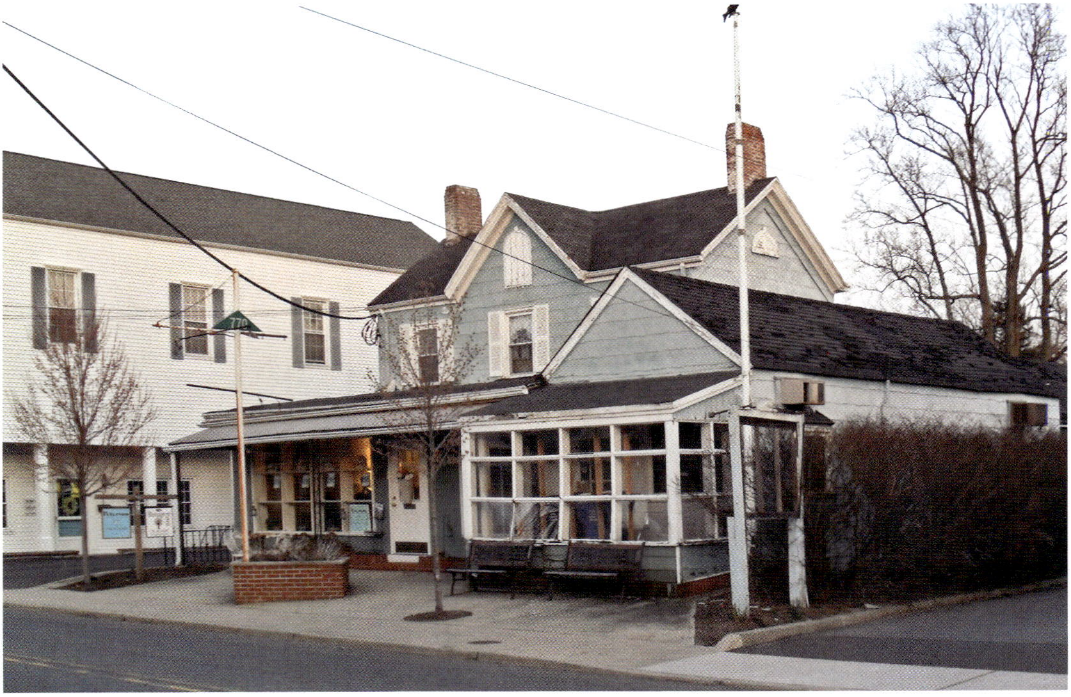

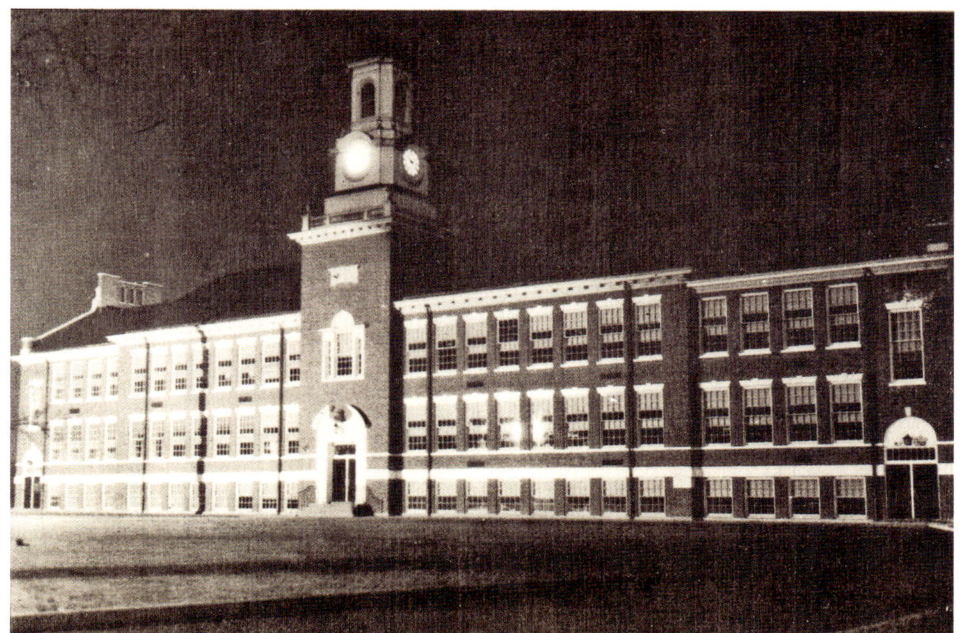

THE RUMSON FAIR HAVEN HIGH SCHOOL: The School was constructed by the Works Progress Act in 1936. The rare night photograph here was taken in 1938. In an odd, and somewhat frightening note, in 2004 military intelligence recovered a CD-rom from the body of an Iraqi insurgent which had detailed information regarding four high schools in the United States, RFH being one of them. Luckily, there were never any further developments to this frightening revelation.

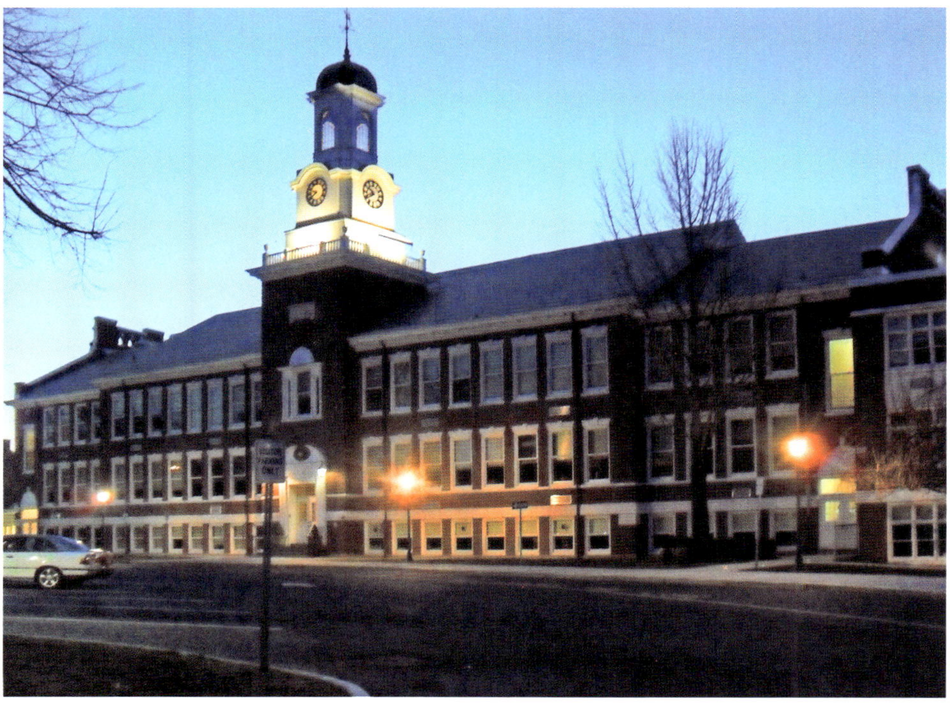

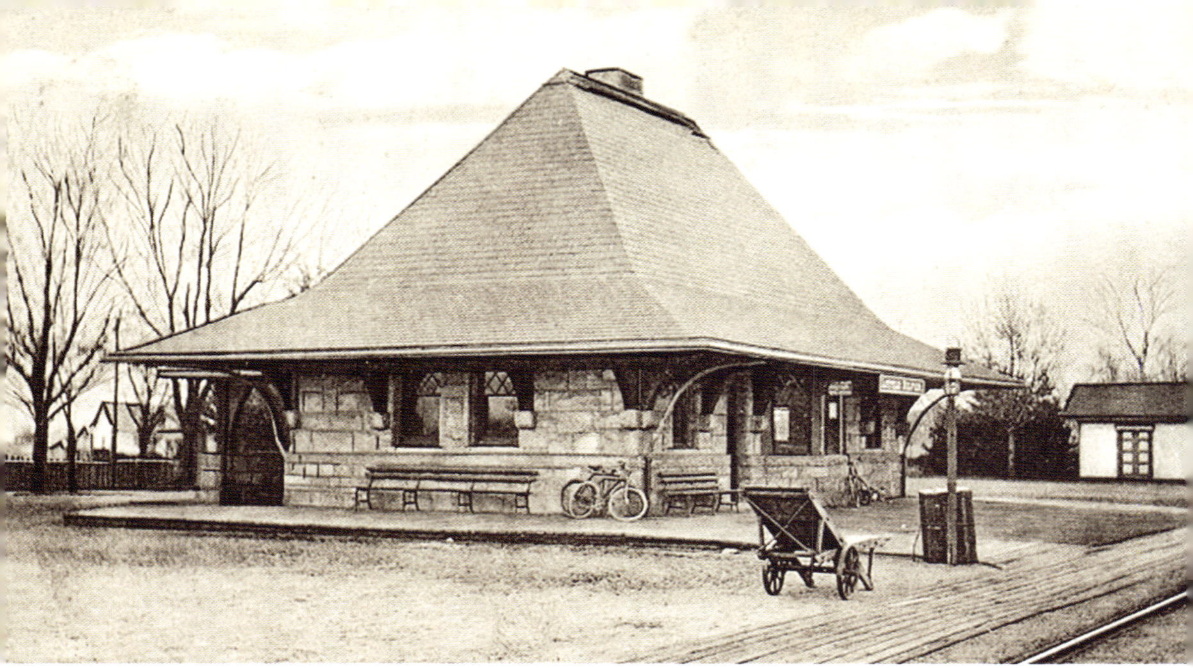

Little Silver Train Station: Completed in 1890 and pictured here in the 1900s, this is one of the final architectural designs by the noted Henry Hobson Richardson prior to his death in 1886. By the end of the 1990s, the station was in disrepair, and faced the threat of demolition. Luckily, funds were secured for the station's renovation, which was undertaken from 2001-3.

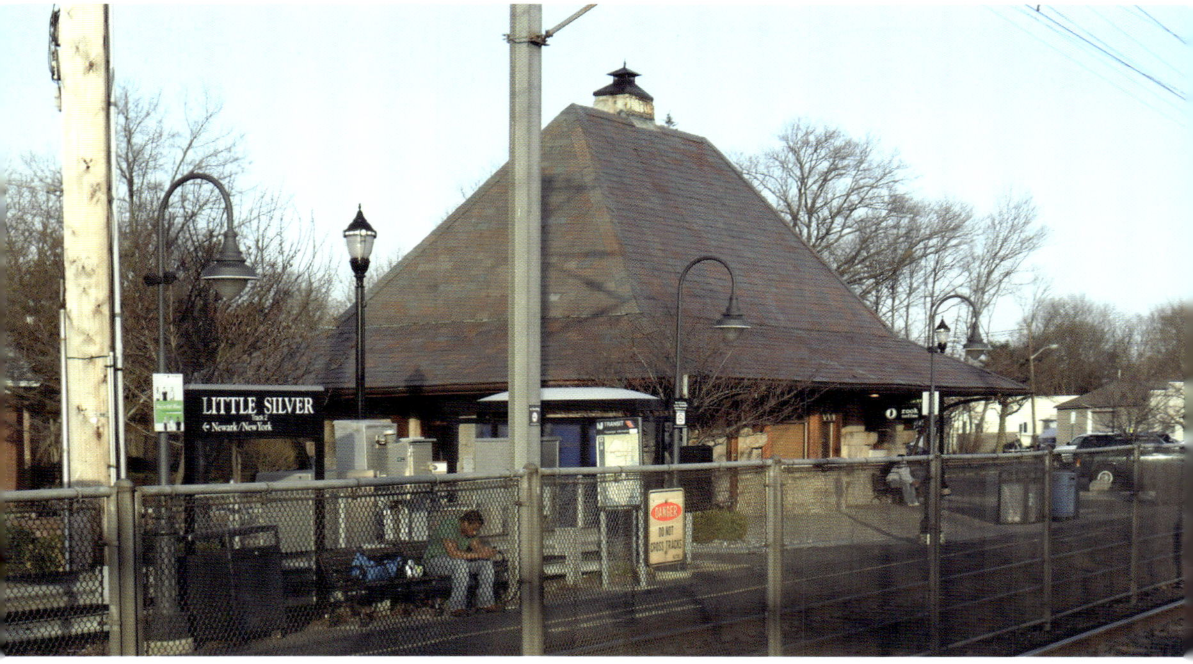

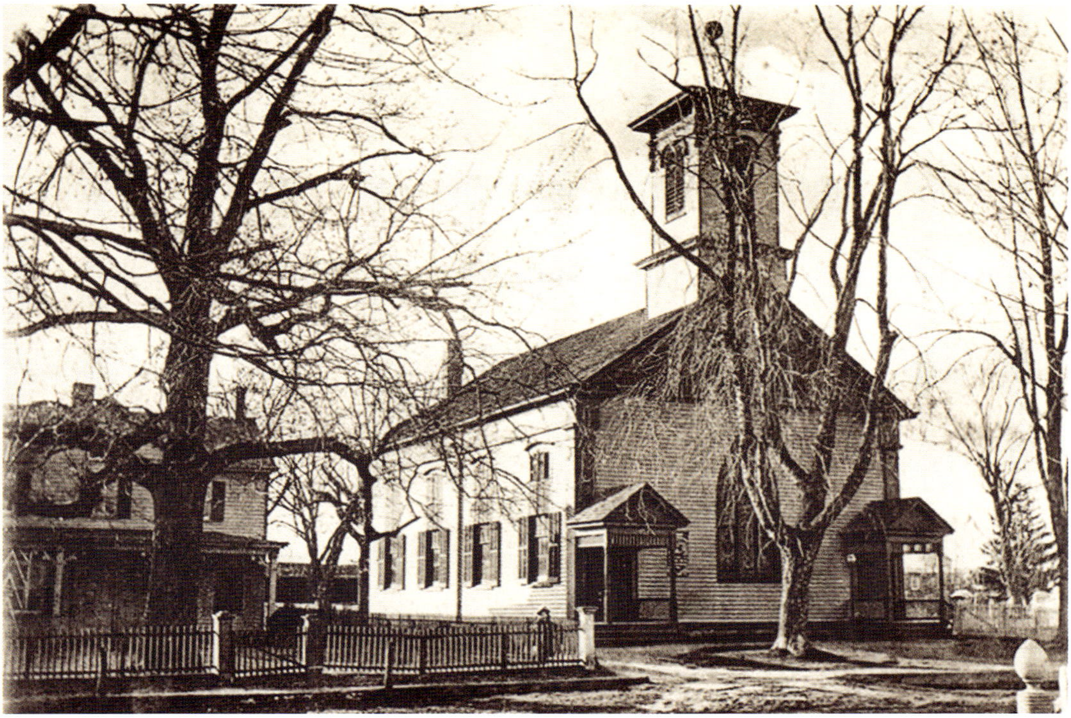

THE EMBURY UNITED METHODIST CHURCH: This is a 1890 view of the Embury United Methodist Church in Little Silver. It was constructed in 1868-9, and was named after Phillip Embury, a pioneer Methodist preacher from New York City. The building was updated and expanded in the 1920s, 1950s, 1960s and again in the 1980s. Throughout all of these renovations, the basic exterior presence has remained unchanged.

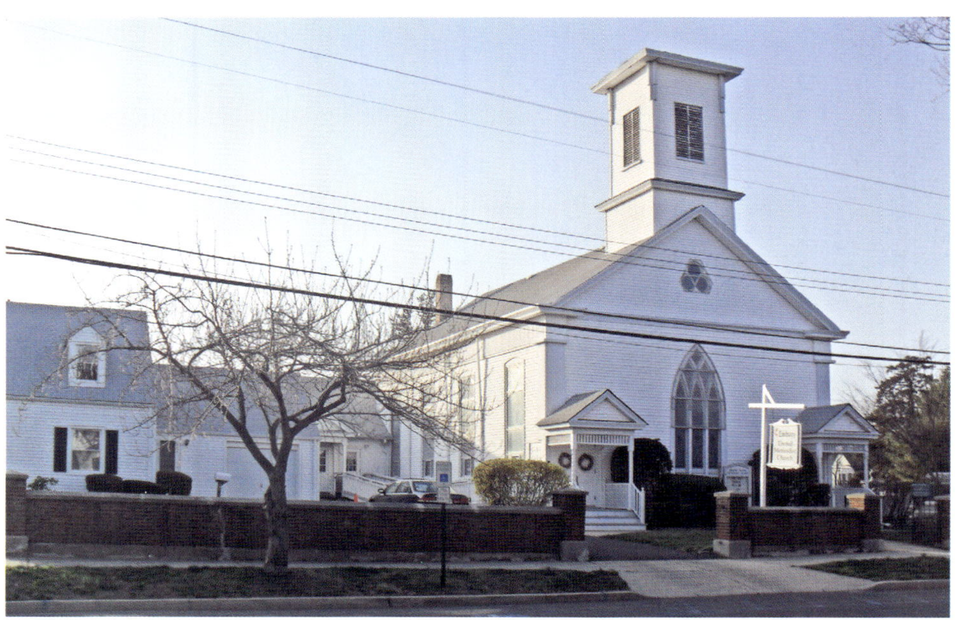

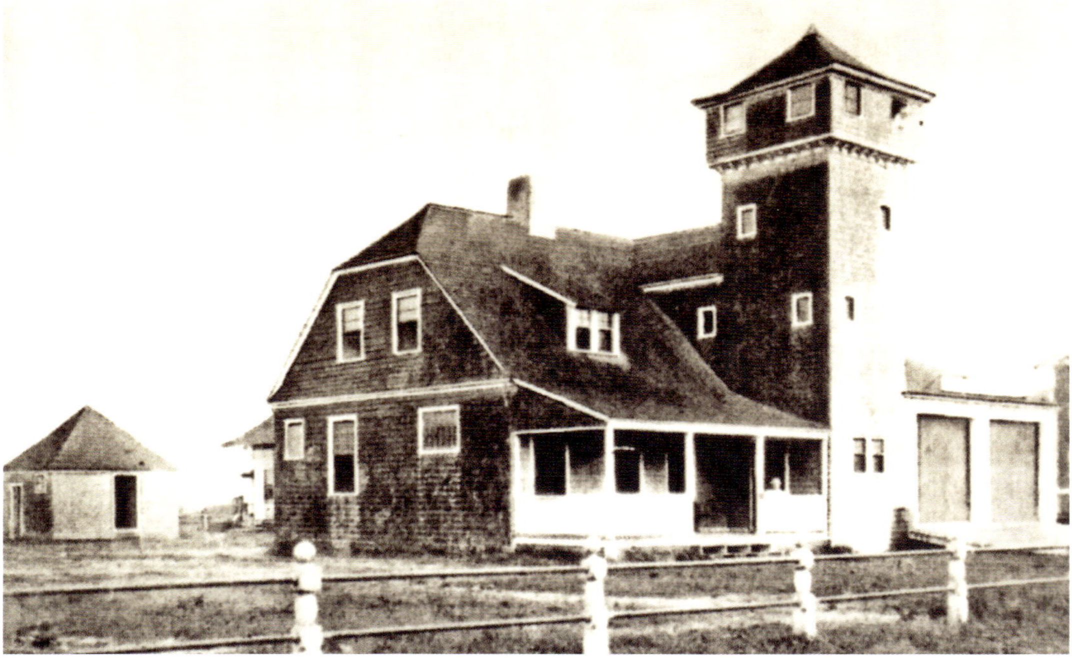

THE 1895 MONMOUTH BEACH LIFE SAVING STATION: Currently serving as a museum, the Station is pictured on a *c.* 1907 postcard. The Life Saving Service built hundreds of these 'Duluth' buildings around the country named after the first example built in Minnesota. As of 2013, there were three remaining in Monmouth County. The design serves as a testament of durability with a commendable number still existing around the country despite so many years of oceanfront embattlement with Mother Nature.

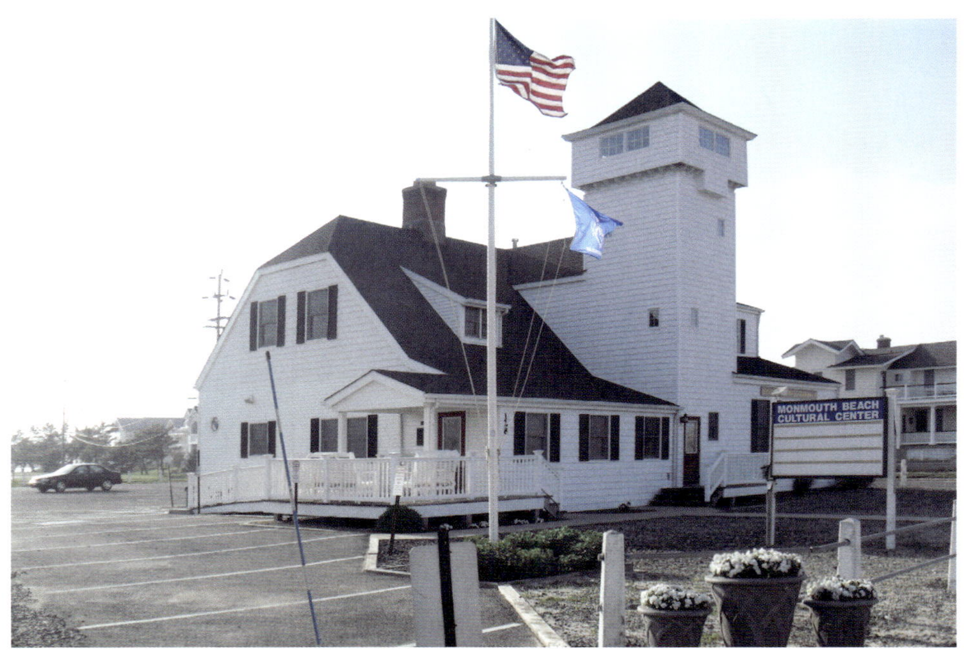

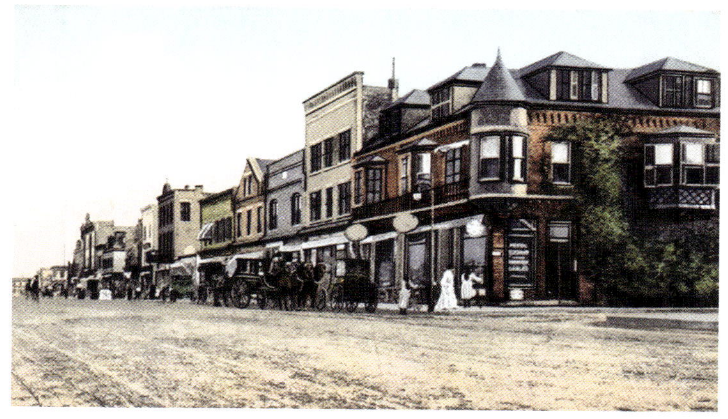

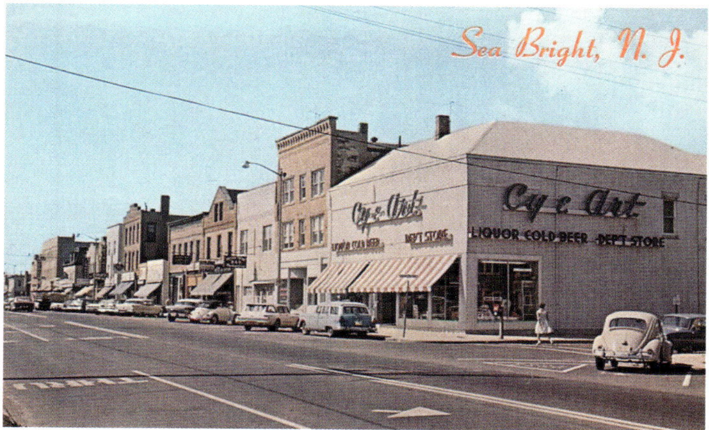

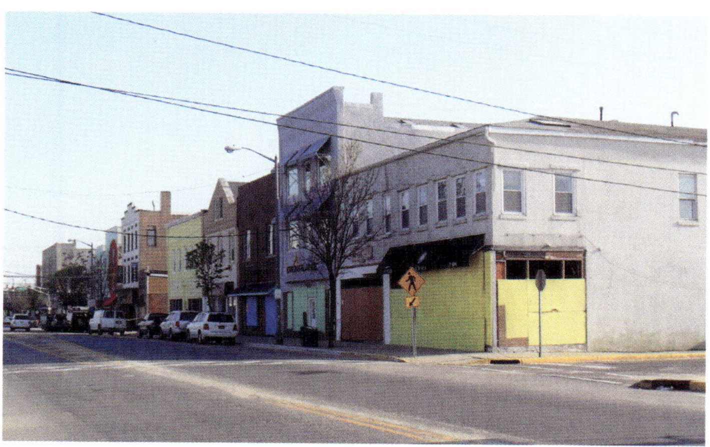

OCEAN AVENUE: The main drag along Ocean Avenue in Sea Bright is pictured in the 1900s, 1960s and 2013. Despite being damaged by Hurricane Sandy, all of the major buildings on the strip survived and are in various stages of repair. This is certainly not the first time these buildings have faced storm damage, and probably will not be the last. Lest we forget the mariners' proverb that, 'you can't fight the sea'.

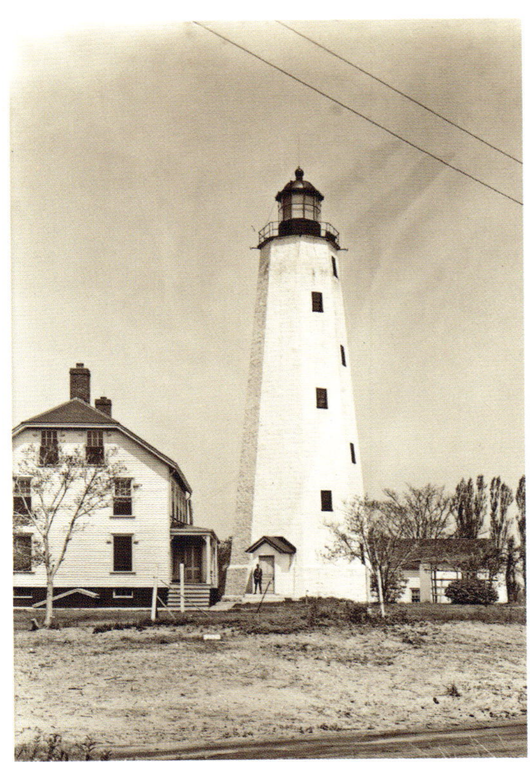

THE SANDY HOOK LIGHTHOUSE: Built in 1764, the Lighthouse is the oldest operating lighthouse in the United States. Pictured here in 1937, the beacon has long guided ships to the entrance of New York harbor. The Fresnal lens installed during the 1857 renovation is still in use. The present keeper's house was constructed in 1883.

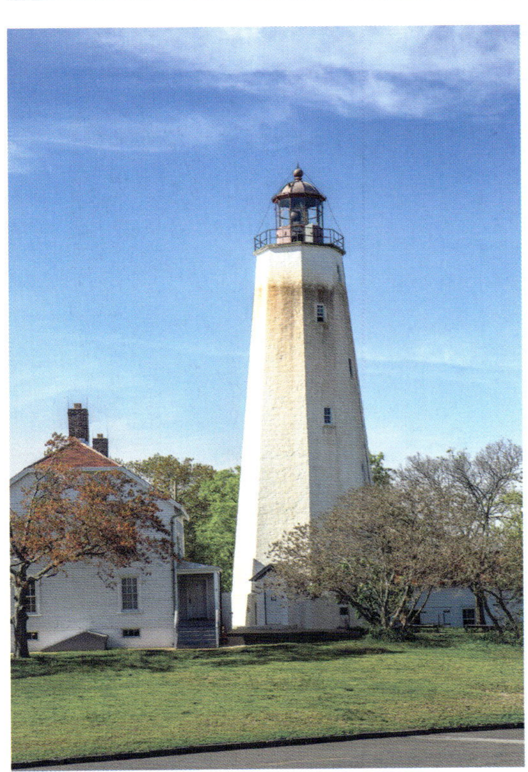

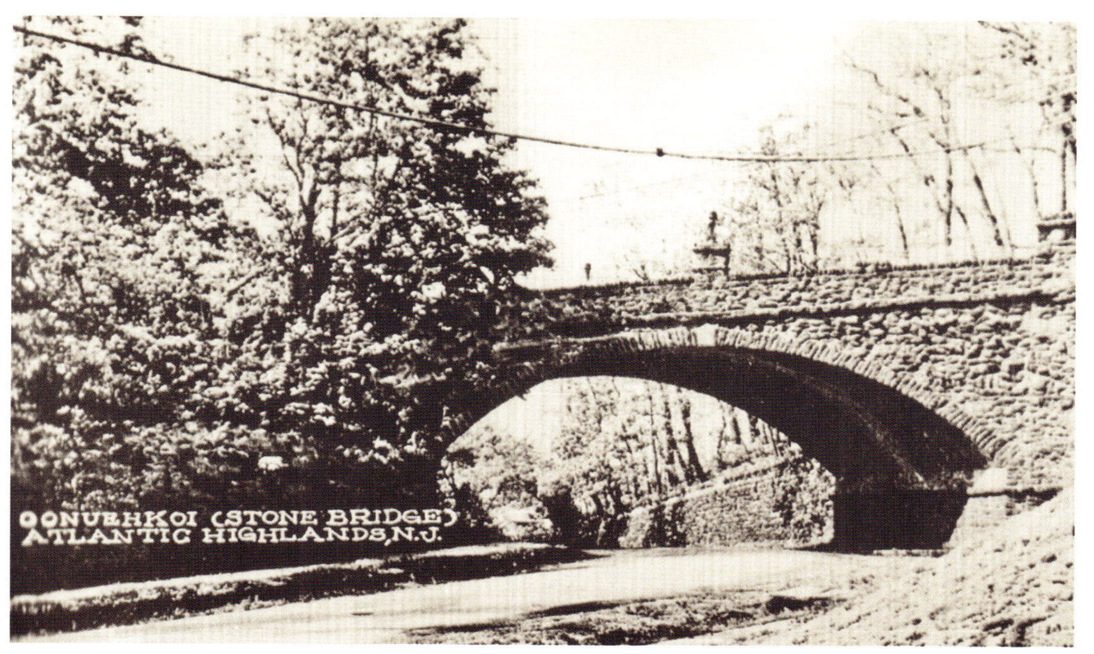

THE BRIDGE OVER GRAND AVENUE: George Lawrie designed and built an attractive stone bridge to carry Mount Avenue traffic over Grand Avenue in Atlantic Highlands in 1895-6. A contemporary history of Monmouth County printed that the bridge was named Oonuehkoi after the local family of Lenape natives, a claim which is unsupported by any existing historical evidence. Modern researchers suggest that Lawrie may have found the name in a history for the Boston-based Natick tribe for whom the word means 'valley'.

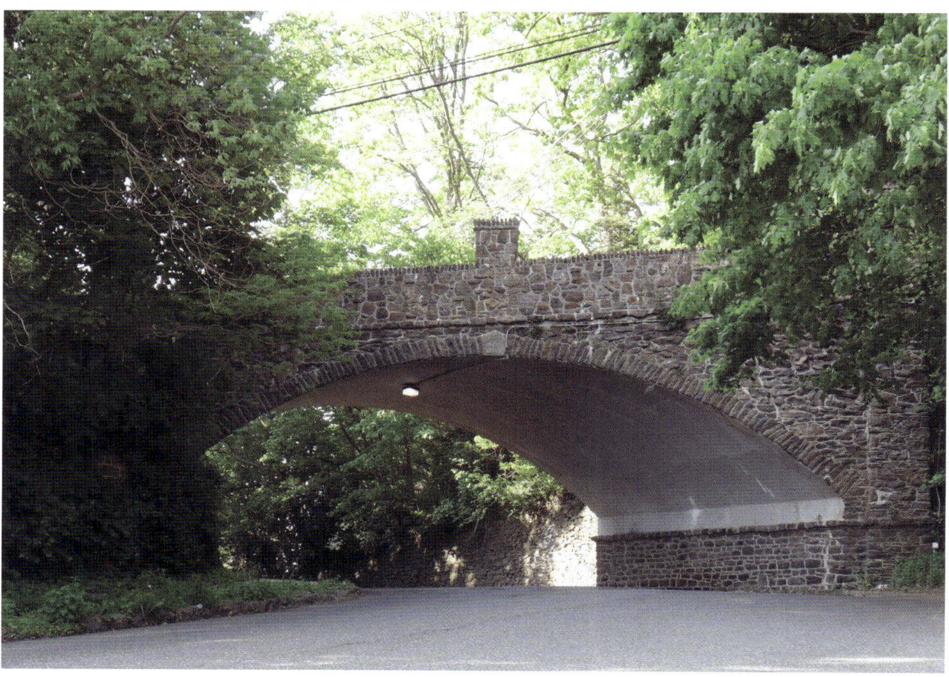

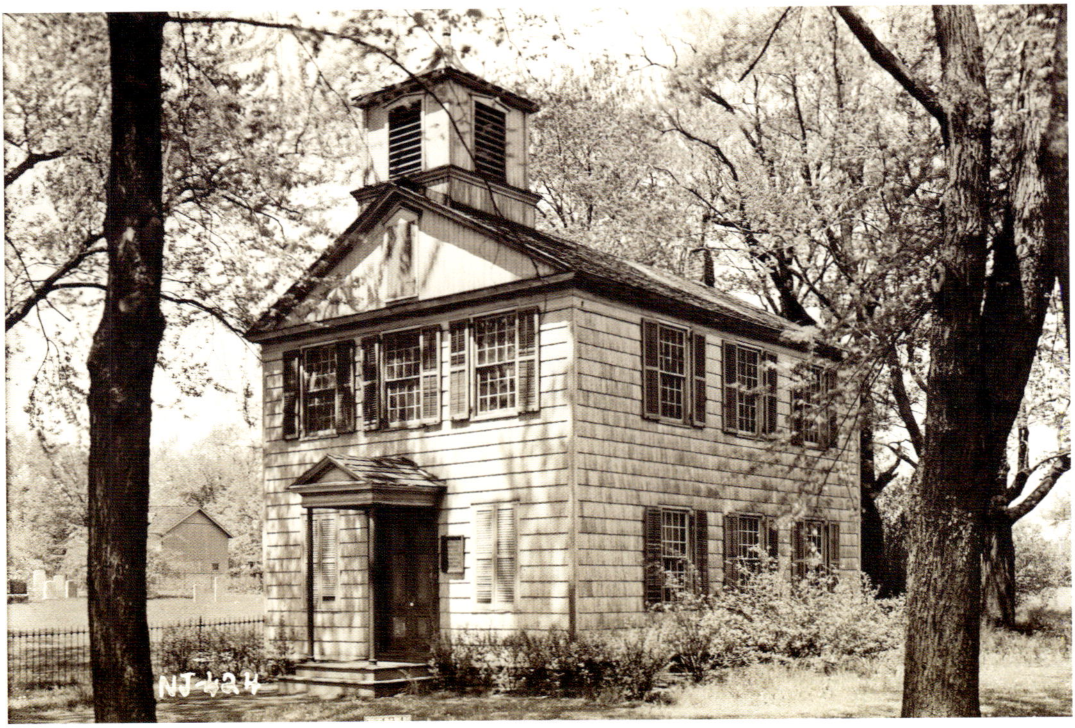

THE FRANKLIN ACADEMY: The Academy on Old Kings Highway in Middletown was built in 1836, and operated until 1851 as a co-ed private school. From 1851 until 1901 the building served as a Middletown public school. Thereafter it was used as a public library and is currently a private residence.

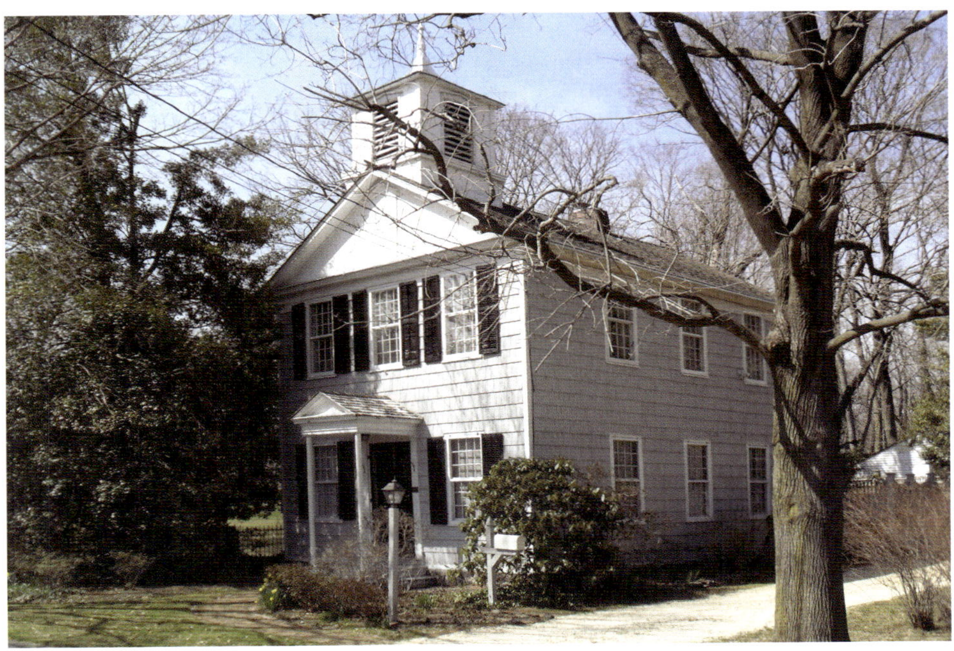

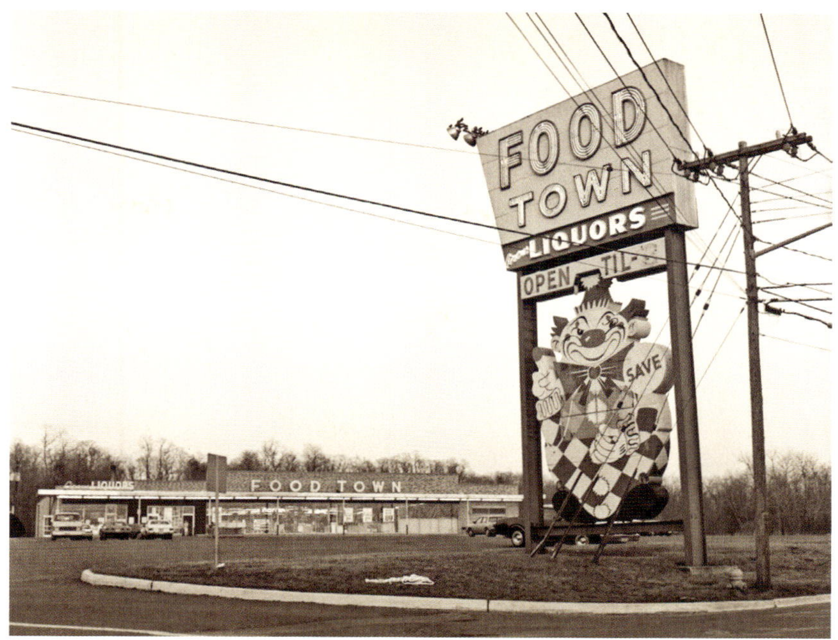

THE SIGN BUILT BY JOSEPH AZZOLINA: The sign was built in 1956 to advertise his supermarket. It has long been known locally as 'the evil clown of Middletown'. For the first few decades of service, the clown rotated within the display. Pictured here in the mid 1980s, 'Calico the Clown' is shown in his original duty, fittingly advertising the Circus Liquor store located within Foodtown. In 1991, the Azzolina family phased out the supermarket at the flagship location and focused exclusively on the liquor business, now operating as a Spirits location.

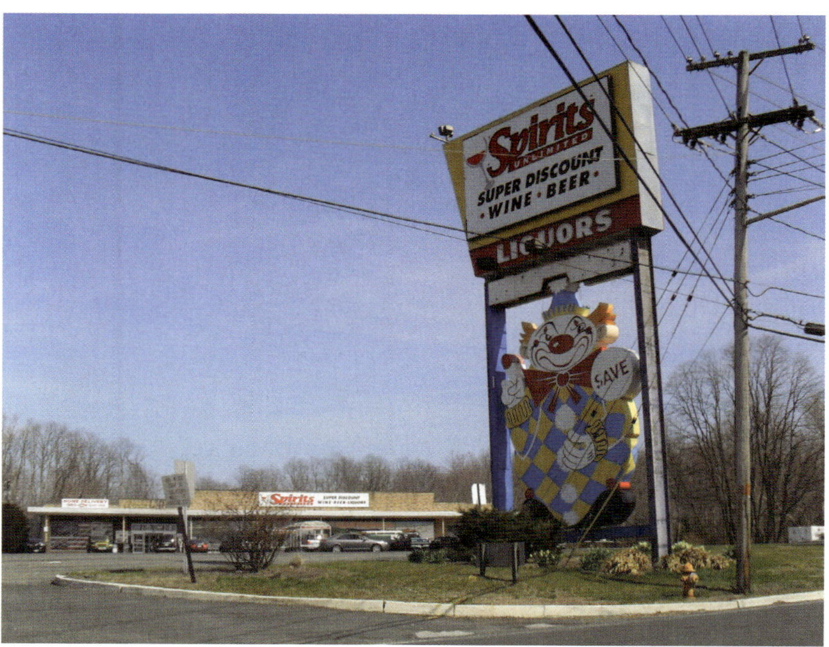

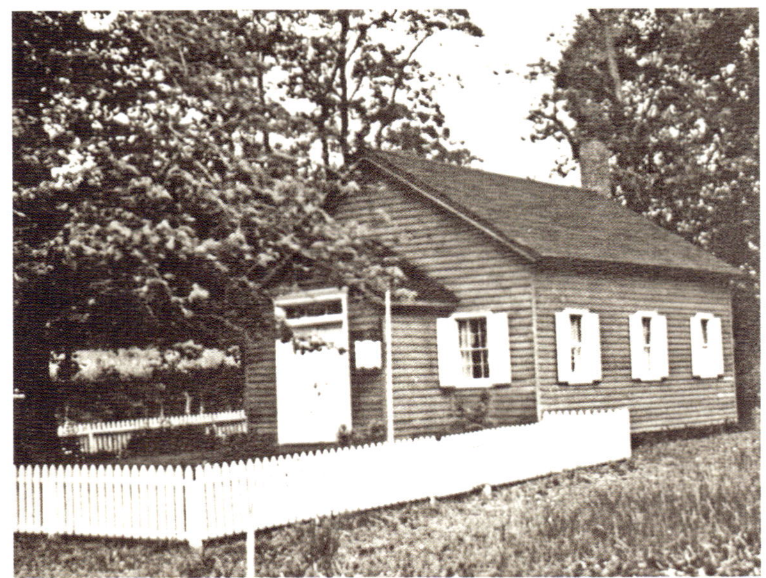

THE 1842 ONE-ROOM SCHOOLHOUSE: The structure in the Nut Swamp section of Middletown was discontinued for educational use in 1907, when a more substantial school was built nearby. The building was used to store farm equipment for nearly fifty years, when its custodianship was passed on to the Rural Free Delivery Garden Club of Holmdel in 1954. Originally utilizing the long-discontinued rural free postal system to deliver sproutlings to local growers, the club, pictured in 1960, continues to maintain the building and host seasonal plant sales.

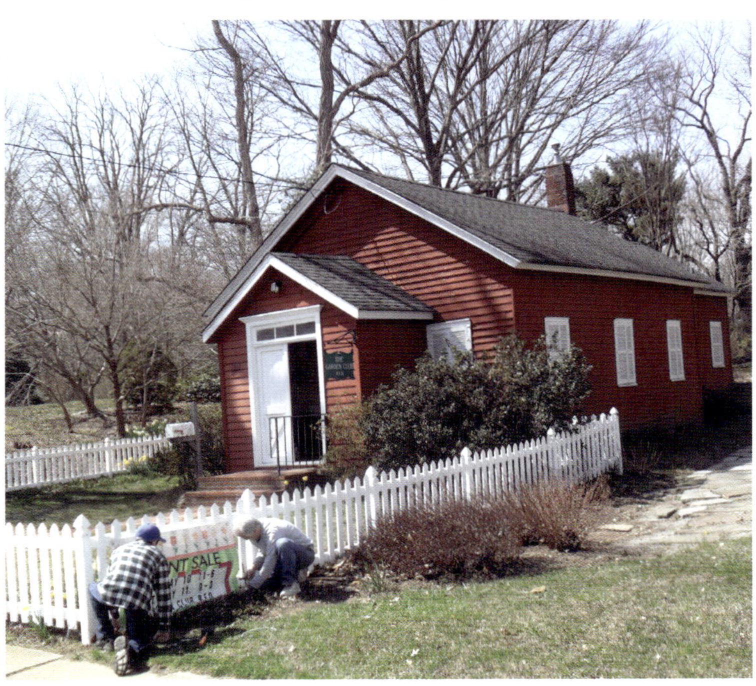

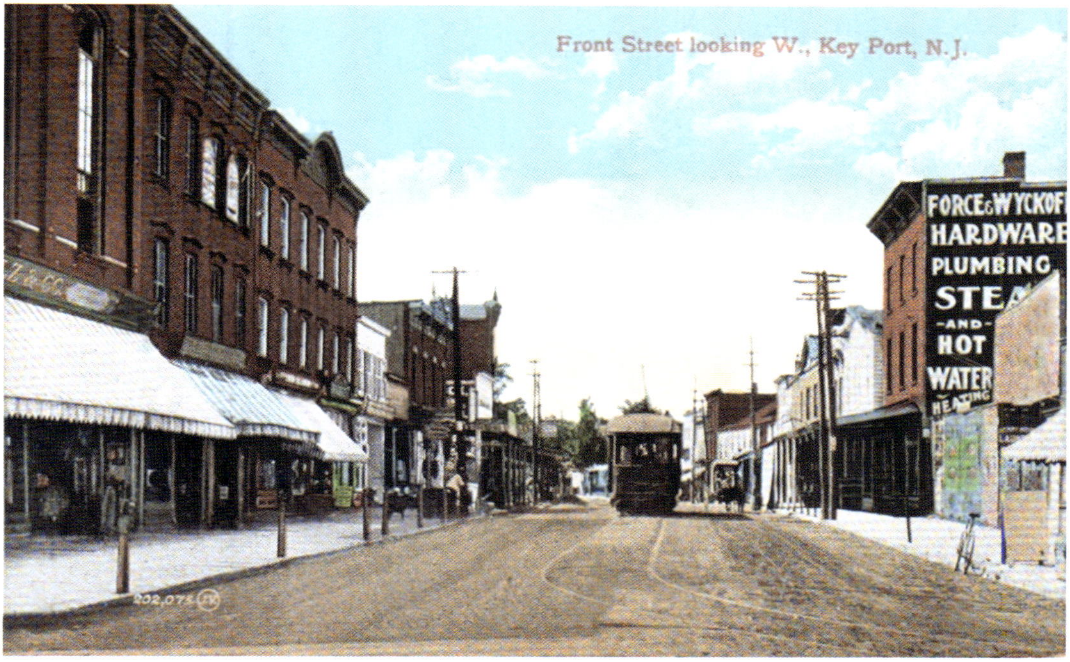

FRONT STREET: The Main Drag in Keyport is shown in this 1910s postcard. Although some of the landmark buildings have been demolished, the scene is completely recognizable, and the daily shuffle continues as it did a century ago.

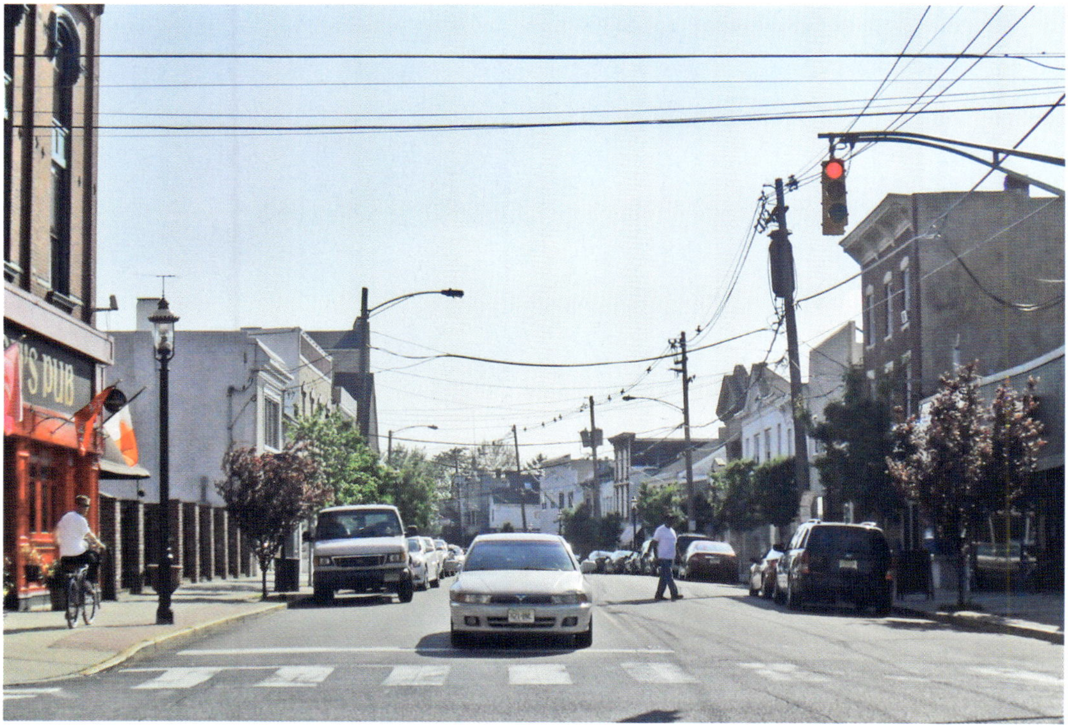

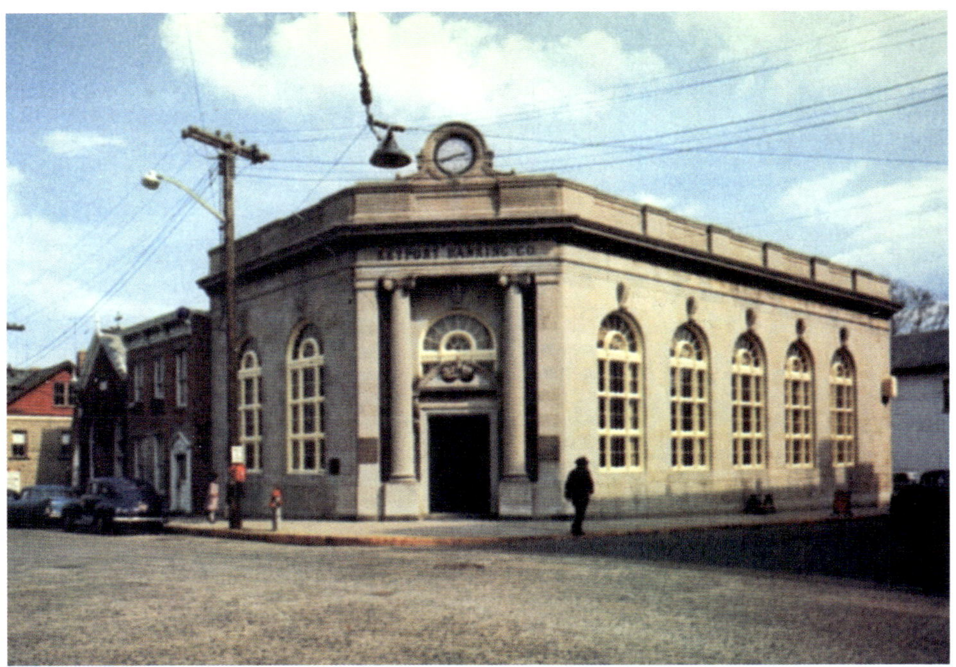

THE 1928 KEYPORT BANKING COMPANY: The building still continues in its original intended use as the main bank in the town of Keyport. Shown here in the late 1940s, the bank was organized in 1889 after a string of previous banking efforts in the town failed. Fittingly, the bank is currently home to a Wells Fargo branch, one of the nation's oldest banking firms, founded by the same men who also started American Express.

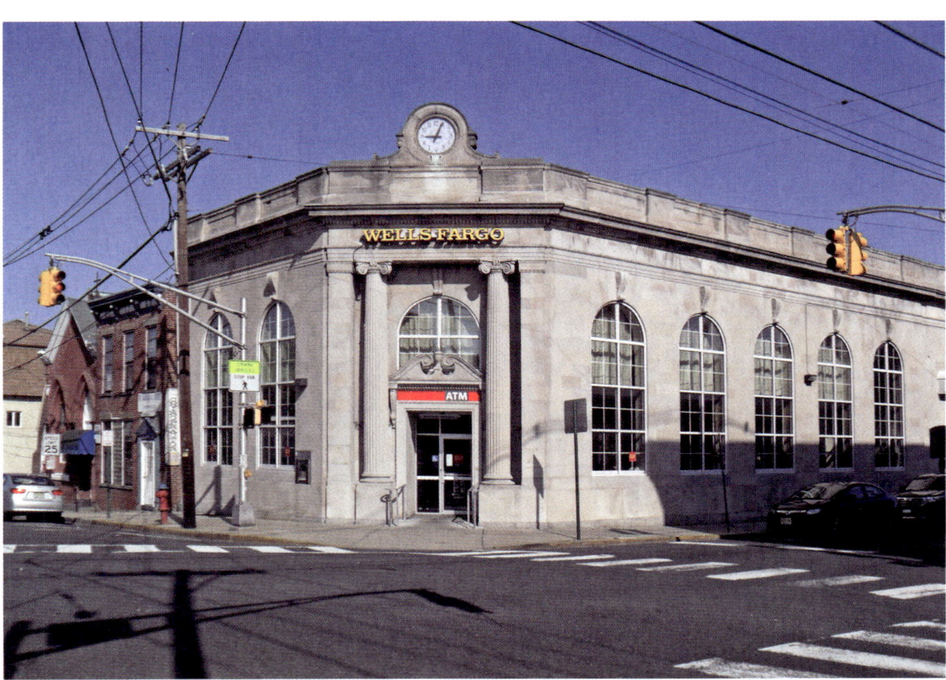

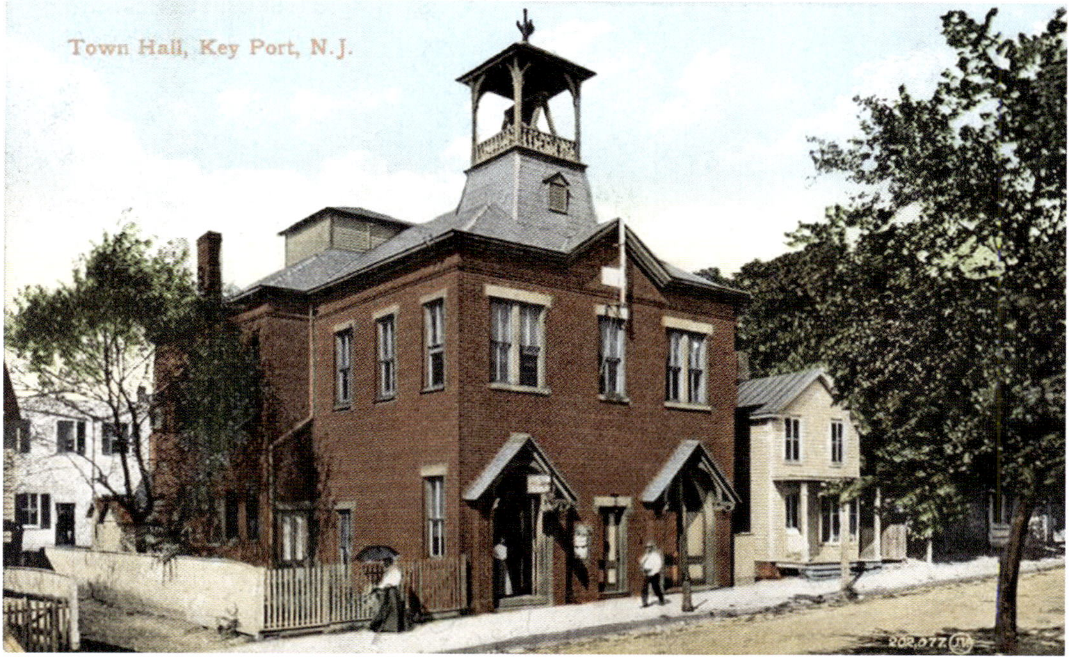

Town Hall, Key Port, N.J.

202,077

KEYPORT TOWN HALL: This 1910s postcard view shows the extant 1885 structure which originally served as the Keyport municipal offices and firehouse. The municipal body relocated in the 1950s, and the location was discontinued for use as a firehouse in 1986. It currently houses residential and retail units.

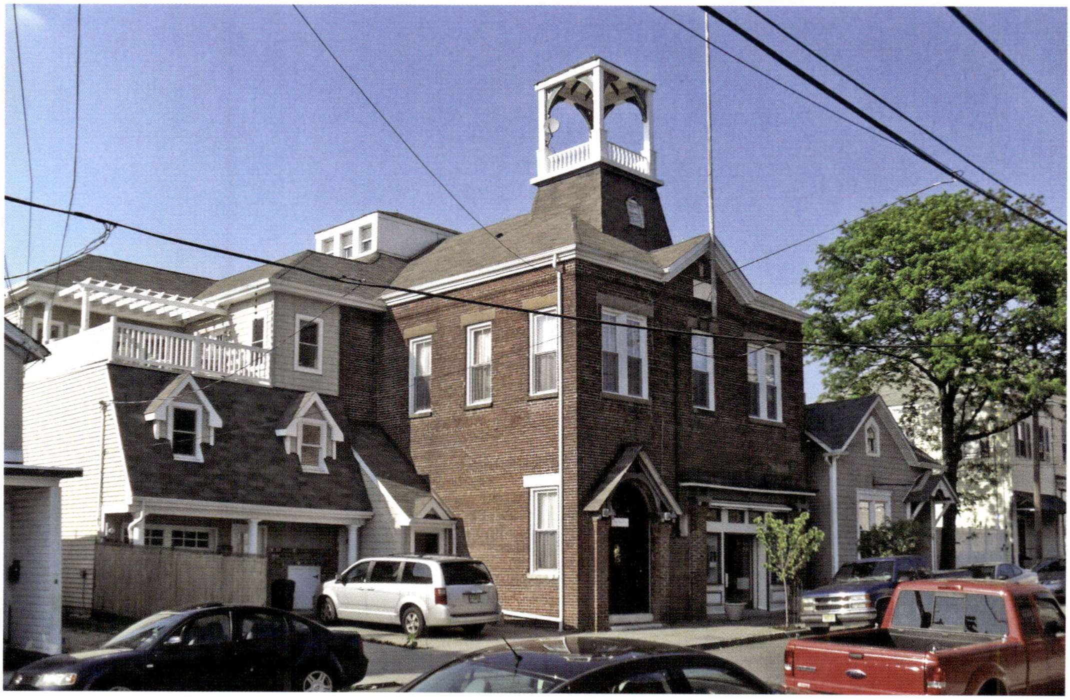

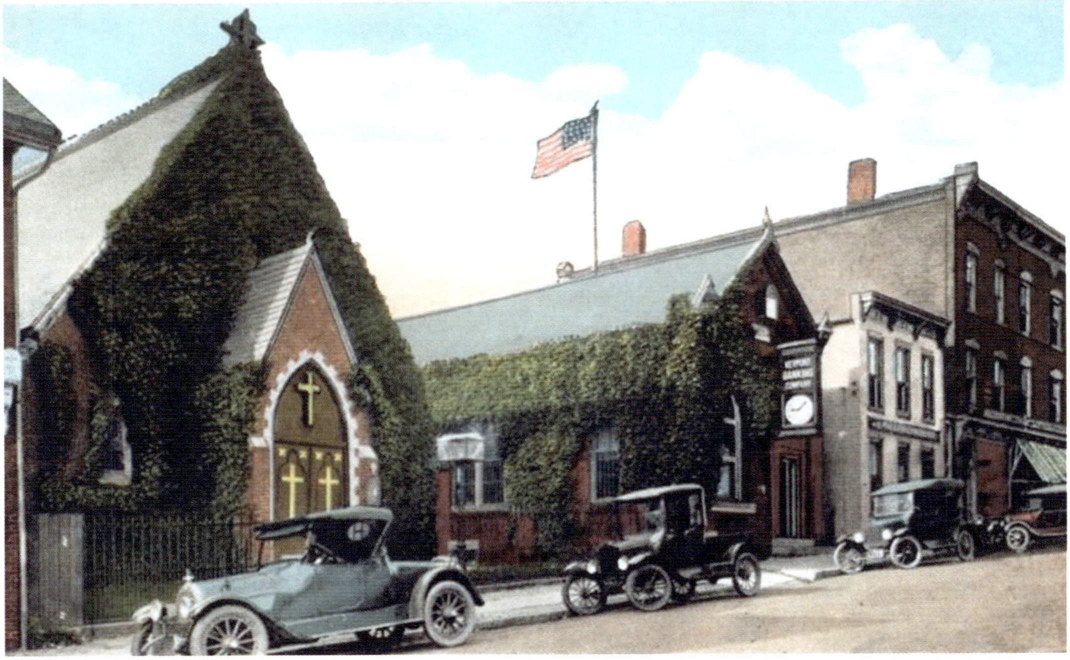

SAINT MARY'S CHURCH: The Church and the original location of the Keyport Banking Company were built in the 1880s, and are pictured here in the early 1920s. The Episcopal congregation was organized in the 1850s and the original structure burned a few decades later.

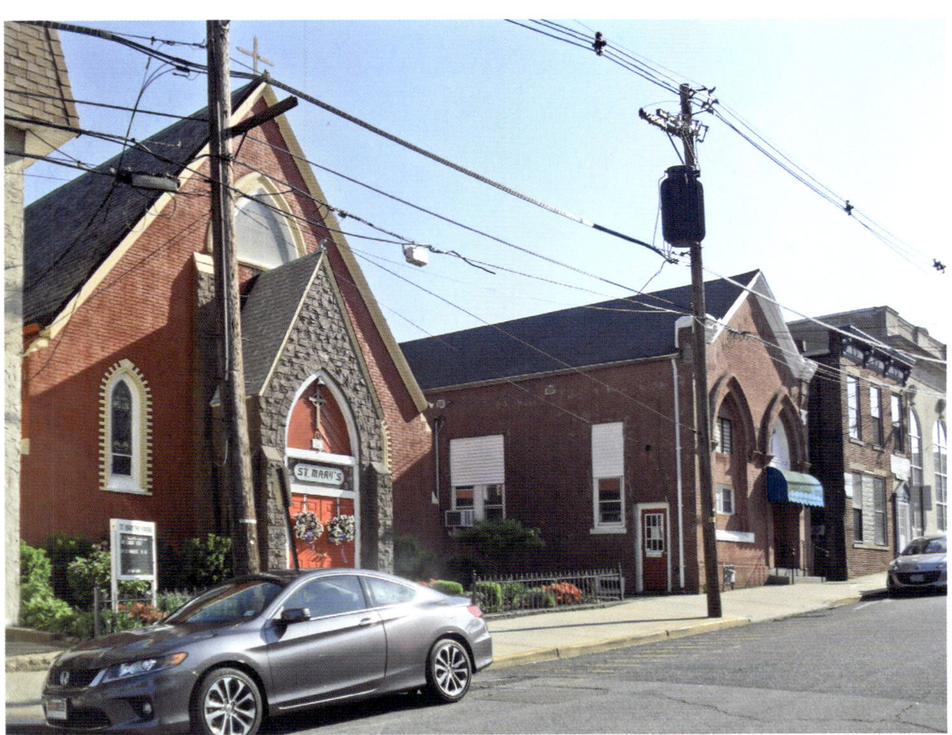

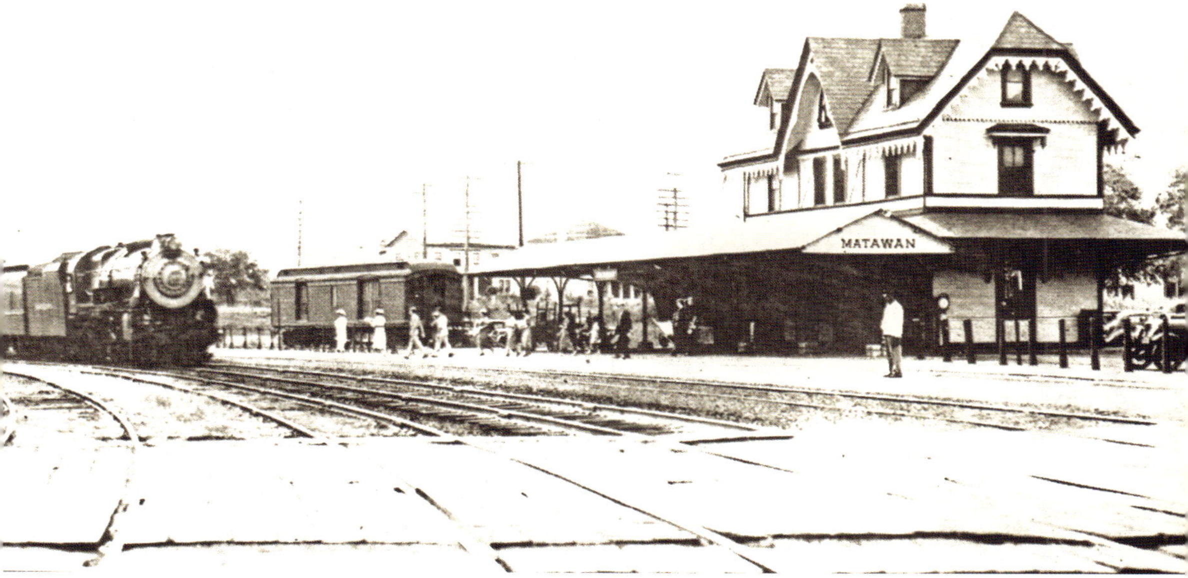

MATAWAN TRAIN STATION IN THE 1930S: Constructed in 1875, this was the first station built on the New York and Long Branch line. The station was expanded and modern platform services were installed on the Aberdeen side of the tracks during the 1990s. Stabilized and repaired by NJ Transit in 2008, the historic station building is currently used as a utility maintenance structure.

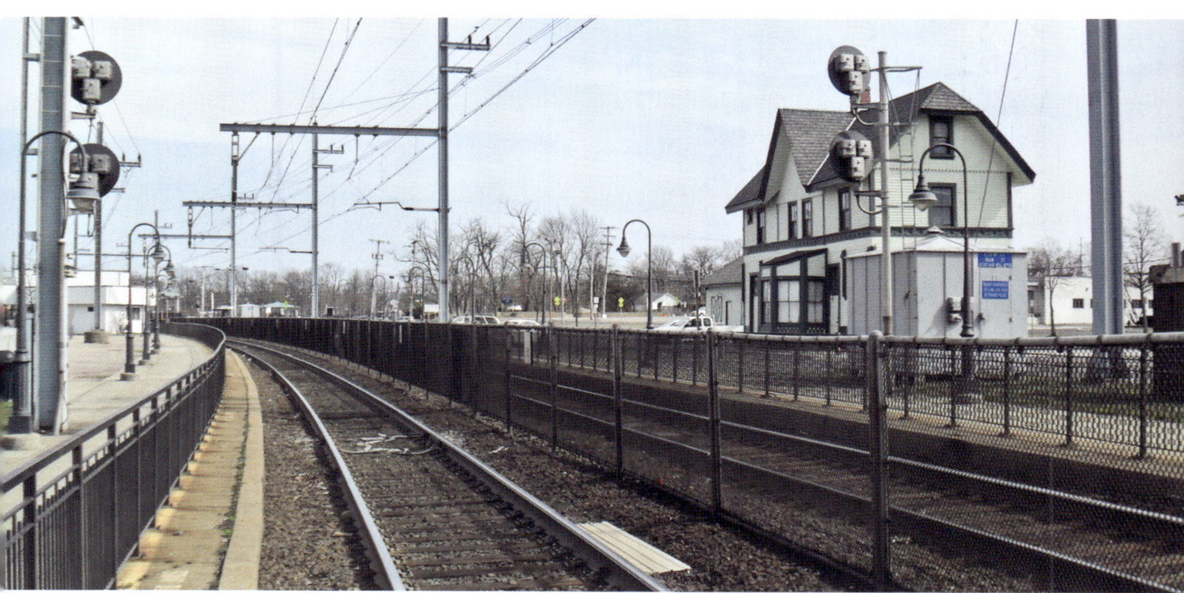

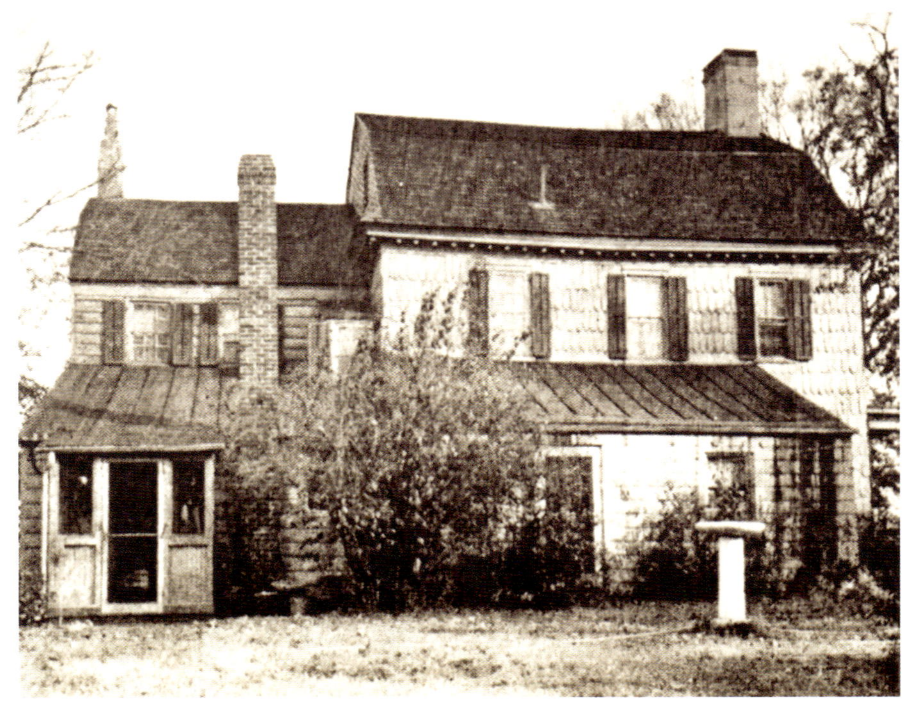

THE BURROWES MANSION: The rarely-pictured rear view of the Burrowes Mansion on Main Street in Matawan as photographed in the 1930s. It was purportedly built in 1723 by John Bowne, the property was purchased by the Burrowes family in 1769. The first miltia mounted in New Jersey during the Revolution and all related mustering activities, occurred right in this backyard. In 1778, loyalists invaded the house and assaulted the beautiful young wife of Captain John Burrowes Jr.

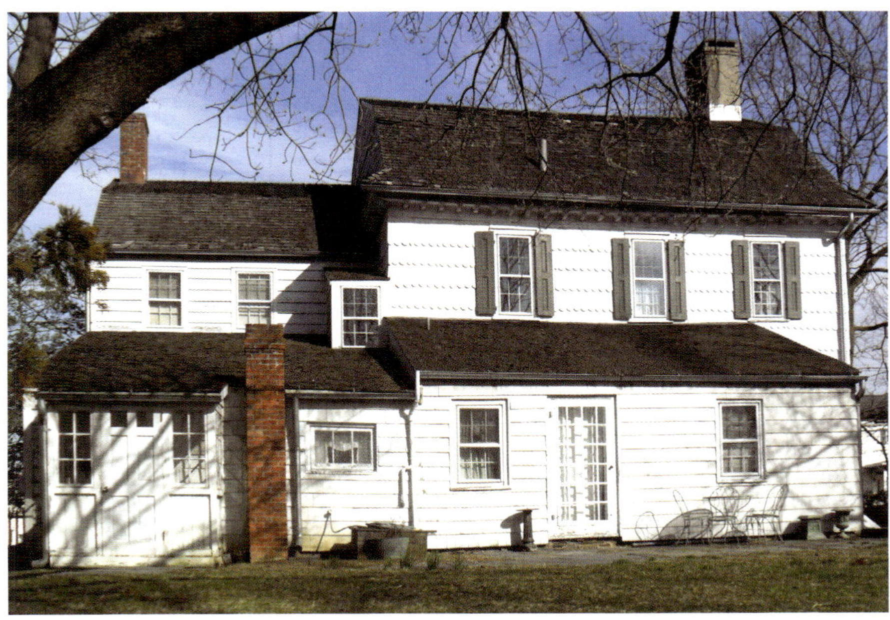

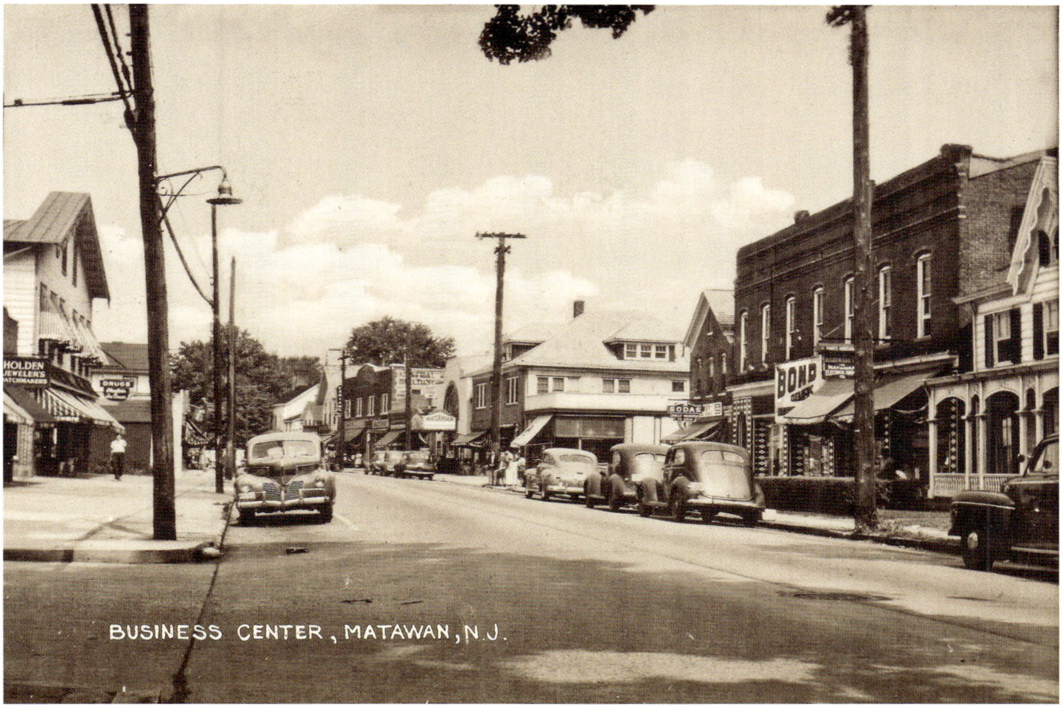

BUSINESS CENTER, MATAWAN, N.J.

MAIN STREET, MATAWAN: This 1940s view of the business district is reproduced directly from the original postcard negative in the author's collection. Although the businesses have changed hands, the integrity of the district remains almost completely intact.

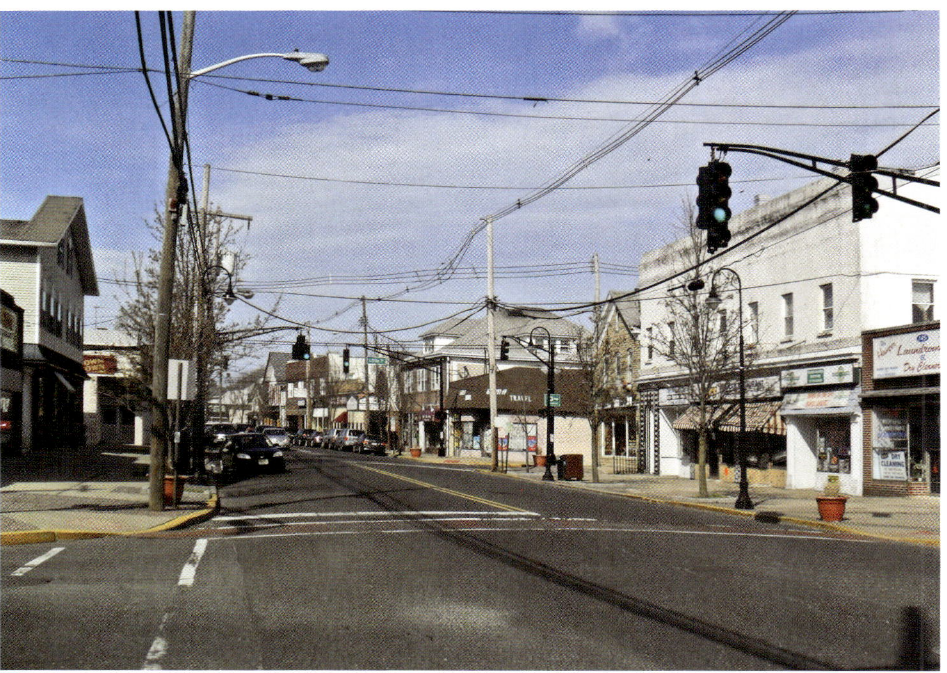

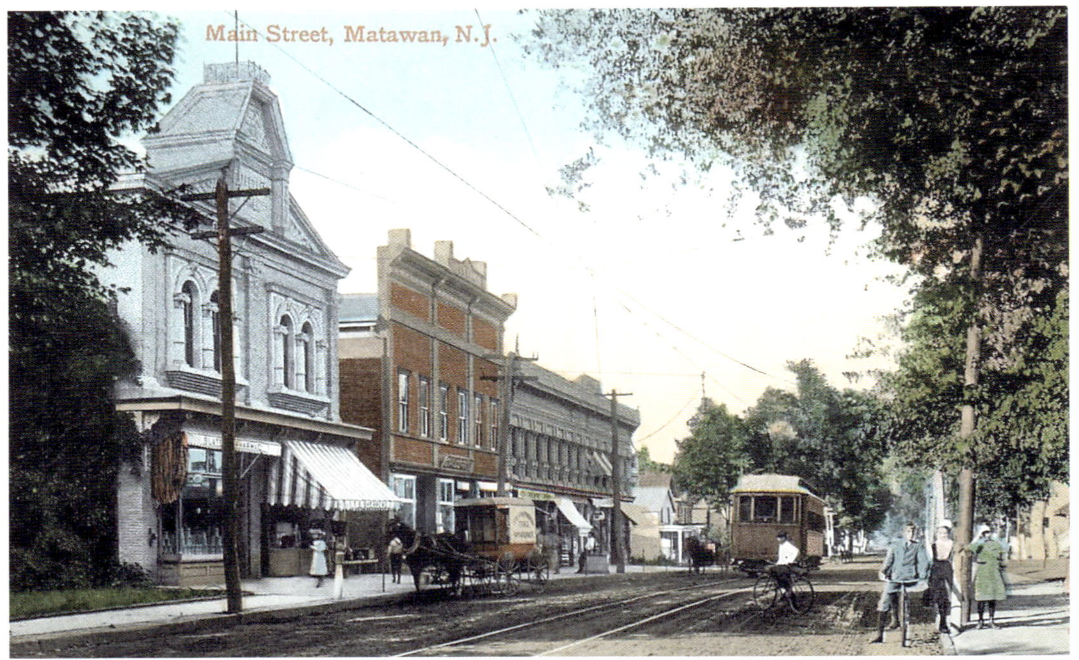

THE MASONIC HALL: The Masonic Hall is the only recognizable survivor in this 1915 view of the far end of Main Street on the edge of the business district. Constituted in 1910, the Matawan Lodge Number 192 of Free and Accepted Masons have always called this building home. In a somewhat mystical coincidence, the street number of the lodge is also 192.

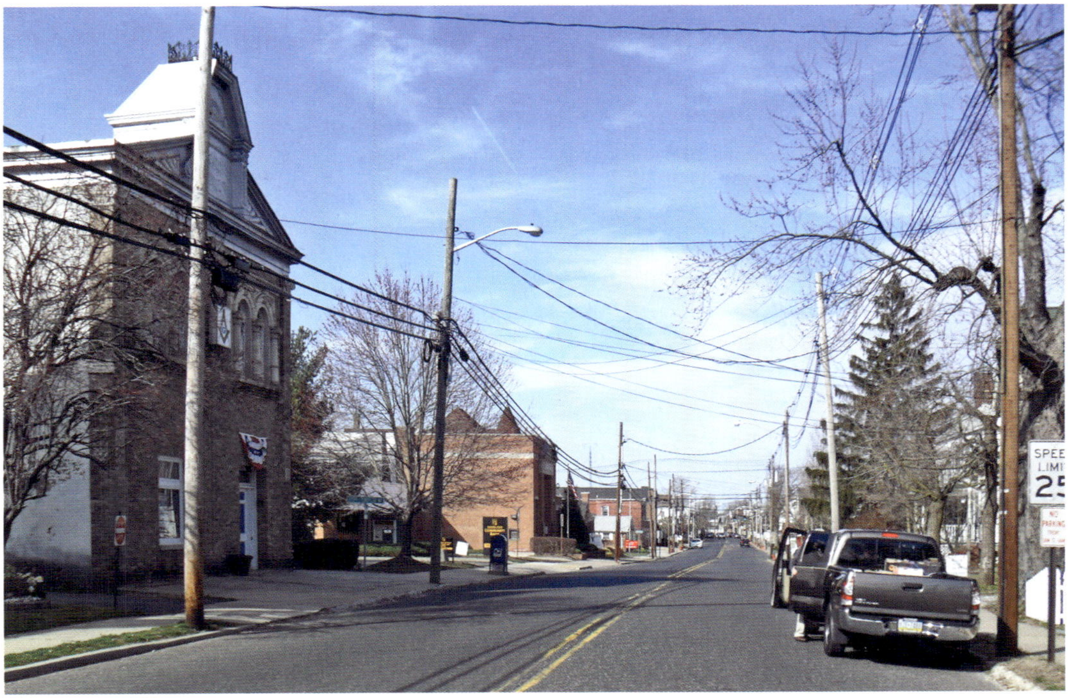

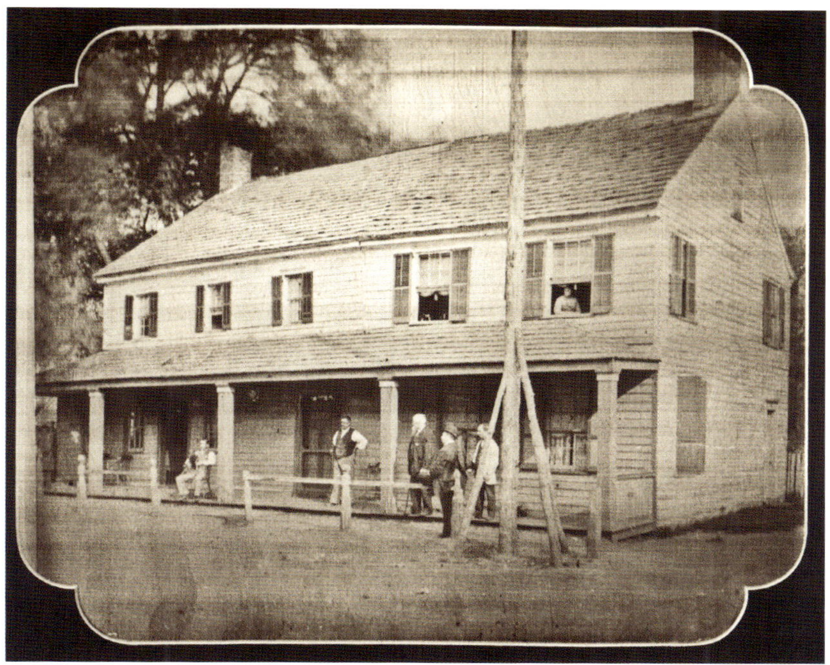

THE VILLAGE INN TAVERN: The Englishtown gentry assemble outside the Tavern in this March, 1882 photo. The section on the left was built before 1750. The building was adapted for use as a tavern and inn prior to the American Revolution, and was certainly a resting point for militia men during the nearby 1778 Battle of Monmouth. The long-standing legend that the location was personally utilized by George Washington seems to have been concocted during the fervor to celebrate the bicentennial of his birth in 1932.

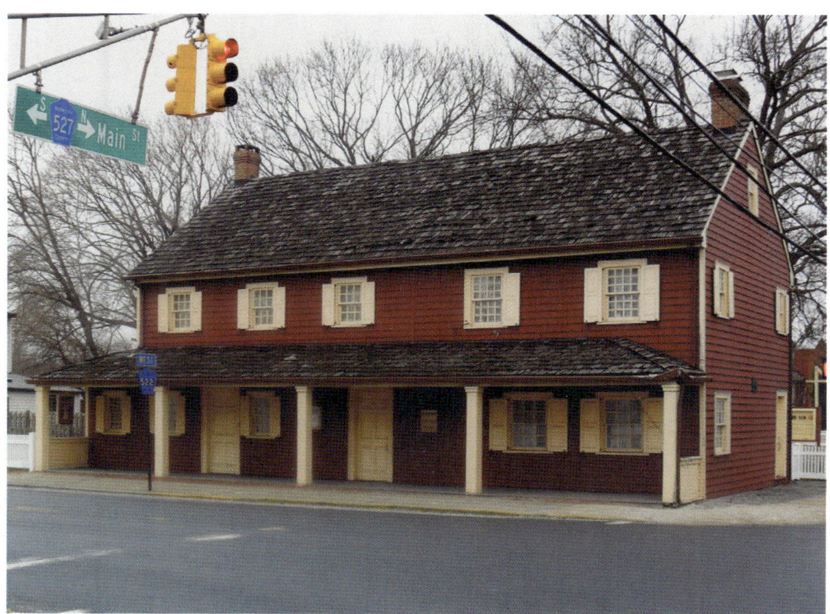

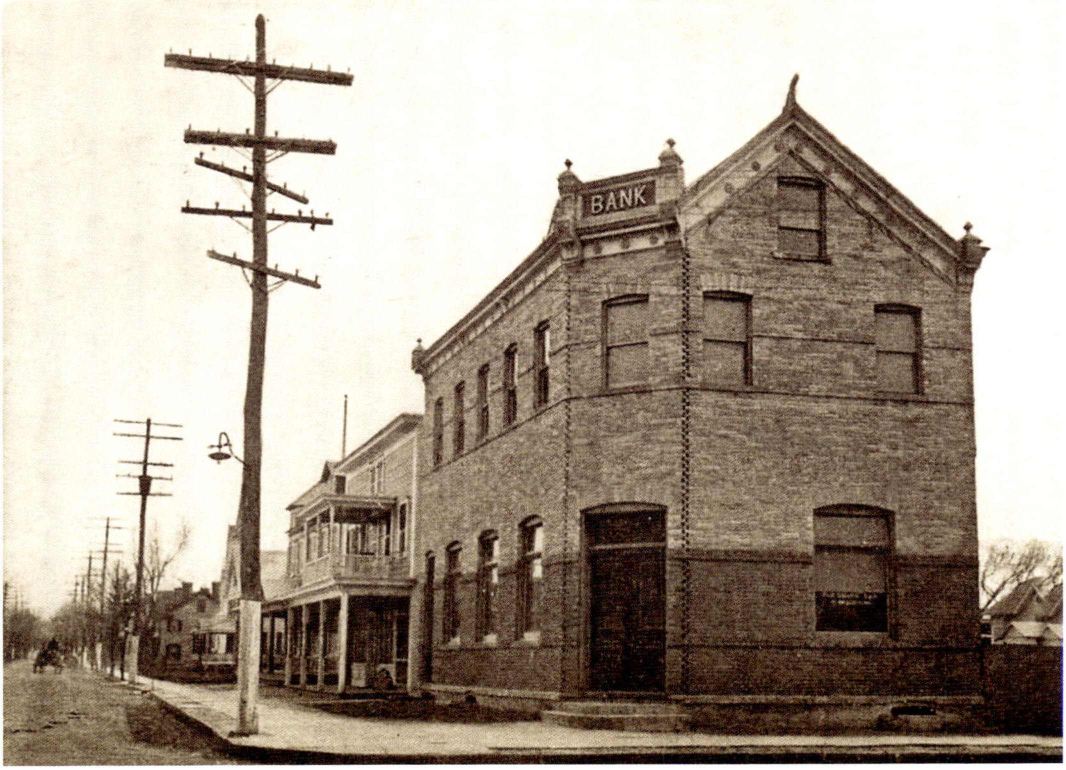

THE FIRST NATIONAL BANK: The handsome building standing directly across the street from the Village Inn was built *c.* 1880. This 1910s postcard view captures the still-present charm of Englishtown's Main Street. The bank building is currently being utilized as a deli.

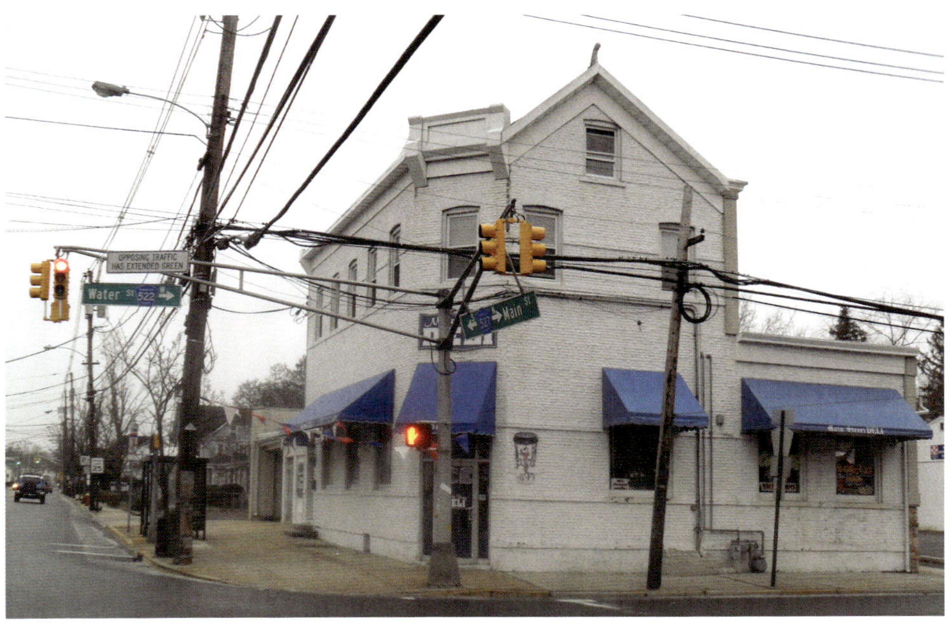

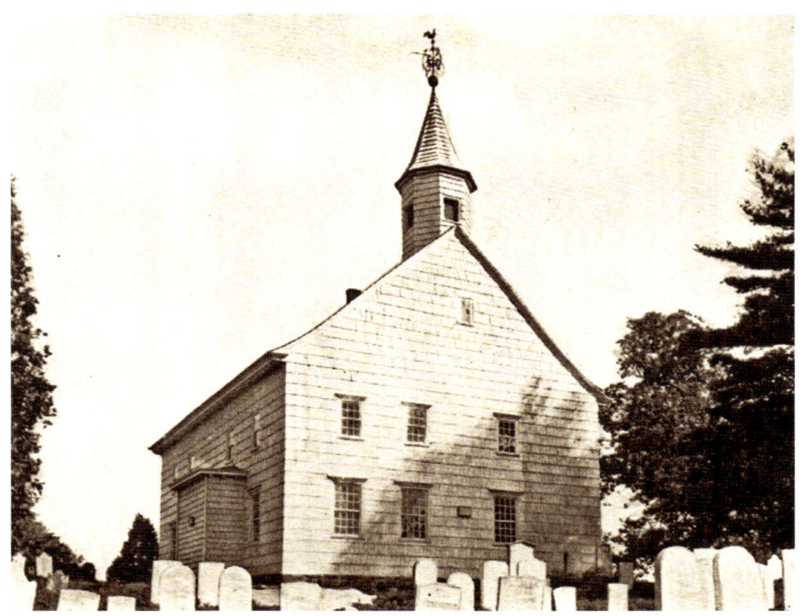

THE TENNENT PRESBYTERIAN CHURCH IN MANALAPAN: The church was built in 1751 and during the Battle of Monmouth in June of 1778 it was used as a field hospital. There are still blood-stained pews with marks from the surgeon's amputation saw. The church was restored in the 1980s, and continues to boast a dedicated, active congregation and Sunday school.

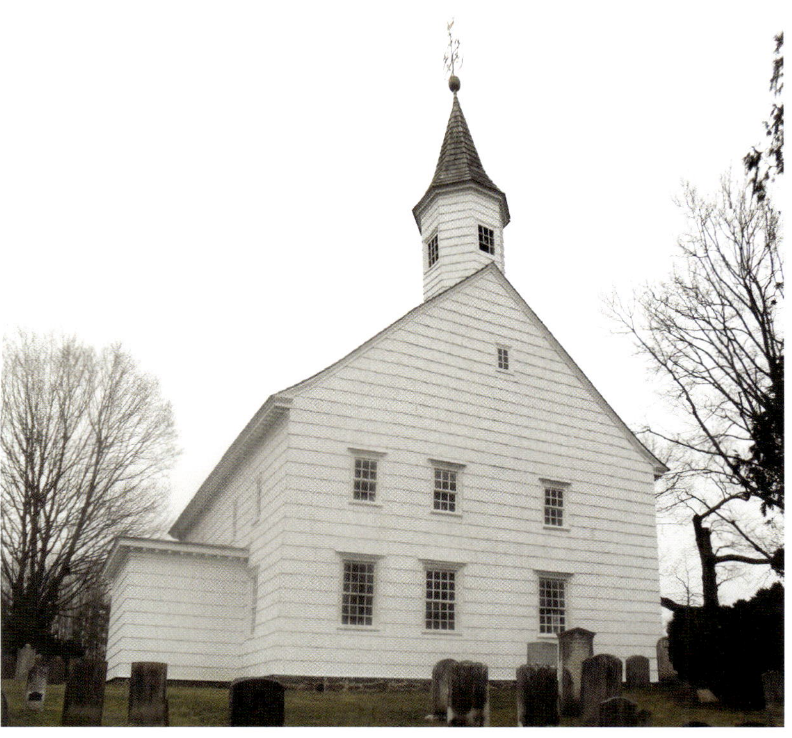

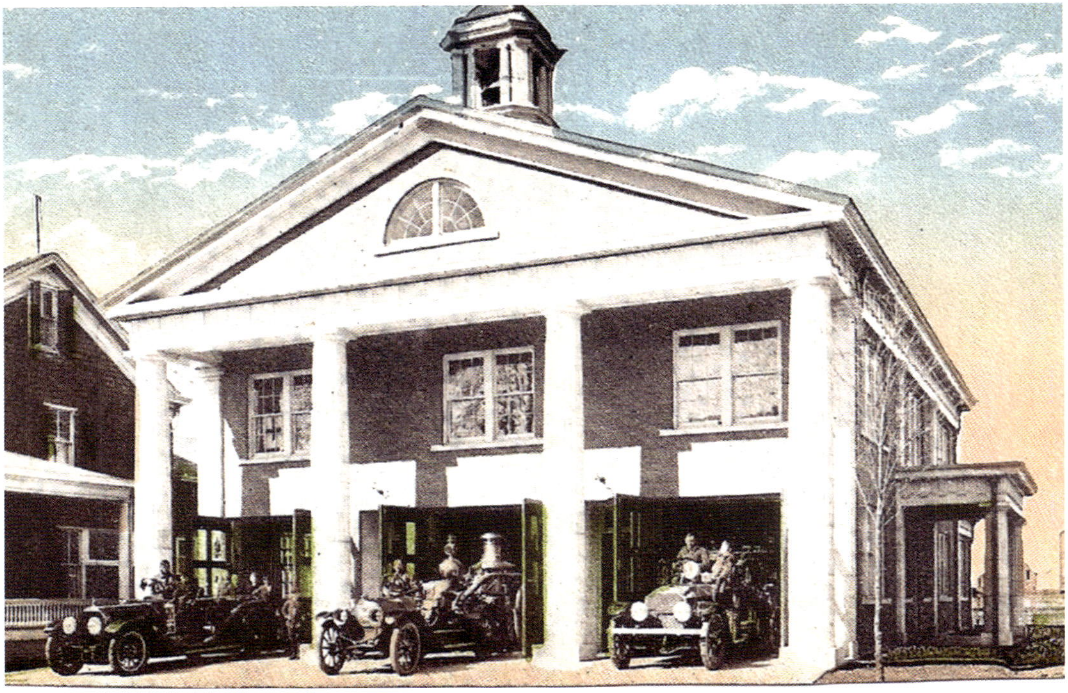

FREEHOLD FIRE DEPARTMENT HEADQUARTERS: The Headquarters are shown during opening ceremonies in this 1922 postcard view. The borough complex is at far left. The 2013 view shows the building dressed in the traditional mourning crêpe for a recently deceased member.

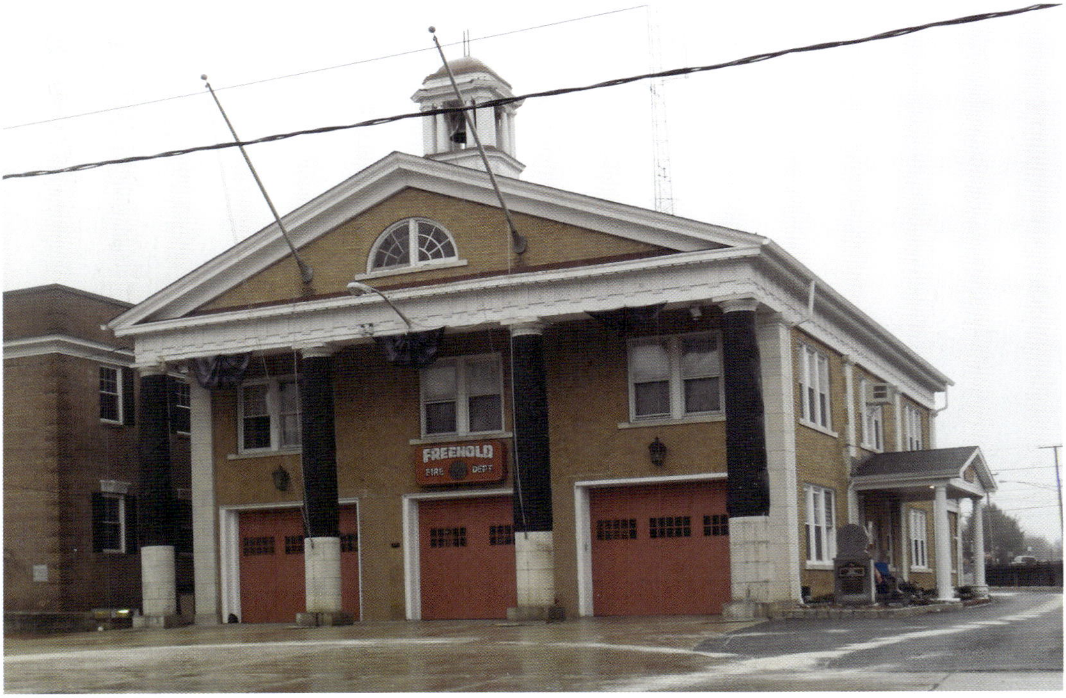

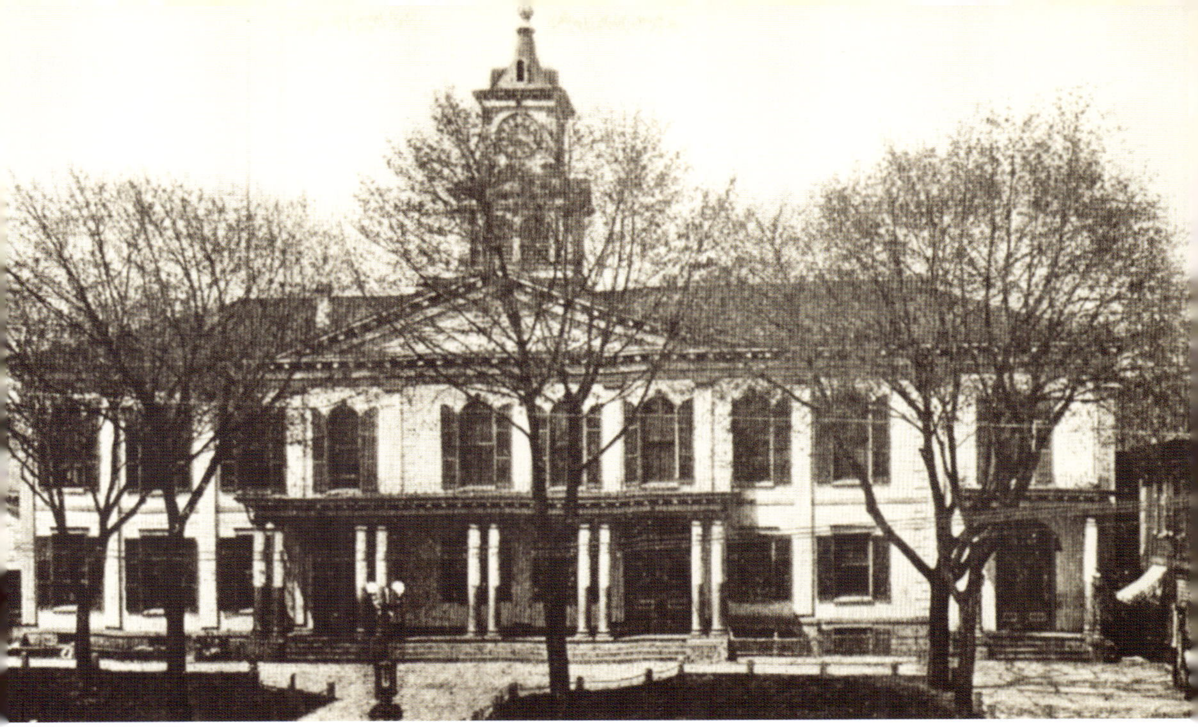

THE OLD MONMOUTH COURTHOUSE ON MAIN STREET IN FREEHOLD: The building has 1806 origins, but major fires in 1855, 1873 and 1930 have resulted in various overhauls and repairs. The vicinage constructed a new elaborate court building in 1954, and this structure, seen in 1922, has since been utilized as the county hall of records.

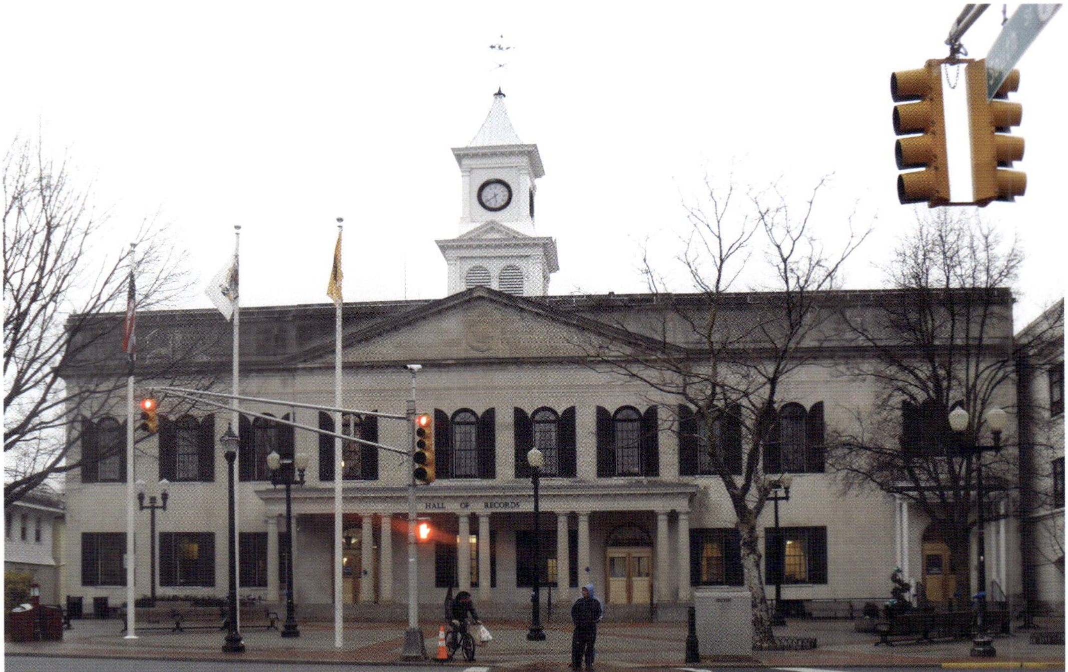

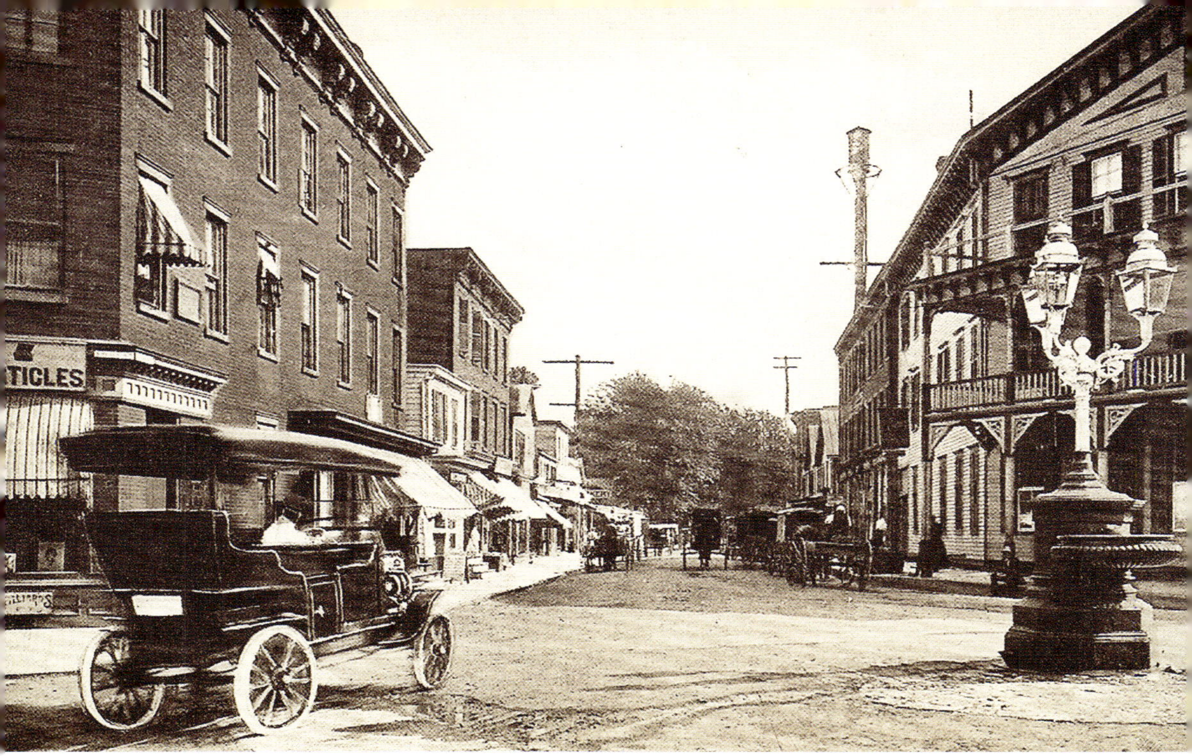

SOUTH STREET: This 1910s view is taken from in front of the courthouse. It shows the century of changes at this important and highly traversed intersection. Most of the extant structures were built in the 1870s-80s. Many towns had similar monuments and fountains installed at notable intersections. Most of these were removed after deadly incidents during the early reckless automotive era.

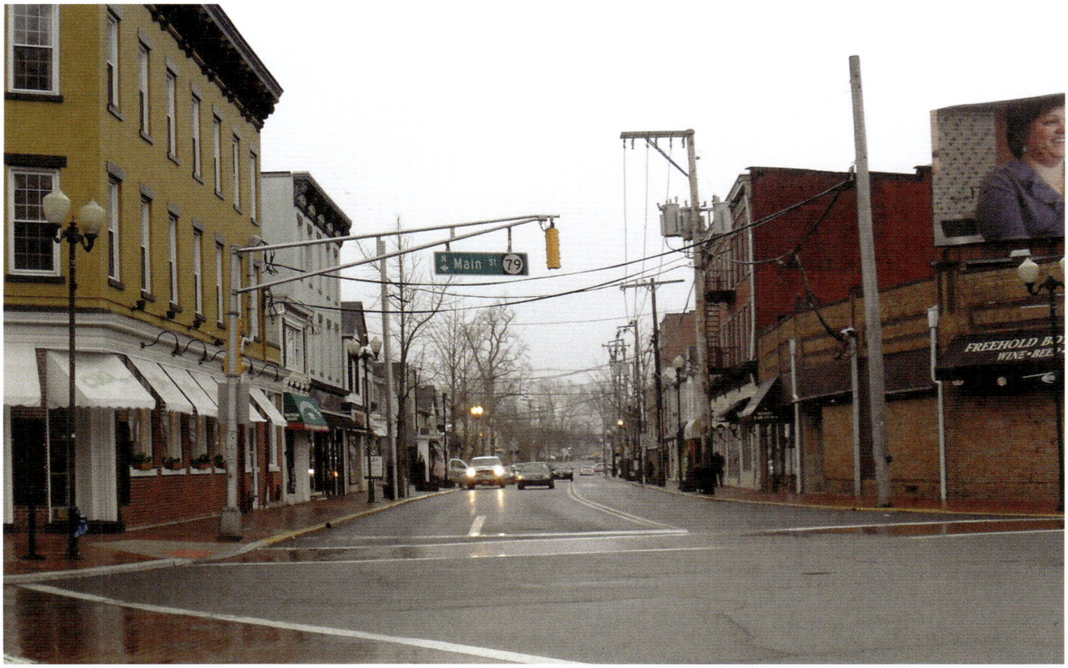

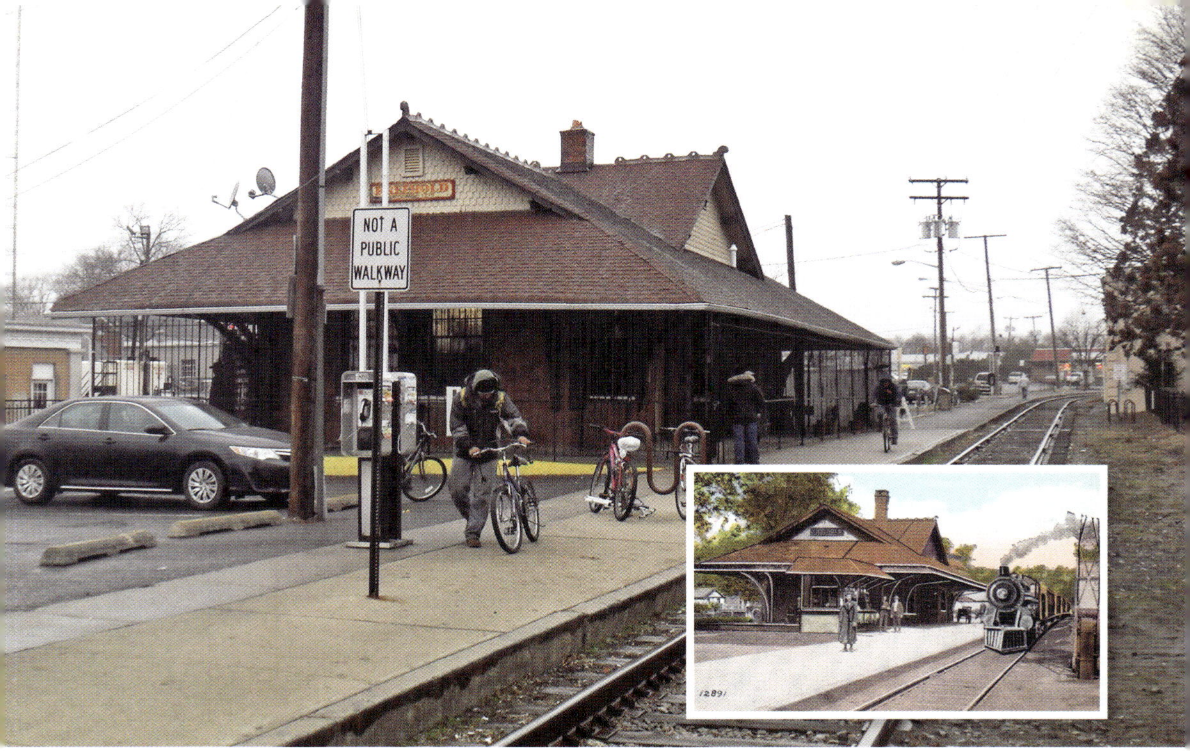

FREEHOLD'S RAIL STATIONS: Both stations exist in their original locations, but neither is an active rail station, or comes in any contact with rail traffic. The Pennsylvania station on Throckmorton Street sits on a very seldom-used freight line, but the location does serve as a regional and local bus station. The Central Rail station was situated near the Karagheusian rug mill, and today serves as a private office.

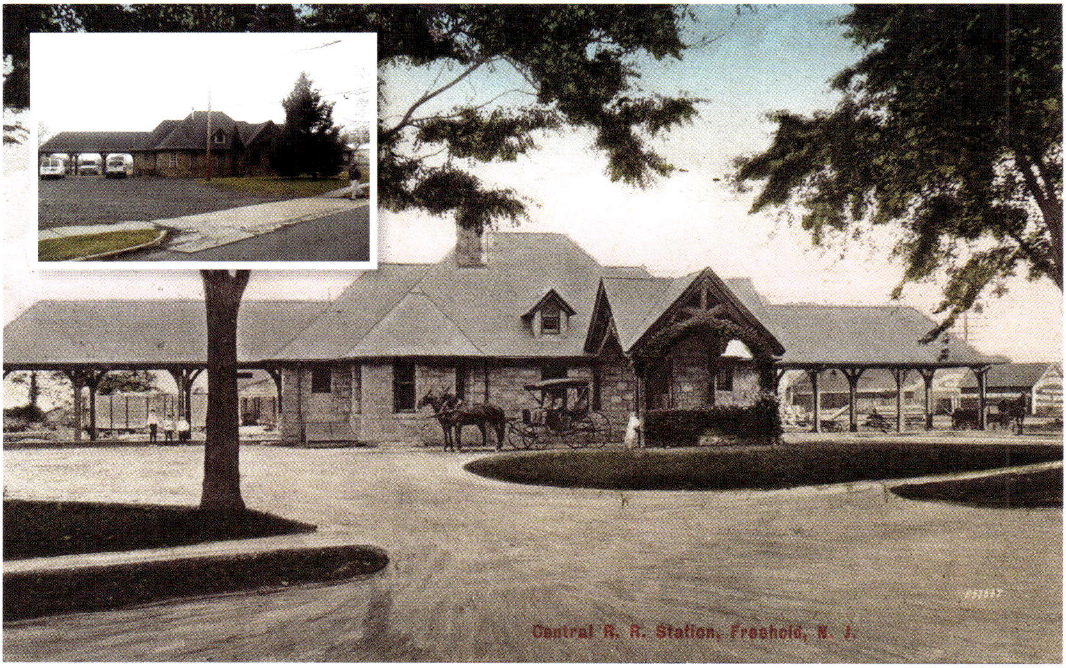

Central R. R. Station, Freehold, N. J.

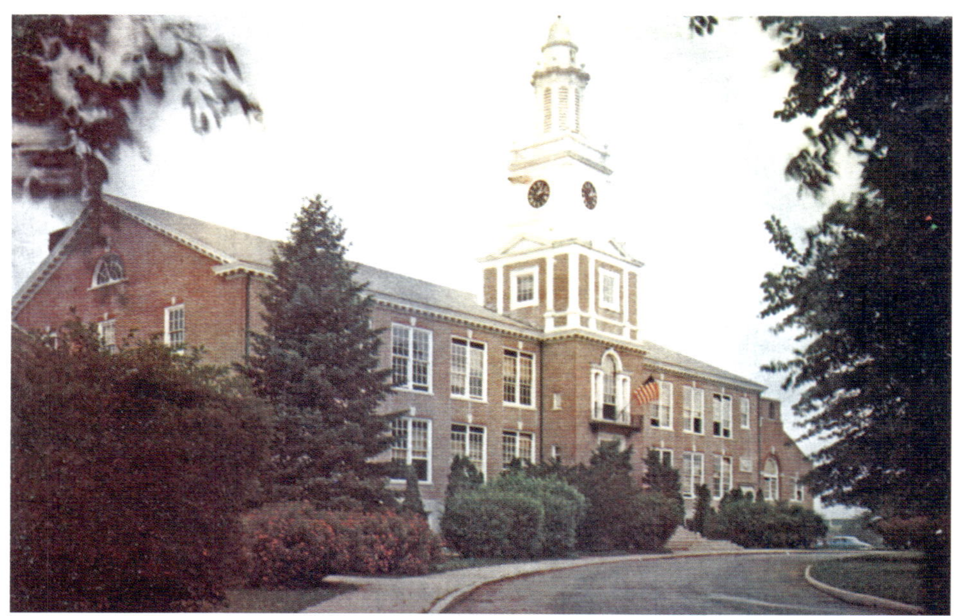

FREEHOLD HIGH SCHOOL This 1955 photo of Freehold High School shows that the school exterior has only undergone very minor changes over sixty years. The 1925 edifice is oldest building currently in use within the Freehold Regional High School District. The Monmouth County scholastic community have long affectionately called the institution 'boro' to distinguish the school from nearby Freehold Township High School.

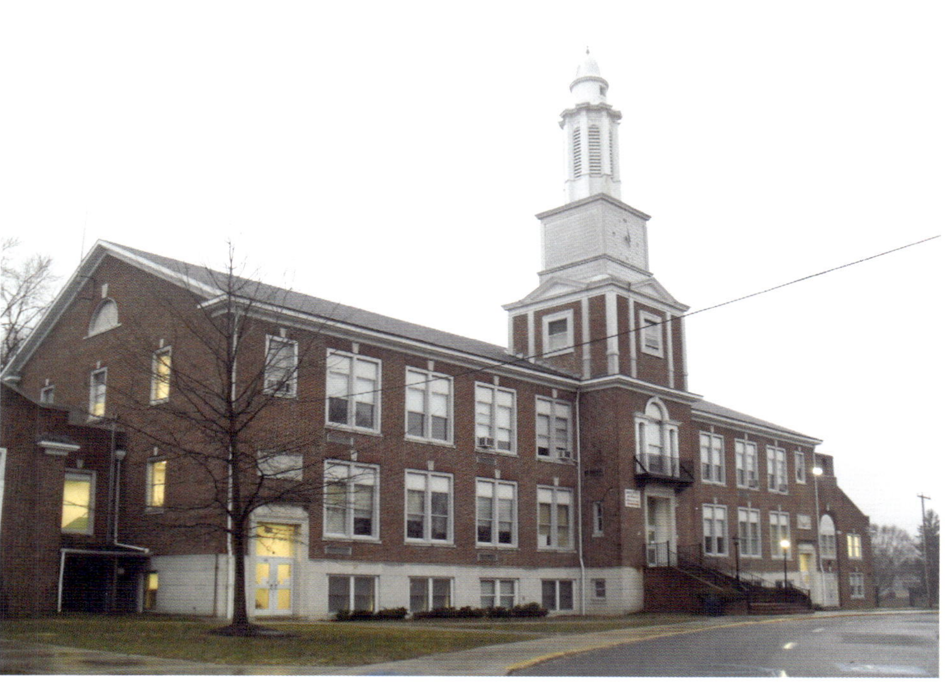

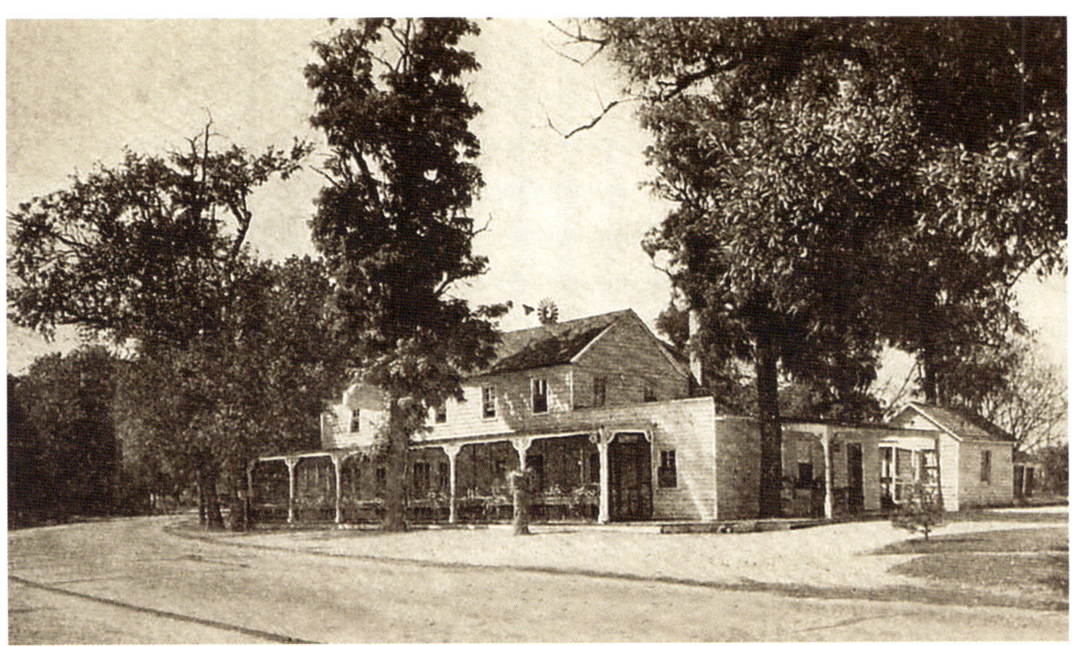

MARRINER'S TAVERN: The Tavern was built in 1747 by George Marriner on the dead man's curve of old Adelphia Road in Farmingdale. In Revolutionary times, the tavern was the hangout for a rough group of outlaws and highwaymen who preyed on the passing stages on the rural back roads. Major Henry Lee captured one of the gang's ringleaders, and hung him in front of the building in 1779. Princeton graduate Lee was the father of Confederate General Robert E. Lee. The facility, seen in the 1930s, has been known as Our House for over a century.

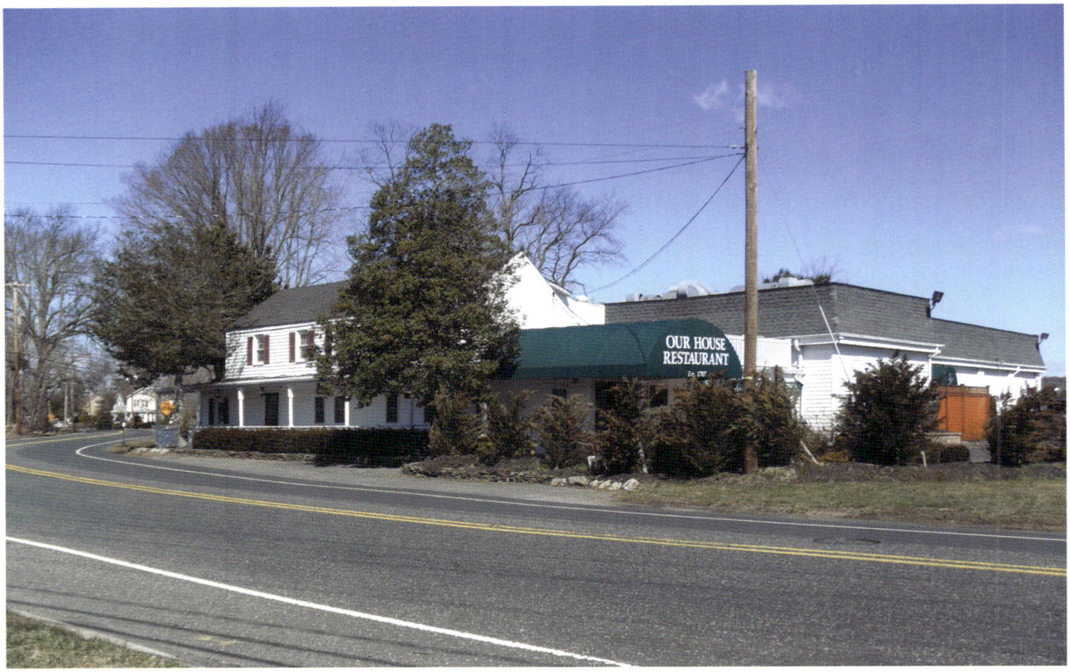

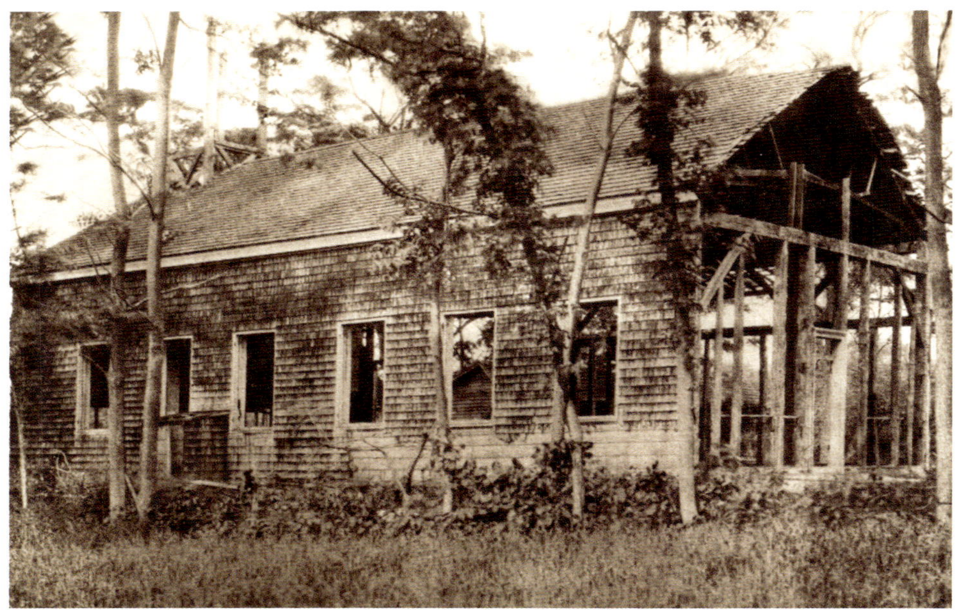

ALLAIRE CHURCH: When famed newspaper editor Arthur Brisbane purchased the Allaire Village Tract in the early twentieth century, the property had already gained fame as an abandoned ghost town. This was the major appeal to Brisbane. Further neglect only heightened the vacant aurora of the ruins. This 1924 newspaper photo shows the deplorable condition of the Allaire church before being restored by the Asbury Park Elks club later that year.

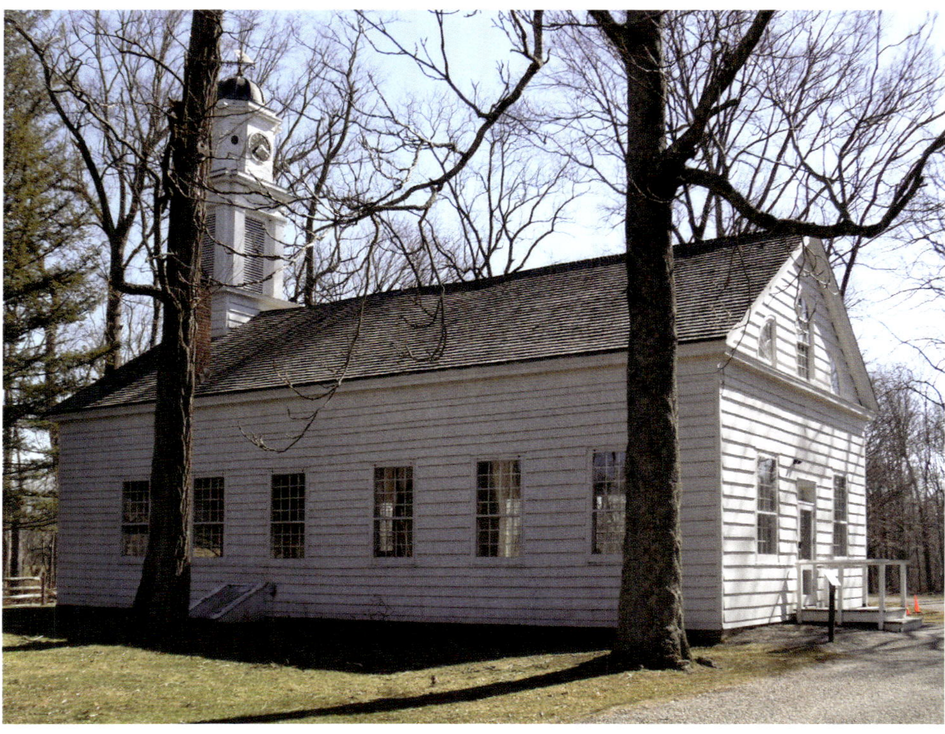

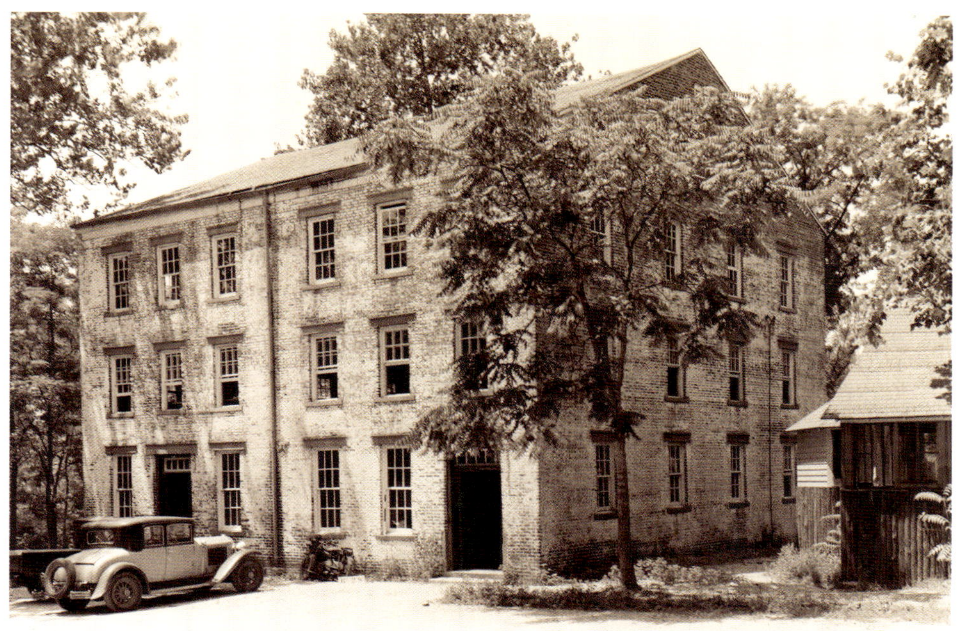

THE HOWELL IRON WORKS COMPANY STORE: The Store had recently celebrated its centennial year in this 1936 photo. James Allaire built a bog iron town off of the winding country road that is currently known as Route 524 in the western Wall swamplands in the 1820s-30s. The store building was one of the few structures that was never long-uninhabited, serving as a factory, restaurant, and residential units during different stretches of the town's abandonment. The village began restoration efforts in the late 1950s.

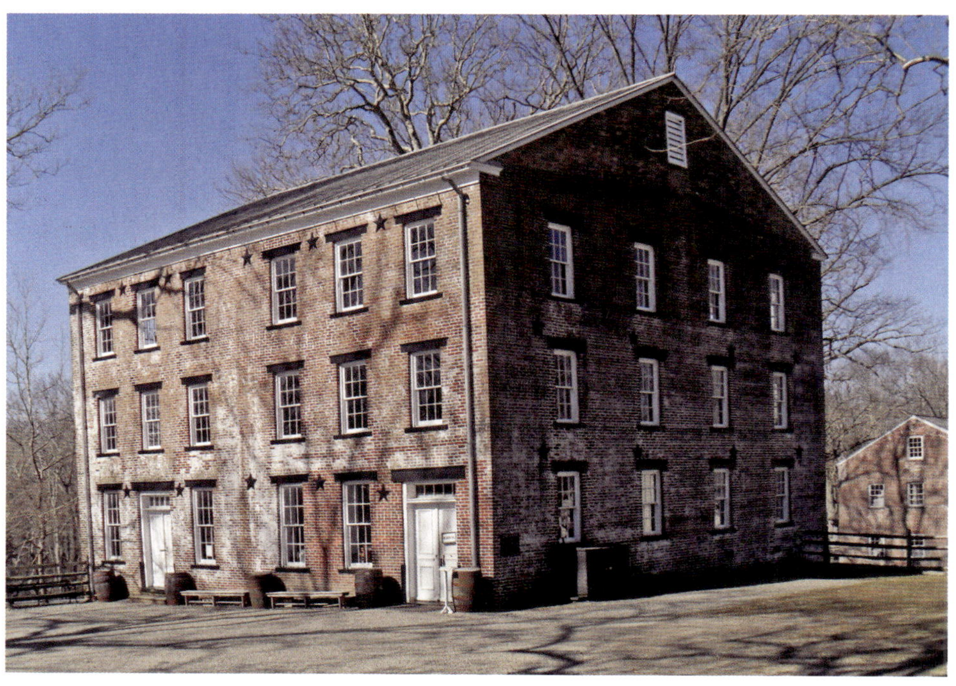

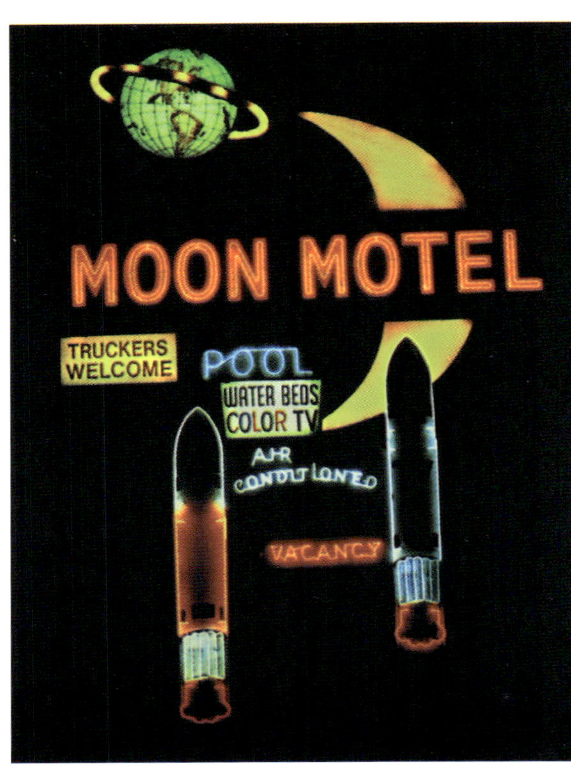

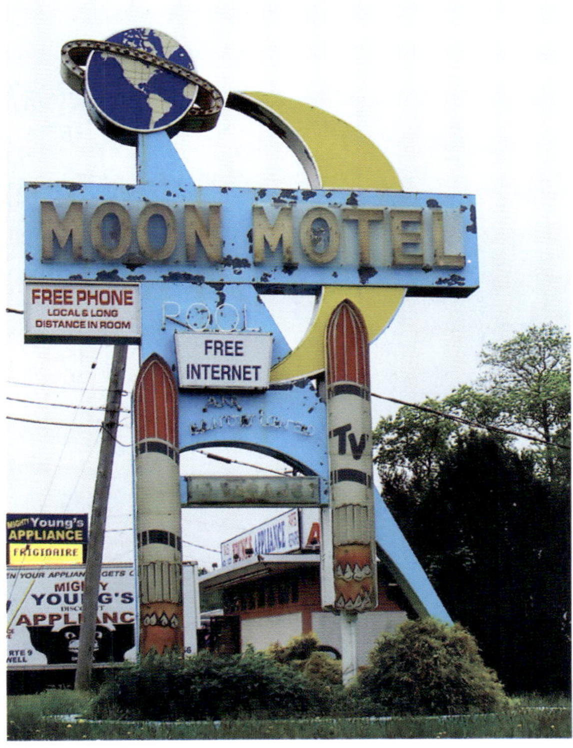

THE MOON MOTEL:
A relic of the Nation's space race was built in 1966 on Highway 9 in Howell Township. The distinctive neon sign, long a siren's song for weary truckers traveling the old inland commercial routes, boasted different modern amenities throughout the years to interest potential late-nite patrons. The motel was seriously damaged in a March 2013 fire.

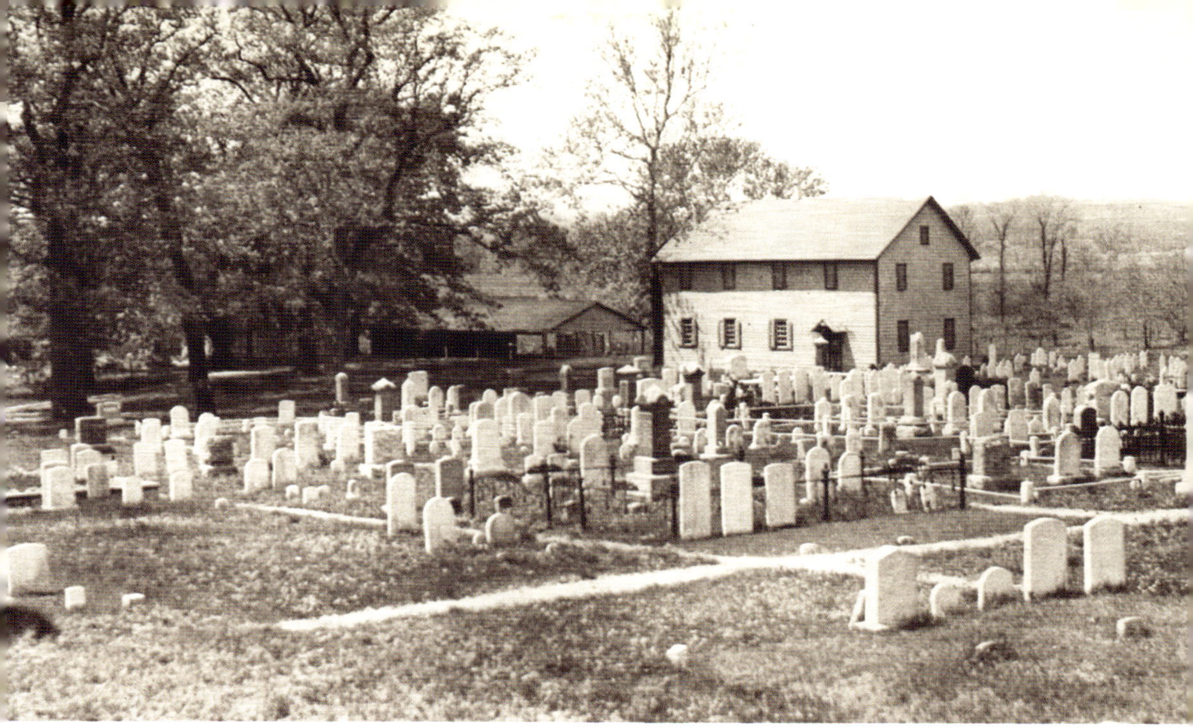

THE OLD YELLOW MEETING HOUSE IN UPPER FREEHOLD: This view is a photo from the 1930s. The Baptist church, built in the 1730s is the oldest existing religious structure in Monmouth County. The Baptist community moved their congregation to Imlaystown in the middle of the nineteenth century. The church eventually fell into a dilapidated state after many years of abandonment. In 1975, a non-profit organization was formed which lovingly restored the structure.

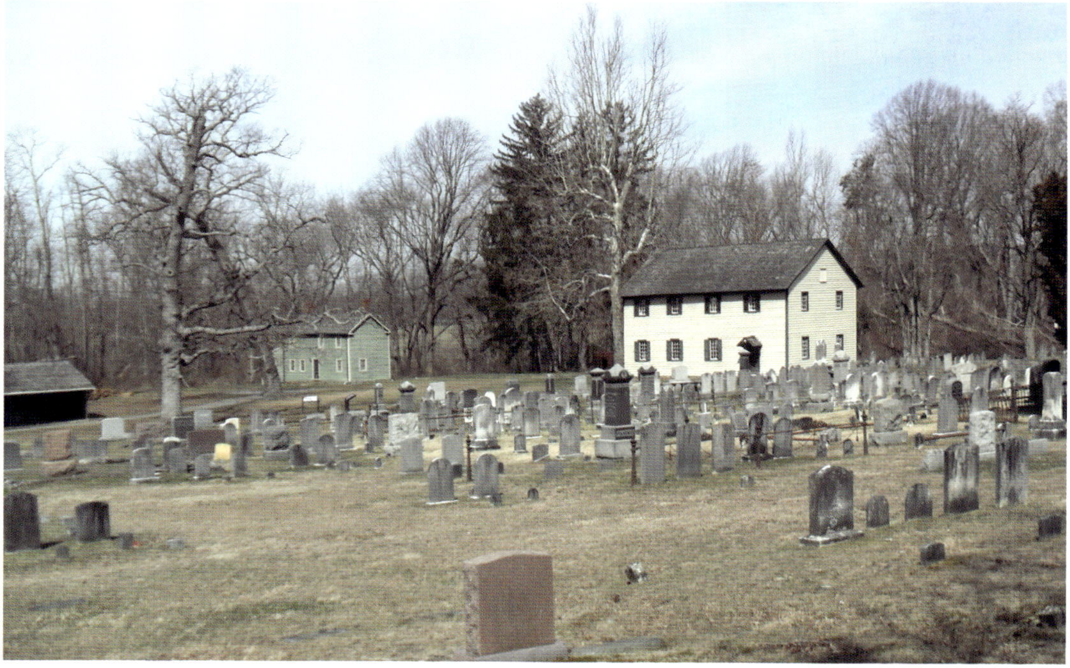

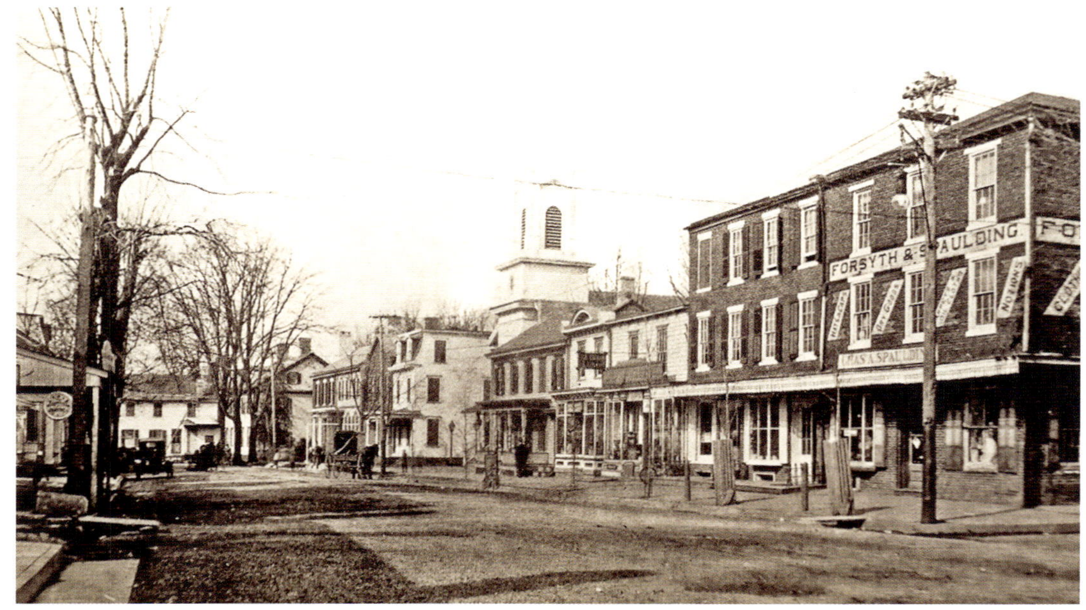

ALLENTOWN: The tiny hamlet of Allentown serves as a time capsule of yesteryear. Located in the hilly, winding country roads in the westernmost section of Monmouth County, many of the buildings found therein date back almost two centuries. This *c.* 1910 view of Main Street in Allentown captures the small-town charm which has survived for many generations.

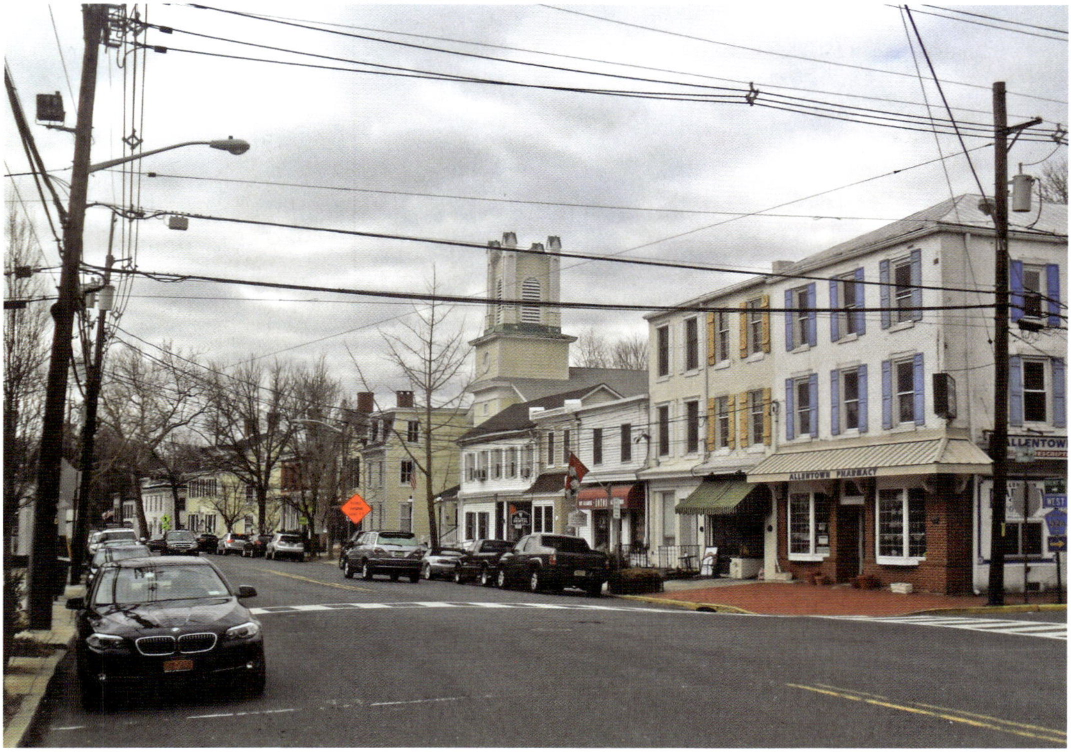

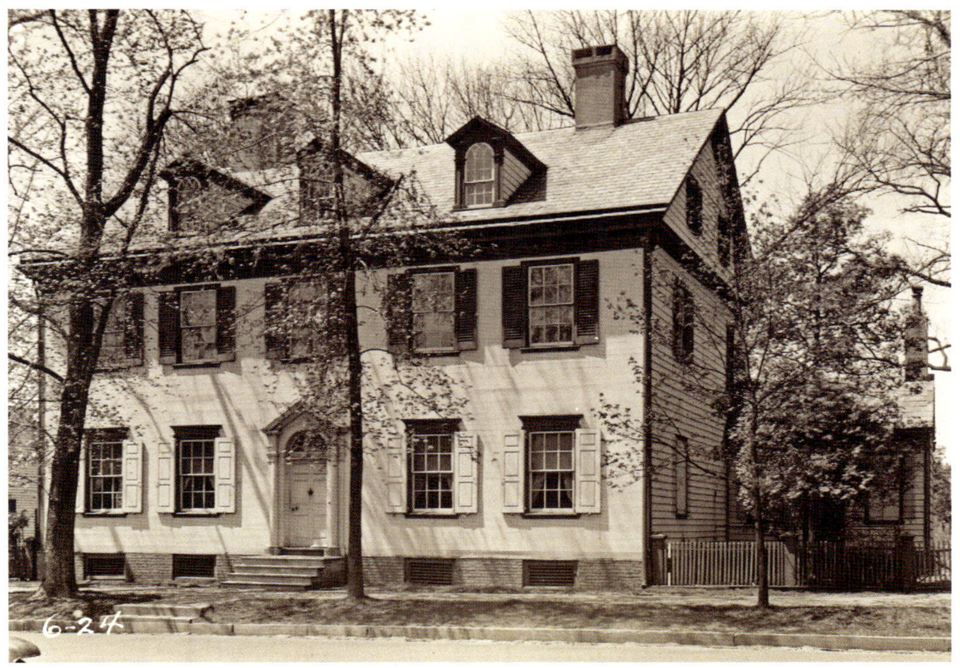

THE IMLAY HOUSE: Wealthy Philadelphia merchant John Imlay began construction of a retirement home on Main Street in Allentown in 1791. Imlay had relations who settled nearby Imlaystown, and fell in love with the neighborhood. Pictured in 1924, many artifacts were sold and removed from the building over the years, as it has never served as a place of public exhibit or museum. It has functioned as a boarding house, a doctor's office, and is currently divided into retail units.

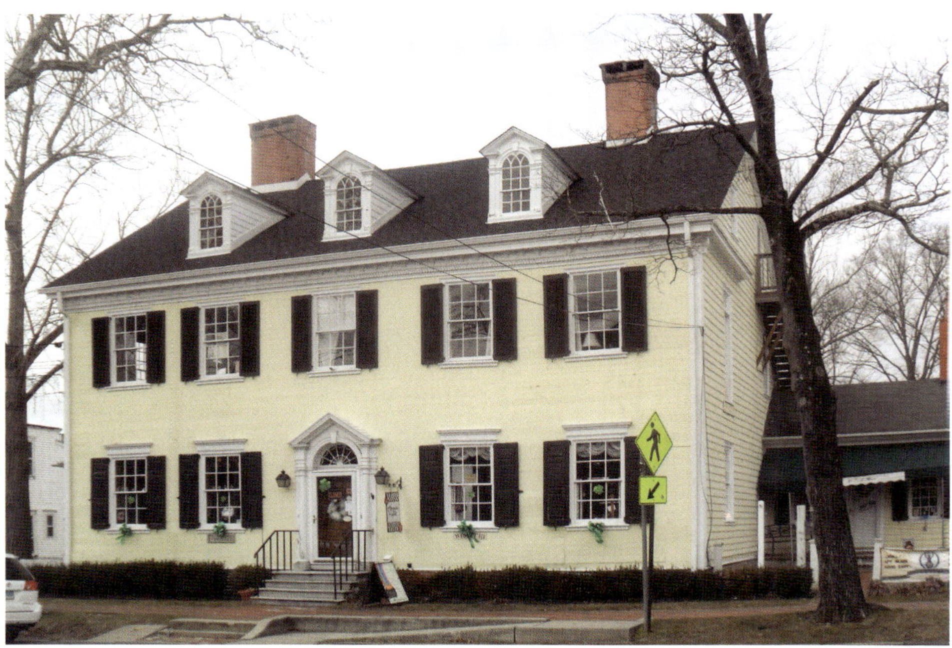

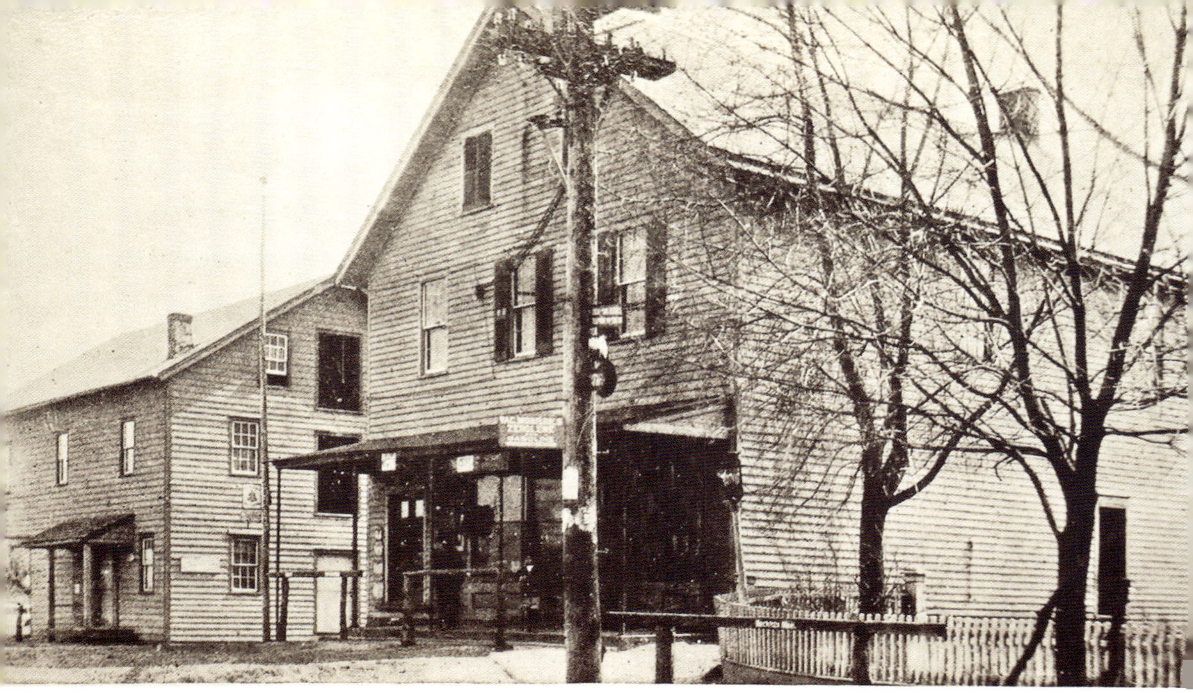

SALTAR'S MILL (ON THE LEFT) AND THE OLD IMLAYSTOWN POST OFFICE: The Mill and Post Office are pictured in this early 1900s postcard view. Richard Saltar built the original mill structure in the late seventeenth century. A major fire in 1793 forced a reconstruction of the building and another extensive remodeling was undertaken in the 1820s. Conversion to office/retail lofts in 2008 revealed that original materials were most likely reused during both reconstruction efforts. Abraham Lincoln was a direct descendant of Richard Saltar.

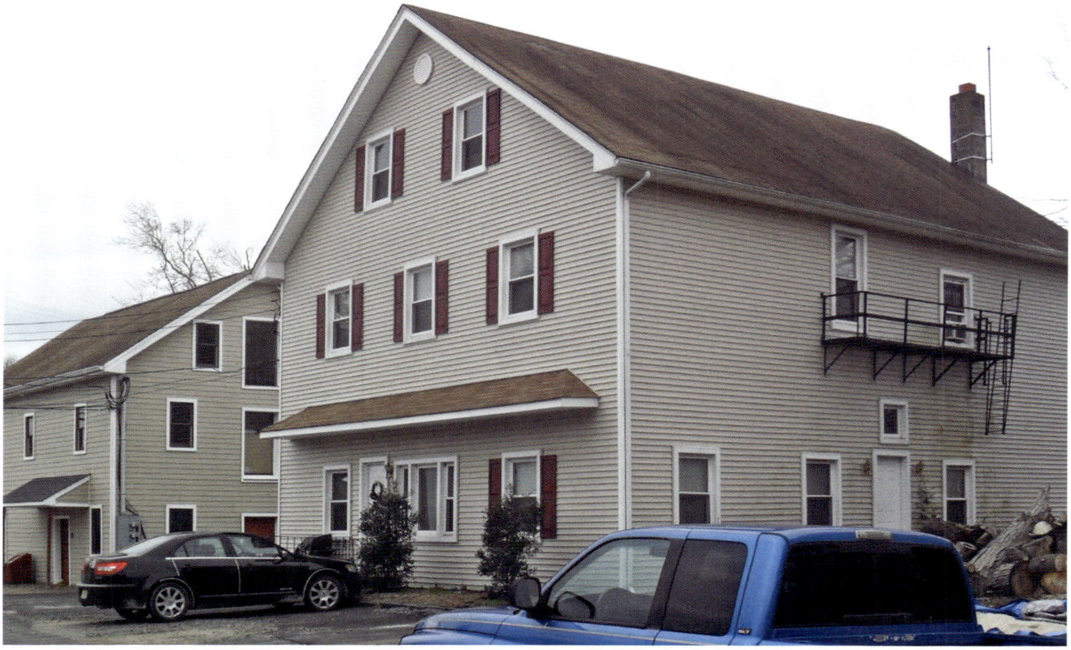

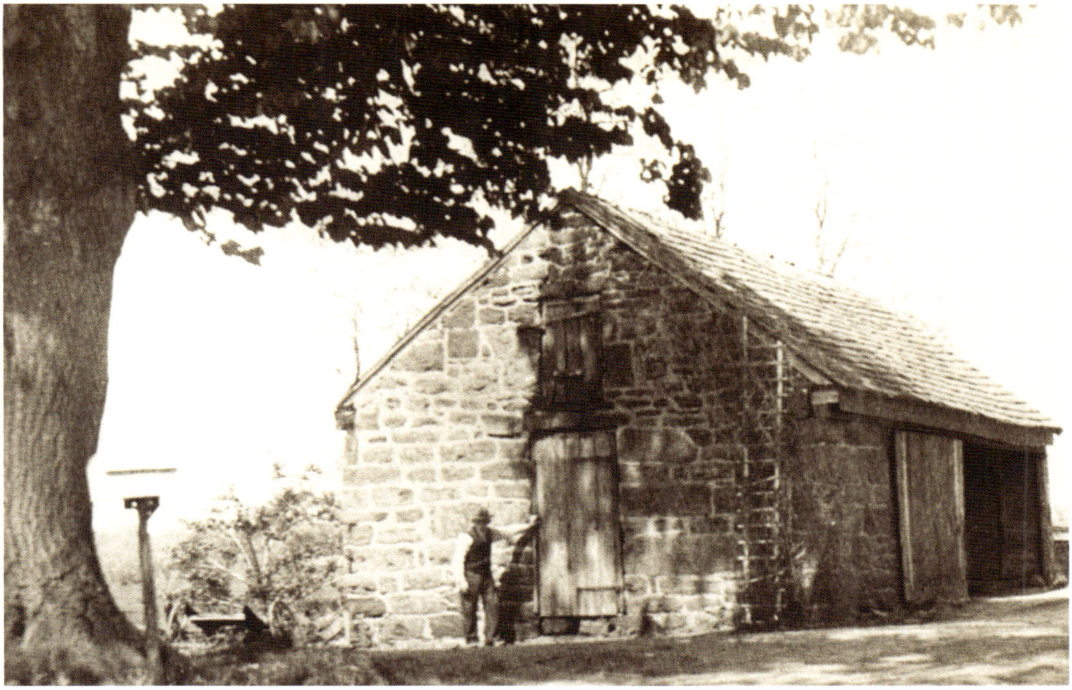

THE BLACKSMITH SHOP: This is the tradtional location where Mordecai Lincoln plied his trade during his residency in Monmouth County, pictured in the 1920s. Anybody who has visited these ancient ruins in the Fillmore section of Upper Freehold will have little doubt as to the age of the sadly crumbling remains. Although there have been attempts to disprove the authenticity of the traditional claims, the fact is that Lincoln was recruited by Saltar specifically for his smithy expertise, as there was a lack of qualified artisans in the area. The shop is very close in proximity to Saltar's Mill. Lincoln married Saltar's daughter and eventually moved to Pennsylvania.

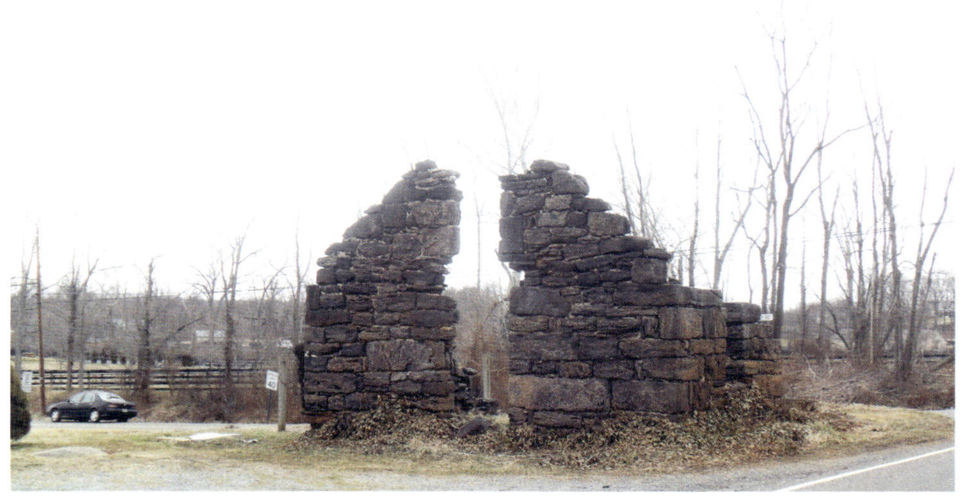

Credits and Acknowledgments

First and foremost, I would like to thank Alan Sutton. A legendary figure and pioneer in the modern local publications genre, Mr. Sutton was always there throughout the endeavor to answer any questions, or to offer his guidance and wisdom.

I would also like to extend my heartiest gratitude to those individuals and organizations which have helped me in completing this volume by providing photos for publication: The Library of Congress has done a great service to the American public by offering a large database of thousands of public domain images available for use, each scanned in high resolution. The vintage images found on pages 25, 35, 66, 68, 89 and 93 are all drawn from this great archive. The wonderful staff at the Belmar Public Library, for the images on pages 13, 15, 16, 17, and 18, Emmett Francois, page 32. My good friend, Vini Lopez for the snapshot on page 33. Vini is not only one of the greatest drummers ever to hail from the Jersey Shore, but served as the caddy master for many years at the facility pictured on page 40. Jim Abels for shooting the cover image as well as the 2013 images on pages 37 and 66. Eric Rudolph for digging through his vast archive for the great photo on page 69. Lora Capozzoli and the Battleground Historical Society for the image on page 79. Young Ski for the modern image on page 90. The copyrights to all above mentioned images are retained by their respective owners, and are used here with permission.

I also would like to thank Delicious Orchards for their help and encouragement, My buddy, Mark Sceurman and the entire Weird NJ staff, Monmouth University, the Bradley Beach Historical Society, the Garden Club RFD of Holmdel, Porta and their awesome staff down on Kingsley Ave, the Asbury Park Public Library, Thomas Appleby, Michael Corio, Raúl Rodriguez, Jeff Harshman and the fellas from the Ocean Monmouth Amateur Radio Club and Infoage. My friend and mentor for many years, Glenn Vogel, all of the pictured businesses and organizations and anyone else who I have erroneously omitted. Thank you.

Finally, I would like to thank my patient and terrific family: my beautiful daughters Leyna and Claire, my Mom and Dad for always encouraging and helping me to do my best, my brothers Michael and Tommy, and to my entire extended family and friends. Above all to my wonderful Rossy for loving and tolerating me. After all, I don't even own a working camera or scanner. I had to borrow hers!